The Bible
of Options
Strategies

The Bible of Options Strategies

The Definitive Guide for Practical Trading Strategies

Guy Cohen

Library of Congress Number: 2004116072

Vice President and Editor-in-Chief: Tim Moore
Executive Editor: Jim Boyd
Editorial Assistant: Kate E. Stephenson
Development Editor: Russ Hall
Marketing Manager: Martin Litkowski
International Marketing Manager: Tim Galligan
Cover Designer: Sandra Schroeder
Managing Editor: Gina Kanouse
Senior Project Editor: Sarah Kearns
Copy Editor: Ben Lawson
Indexer: Larry Sweazy
Compositor: Interactive Composition Corporation
Manufacturing Buyer: Dan Uhrig

FT Press offers excellent discounts on this book when ordered in quantity for bulk purchases or special sales. For more information, please contact U.S. Corporate and Government Sales, 1-800-382-3419, corpsales@pearsontechgroup.com. For sales outside the U.S., please contact International Sales at international@pearsoned.com.

Fourteenth Printing: September 2013

ISBN: 0-13-171066-4

Pearson Education LTD.
Pearson Education Australia PTY, Limited.
Pearson Education Singapore, Pte. Ltd.
Pearson Education North Asia, Ltd.
Pearson Education Canada, Ltd.
Pearson Educatión de Mexico, S.A. de C.V.
Pearson Education—Japan
Pearson Education Malaysia, Pte. Ltd.

To Dominic and Lulu, who keep reminding me of their omission from the Acknowledgments of my first book!

Table of Contents

Find Your Strategy

By Chapter

Find Your Strategy
By Proficiency

The following strategies are appropriate for novice traders:

The following strategies are appropriate for intermediate traders:

The following strategies are appropriate for advanced traders:

The following strategies are appropriate for expert traders:

Find Your Strategy
By Direction

The following strategies are bullish:

The following strategies are bearish:

The following strategies are direction neutral:

Find Your Strategy
By Volatility

The following strategies benefit from high volatility once you are in the trade:

The following strategies benefit from low volatility once you are in the trade:

Low Volatility	Chapter	Page
Bear Call Ladder	*3*	*109*
Bull Call Ladder	*3*	*99*
Long Call Butterfly	*5*	*188*
Long Call Condor	*5*	*198*
Long Iron Butterfly	*2 and 5*	*36, 217*
Long Iron Condor	*2 and 5*	*41, 217*
Long Put Butterfly	*5*	*193*
Long Put Condor	*5*	*203*
Modified Call Butterfly	*5*	*208*
Modified Put Butterfly	*5*	*212*
Ratio Call Spread	*6*	*229*
Ratio Put Spread	*6*	*233*
Short Call Synthetic Straddle	*7*	*263*
Short Guts	*5*	*184*
Short Put Synthetic Straddle	*7*	*267*
Short Straddle	*5*	*176*
Short Strangle	*5*	*180*

Find Your Strategy
By Risk / Reward

The following strategies have a capped risk profile:

The following strategies have an uncapped risk profile:

The following strategies offer only a capped reward profile:

The following strategies offer an uncapped reward potential:

Find Your Strategy
By Type

The following strategies enable to you capture a regular income:

The following strategies are for capital gain:

Preface

How to Use This Book

Options give investors so much flexibility that when it came to writing a book named *The Bible of Options Strategies*, I found myself cursing just how flexible they can be! Sixty strategies is a lot of ground to cover, but in reviewing them all again (I've done it several times already!), I was reminded of the beauty of these amazing trading instruments.

Options give us the ability to do so many things—they enable us to configure our investment aims in any way we like. The benefits of options are often trotted out to new students or prospective customers as the first salvo of an up-sell campaign, but they're worth looking at again, this time from a *practical* point of view.

Options enable us to:

- **Control more assets for less money.**

    One option contract represents 100 shares of stock and is usually a fraction of the cost of what you'd pay for the equivalent number of shares.

    For example, ABCD stock is priced at $26.20 on June 2, 2004.

    An option to *buy* ABCD shares (a call option) might be priced at $2.60. Because one contract represents 100 shares, we can therefore buy one ABCD call contract for $260.00 [100 * 2.60]. The alternative would be to buy 100 shares of the stock for a total sum of $2,620. So, in this example, we can buy ABCD calls options for around 10% of the stock price in order to control $2,620 of ABCD stock until the appropriate expiration date of the option.

- **Trade with leverage.**

    Because our cost basis is so low, the position is much more sensitive to the underlying stock's price movements, and hence our percentage returns can be so much greater.

- **Trade for income.**

    We can design strategies specifically for the purpose of generating income on a regular basis.

■ **Profit from declining stocks.**

We can use puts and calls to ensure that we can make money if the stock goes up, down, or sideways.

■ **Profit from volatility or protection against various factors.**

Different options strategies protect us or enable us to benefit from factors such as time decay, volatility, lack of volatility, and more.

■ **Reduce or eliminate risk.**

Options enable us to substantially reduce our risk of trading, and in certain rare cases, we can even eliminate risk altogether, albeit with the trade-off of very limited profit potential!

So, with all the different benefits of options, why on earth would traders *not* be curious to learn more about them? Well, for a start, the initial barrier to entry is quite high, in that options are reasonably complex instruments to understand for the first time. After you're over that hurdle, though, they become more and more fascinating! The other reason is that there is such a multitude of other investment securities for people to choose from, many will pick what seems like the simplest, rather than what may fit their investment aims the best.

Given that options can be a challenge, it's my job to make life as simple as possible for you. One of the ways in which I do this is to break things down into pictures so we can *see* what we're doing. As soon as we can see what we're doing, life becomes much clearer when you're creating options strategies. Everything to do with OptionEasy and all my material is designed to be visual-friendly. This goes back to when I started to learn all about options and the fact that the penny only started to drop when I converted the concepts into pictures. All of a sudden, everything fit into place, and I started to be able to extend logic faster and further than before.

This book is designed to be a reference book, one that you can pick up any time to learn about and understand a strategy. It isn't an academic workbook. It's a practical book, written for traders, designed to work interactively with your trading activities. As the title suggests, it's a book about options strategies, of which we take on 58! That's not to say you need to learn about each and every one of them, but at least you have the choice!

In order to make life easier for you, we categorize the strategies into different descriptions for the following criteria:

Proficiency Level

Each strategy is assigned a "value" in term of its suitability for different levels of trader. Each level is given an associated icon.

    Strategies suitable for novices

    Strategies suitable for intermediates

Strategies suitable for advanced traders

 Strategies suitable for expert traders

The allocations are defined according to a subjective view of complexity, risk, and desirability of the strategy. Therefore, some highly risky and undesirable strategies have been put into the *Expert* basket in order to warn novices and intermediates away. Also *Novice* strategies are not exclusive to novice traders. It's simply a question of suitability, and novice strategies are highly relevant and suitable to all levels of trader.

In some cases, the strategy is not complex at all but is considered unacceptably risky for novice and intermediate traders (at least without a warning). I have tried to be objective here, but I'm mindful not just of my own experiences but also the many students who regularly show me their trading disasters! Conservative by nature, I'm a believer that *loss of opportunity is preferable to loss of capital* (Joe DiNapoli), and perhaps some of these rankings bear testimony to this philosophy.

Market Outlook

This is where we define whether a strategy is suitable to bullish, bearish, or direction neutral outlooks.

 Strategies suitable for bullish market conditions

 Strategies suitable for bearish market conditions

 Strategies suitable for sideways market conditions

Volatility

Volatility is one of the most important factors affecting option pricing and therefore option trading. You really should familiarize yourself with the concept, which, forgive the plug, is dealt with in my first book, *Options Made Easy*.

Here, we define whether a strategy is suitable for trades anticipating high volatility or low volatility in the markets. Some strategies, such as Straddles, require high volatility after you've placed the trade, so a Straddle would fall into the High Volatility category.

 Strategies suitable for high volatility markets

 Strategies suitable for low volatility markets

Risk

With any trade you're looking to make, you must be aware of your potential risk, reward, and breakeven point(s).

Some strategies have unlimited risk; others have limited risk, even if that "limited" risk means 100% of the trade. Believe it or not, sometimes with options it's possible to lose more than 100%. In such cases, or when there is no definable stop to the potential risk of a trade, you're well advised to be aware of such a position in advance!

Here, we show you which strategies have capped or uncapped risk. Strategies with uncapped risk aren't necessarily all bad, but you should at least be aware of what you are getting into. Often you can mitigate such risk with a simple stop loss provision, in which case you're not going to be liable to uncapped risk. Often, such uncapped risk scenarios only occur if the stock falls to zero or rises to infinity, which mostly are rare circumstances, but you're better off being aware!

  Strategies with capped risk

  Strategies with uncapped risk

Reward

Following the risk scenarios described previously, the strategies also have potential reward scenarios, too.

Just because a strategy has unlimited reward potential doesn't mean that it's necessarily a great strategy, and just because it may have capped reward doesn't mean it's necessarily a bad strategy.

  Strategies with capped reward

  Strategies with uncapped reward

Strategy Type

Strategies can be used for income purposes (usually short-term) or to make capital gains. Many traders like the Covered Call because it's suitable for novices and because it's an income strategy that they can use every month.

Income strategies

Capital gain strategies

Strategy Legs

Each strategy contains different legs. Some have just one, and others have up to four. Each leg must be composed of any one of the basic four option strategies (long or short call or put) or a long or short stock position. Here's how we identify them:

Long stock

Short stock

Long call

Short call

Long put

Short put

All strategies contain real-life examples at the end of each guide.

Chapter by Chapter

In terms of structure, I've tried to make this book as easily navigable as possible, and much of that is solved by matrix-style tables of contents.

Each chapter contains strategies that are commensurate with a specific style of options trading. Inevitably there's some overlap between chapters for certain strategies, which we address in the appropriate places.

Chapter 1 addresses the basic strategies, including buying and selling stocks and then buying and selling calls and puts. After you understand those cornerstones and how the pictures relate to each strategy, then you can fast-forward to any part of the book and any strategy you like. All strategy guides are modular and follow the same format, so that you can become familiar with the style and structure of the content.

Chapter 2 is all about income strategies. An income strategy is when you're effectively a net seller of short-term options, which generates (monthly) income. You have to be careful, though, not to expose yourself to unlimited risk scenarios, which is why we use icons to identify excess risk.

In Chapter 3, we cover "vertical spreads." A vertical spread is where we buy and sell the same numbers of the same options (calls or puts) but with different strike prices. Obviously, there's some overlap here with other chapters, which is why the chapter is comparatively small.

Chapter 4 goes into volatility strategies and is bound to be as popular as the income strategies chapter! Here we address those strategies that benefit from increasing volatility *after you've placed the trade*.

In Chapter 5, we reverse this and explore those strategies that benefit from decreasing volatility *after you've placed the trade*. So here we're looking for stocks that we think will be rangebound for some time. Typically these are short-term strategies.

Chapter 6 identifies the ratio spreads and backspreads, where you're using increasing leverage to increase your returns. These are for advanced and experienced traders only!

In Chapter 7, we look at synthetic strategies that mainly mimic other strategic goals, using a combination of stock legs, call legs, and put legs. For example, we can replicate owning a stock purely by buying and selling calls and puts in such a way that we hardly pay any cash out. In other words, we've simulated the risk of owning the stock, but with no cash outlay. We can also synthetically re-create straddle positions and other strategies.

Lastly, in Chapter 8, we investigate some of the taxation issues that will confront you during your trading careers. This is not a definitive tax guide but rather more a flag raiser.

Strategy by Strategy

Each strategy is presented in a modular format. In this way, the book should be easy to navigate. The modules are numbered, and the numbering system applies throughout each chapter and each strategy:

■ The first number refers to the chapter itself. So, all headings in Chapter 2 will start with "2."

■ The second number refers to the strategy in question. So, 2.1 refers to the first strategy (Covered Call) in Chapter 2.

■ The third number refers to the module. So, 2.1.1 refers to the "Description" module for the first strategy (Covered Call) in Chapter 2. Because the modules are identical throughout the book, each module number is the same throughout all the strategies. Therefore, module "1," which appears as the third decimal place, is always "Description." The modules are outlined as follows:

■ x.y.**1**   Description

Here, we describe the strategy in both words and pictures. We identify the steps for each leg and some general comments about what the overall position will mean to you.

■ x.y.**2**   Context

This section describes the *outlook* and *rationale* for the strategy. We also highlight the *net position* in your account as a result of the trade as well as identify the effect of *time decay* and the *appropriate time period* for the strategy. *Stock* and *option-leg selection* are important elements of any trade, so these are covered as well.

■ x.y.**3**   Risk Profile

This section provides, where possible, simple calculations for you to evaluate the *risk, reward,* and *breakeven* points for each strategy.

■ x.y.**4**   Greeks

This is where we graphically explain each of the "Greeks." The Greeks are simply sensitivities of options to various factors, such as price movement, time decay, volatility, and interest rates. The Greeks are as follows:

Delta:

The movement of the option position relative to the movement of the underlying (say, stock) position. The resulting figure gives us an indication of the *speed* at which the option position is moving relative to the underlying stock position. Therefore, a Delta of 1 means the option position is moving 1 point for every point the stock moves. A Delta of –1 means the option position is moving –1 point for every point the underlying stock moves.

Typically, at-the-money options move with a Delta of 0.5 for calls and –0.5 for puts, meaning that ATM options move half a point for every 1 point that the underlying asset moves. This does not mean the option leg is moving slower in percentage terms, just in terms of dollar for dollar.

Delta is another way of expressing the probability of an option expiring in-the-money. This makes sense because an ATM call option has a Delta of 0.5; i.e., 50%, meaning a 50% chance of expiring ITM. A deep ITM call will have a Delta of near 1, or 100%, meaning a near 100% chance of expiration ITM. A very out-of-the-money call option will have a Delta of close to zero, meaning a near zero chance of expiring ITM.

So, Delta can be interpreted both in terms of the *speed* of the position and the probability of an option expiring ITM. Some advanced traders like to trade with the sum of their portfolio Delta at zero, otherwise known as Delta-Neutral trading. This is by no means a risk-free method of trading, but it is a style that enables profits to be taken regardless of the direction of market movement. However, this is only really suited to professional-style traders who have the very best technology solutions and a lot of experience.

Gamma:

Gamma is mathematically the second derivative of the underlying asset's price, or the first derivative of Delta, and can be viewed in two ways: either as the *acceleration* of the option position relative to the underlying stock price, or as the *odds* of a change in probability of the position expiring ITM (in other words, the odds of a change in Delta). Gamma is effectively an early warning to the fact that Delta could be about to change. Both calls and puts have positive Gammas. Typically, deep OTM and deep ITM options have near zero Gamma because the odds of a change in Delta are very low. Logically, Gamma tends to peak around the strike price.

Theta:

Theta stands for the option position's sensitivity to *time decay.* Long options (i.e., options that you have bought) have negative Theta, meaning that every day you own that option, time decay is eroding the Time Value portion of the option's value. In other words, time decay is *hurting* the position of an option holder. When you short options, Theta is positive, indicating that time decay is *helping* the option writer's position.

Vega:

Vega stands for the option position's sensitivity to *volatility.* Options tend to increase in value when the underlying stock's volatility increases. So, volatility *helps* the owner of an option and *hurts* the writer of an option. Vega is positive for long option positions and negative for short option positions.

Rho:

Rho stands for the option position's sensitivity to *interest rates.* A positive Rho means that higher interest rates are *helping* the position, and a negative Rho means that higher interest rates are *hurting* the position. Rho is the least important of all the Greeks as far as stock options are concerned.

■ x.y.5   Advantages and Disadvantages

As indicated, this section highlights the strengths and weaknesses of the strategy in question and the context of suitability for the trader.

■ x.y.6   Exiting the Trade

This module indicates the steps required to *exit the position* or to *mitigate a loss*.

■ x.y.7   Example

Every strategy ends with an illustrated example. The examples are all taken from real stocks using real data. However, because they are intended to be objectively indicative of how the strategies work, I have renamed the stock "ABCD" for every example. This helps us keep our minds focused on the structure of the strategy and avoid any preconceived prejudices against the actual stocks that were selected.

Tables of Contents

With so many strategies to choose from, it's crucial that you don't get lost! The multi-tables of contents are designed so that you can find the appropriate strategy easily, without having to thumb your way through the entire book to get there first. Familiarize yourself with this area because it's going to save you a lot of time as you use it later on. In print, we're restricted to two dimensions, but on the web site, you can use the Strategy Matrix completely interactively.

Free Software for Analyzing Strategies

You can use the free Strategy Analyzers on www.optioneasy.com to analyze any strategy in this book. The dynamic Analyzers help you see the impact of changing any parameters (such as time decay and volatility) in a user-friendly and visual form. Creating these Analyzers enabled me to hone my expertise with numerous options strategies in a very quick time, and will do the same for you.

General Comments

Within the strategy modules, there are references to concepts and definitions that you'll be able to find in the Glossary. For example, "Trading Plan" is referred to throughout the guides and is defined in the Glossary.

As options traders, we should definitely acquaint ourselves with the concepts of fundamental and technical analysis. Fundamental analysis involves the interpretation of how economies, sectors, and individual corporations are performing in terms of assets, liabilities, revenues, and profits.

Technical analysis involves the interpretation of price charts for securities. We really should understand the basic chart patterns such as pennants, flags, head and shoulders, support, resistance, and Fibonacci retracements. Remember, an option is a *derivative*—it is *derived* from an underlying security. Therefore, it makes sense for us to understand how that underlying security is likely to move and why.

I hope you enjoy this reference book and use it for many years to come. By all means, read it from cover to cover, but you'll probably get the best value by dipping in whenever the need arises.

Good luck.

Guy Cohen

Acknowledgments

First, to my colleagues at FlagTrader, whose diligence and ability have enabled us to create institutional grade tools.

To Lulu and Dominic for being extraordinary family friends.

And finally, to the students who have attended my workshops. I have learned so much from you.

About the Author

Guy Cohen BSc ARIC MBA, is developer of OptionEasy, the world's most comprehensive and user-friendly online options trading and training application. A successful private investor and trader, Guy has developed a global reputation for teaching technical analysis, options strategies, and trading psychology.

Guy is author of the global bestseller *Options Made Easy*, the definitive plain-English guide to options trading for private investors. He holds an MBA in finance from City University (Cass) Business School, London, UK.

For more information, go to www.optioneasy.com.

For all inquiries, write to enquiries@optioneasy.com.

The Four Basic Options Strategies

Introduction

The easiest way to learn options is with pictures so that you can begin to piece together strategies step-by-step. However, first we need to understand the four basic strategies. From that point, logic kicks in, and our learning can progress exponentially.

A risk profile chart shows us our profit/loss position for each trade. It differs from a standard price/time chart that we're used to seeing to monitor stock prices.

There are four easy steps to creating a risk profile chart:

Step 1: Y axis for profit/loss position

Step 2: X axis for underlying asset price range

Step 3: Breakeven line

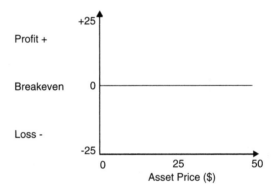

Step 4: Risk Profile line

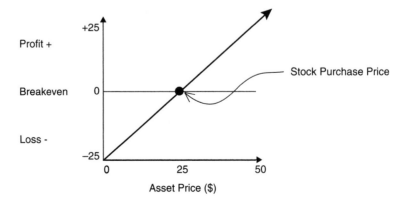

This chart shows our risk profile for a long stock position. As the asset price rises above our purchase price (along the x-axis), we move into profit. Our risk is capped to what we paid, as is our breakeven point, and our potential reward is uncapped.

The reverse position is when we short a stock, in which case the opposite occurs. Here, as the stock price rises above our short price, our short position shows a loss, which can be unlimited as the stock continues to rise. Our risk is uncapped as the stock rises, and our potential reward is the price we shorted at, as is our breakeven point.

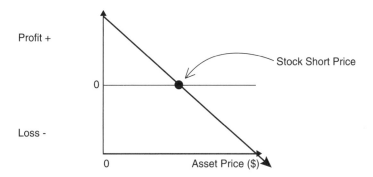

Now that we know how to interpret a risk profile chart, we can proceed with analyzing each strategy.

The four basic strategies that underpin your entire options trading knowledge are:

- Long Call

- Short Call

- Long Put

- Short Put

We should already know that owning an option exposes us to time decay, so typically we like to own options with expiration dates that are reasonably far away to give us a chance of our option increasing in value.

With options, we have the "Rule of the Opposites," where if one thing isn't true, then the opposite must be true. Therefore, if time decay *hurts* us when we buy options, it must *help* us when we sell options. Because time value decreases (or time decay increases) exponentially during the last month to expiration, we typically don't like to own options into that last month, but we *do* like to sell options with one month left to expiration.

With these four strategies, we would buy calls and puts with at least three months (or more) left to expiration, thereby looking for the options to increase in value during that time.

We would short calls and puts with a month or less to expiration, thereby looking for short-term income as the option hopefully expires worthless.

The Four Basic Options Risk Profiles

Imagine that the dotted lines are mirrors and see how each strategy is the opposite of the one on the other side of the mirror.

Buying a Call

- Belief that stock will rise (bullish outlook)
- Risk limited to premium paid
- Unlimited maximum reward

Buying a Put

- Belief that stock will fall (bearish outlook)
- Risk limited to premium paid
- Unlimited maximum reward up to the strike price less the premium paid

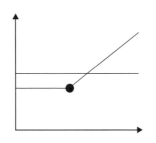

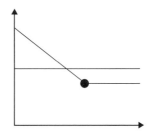

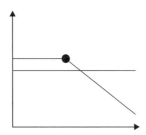

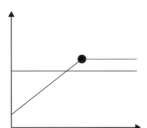

Writing a Call

- Belief that stock will fall (bearish outlook)
- Maximum reward limited to premium received
- Risk potentially unlimited (as stock price rises)
- Can be combined with another position to limit the risk

Writing a Put

- Belief that stock will rise (bullish outlook)
- Risk "unlimited" to a maximum equating to the strike price less the premium received
- Maximum reward limited to the premium received
- Can be combined with another position to limit the risk

1.1 Long Call

Proficiency	Direction	Volatility	Asset Legs	Max Risk	Max Reward	Strategy Type
Novice	Bullish	N/A	Long Call	Capped	Uncapped	Capital Gain

1.1.1 Description

Buying a call is the most basic of all option strategies. For many people, it constitutes their first options trade after gaining experience buying and selling stocks.

Calls are easy to understand. A call is an option to buy, so it stands to reason that when you buy a call, you're hoping that the underlying share price will rise.

ITM	In the Money	stock > call strike price
ATM	At the Money	stock = call strike price
OTM	Out of the Money	stock < call strike price

Buy call

Steps to Trading a Long Call

1. Buy the call option.

   - Remember that for option contracts in the U.S., one contract is for 100 shares. So when you see a price of $1.00 for a call, you will have to pay $100 for one contract.

   - For S&P Futures options, one contract is exercisable into one futures contract. If the option price is $1.00, you will pay $250 for one futures contract upon exercise.

   Steps In

   - Try to ensure that the trend is upward and identify a clear area of support.

   Steps Out

   - Manage your position according to the rules defined in your Trading Plan.

   - Sell your long options before the final month before expiration if you want to avoid the effects of time decay.

   - If the stock falls below your stop loss, then exit by selling the calls.

1.1.2 Context

Outlook

- With a Long Call, your outlook is **bullish.** You expect a rise in the underlying asset price.

Rationale

- To make a better return than if you had simply bought the stock itself. Do ensure that you give yourself enough time to be right; this means you should go at least six months out, if not one- or two-year LEAPs. If you think these are expensive, then simply divide the price by the number of months left to expiration and then compare that to shorter-term option prices. You will see that LEAPs and longer-term options are far better value on a per month basis, and they give you more time to be right, thus improving your chances of success. Another method is to buy only shorter-term deep ITM options.

Net Position

- This is a **net debit** transaction because you pay for the call option.
- Your maximum risk is capped to the price you pay for the call.
- Your maximum reward is uncapped.

Effect of Time Decay

- Time decay works against your bought option, so give yourself plenty of time to be right.
- Don't be fooled by the false economy that shorter options are cheaper. Compare a one-month option to a 12-month option and divide the longer option price by 12. You will see that you are paying far less per month for the 12-month option.

Appropriate Time Period to Trade

- At least three months, preferably longer, depending on the particular circumstances.

Selecting the Stock

- Choose from stocks with adequate liquidity, preferably over 500,000 Average Daily Volume (ADV).
- Try to ensure that the trend is upward and identify a clear area of support.

Selecting the Option

- Choose options with adequate liquidity; open interest should be at least 100, preferably 500.

- **Strike**—Look for either the ATM or ITM (lower) strike below the current stock.

- **Expiration**—Give yourself enough time to be right; remember that time decay accelerates exponentially in the last month before expiration, so give yourself a minimum of three months to be right, knowing you'll never hold into the last month. That gives you at least two months before you'll need to sell. Longer would be better, though.

1.1.3   Risk Profile

- **Maximum Risk**   [Call premium]

- **Maximum Reward**   [Uncapped]

- **Breakeven**   [Call strike + call premium]

1.1.4   Greeks

Key:
Expiration   ....
Today – 6 months   ————
Time(t) – 1 month   – – -

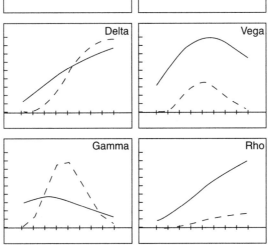

Risk Profile
As the stock price rises, the long call moves into profit more and more quickly, particularly when the stock price is greater than the strike price.

Delta
Delta (speed) is positive and increases at its fastest rate around the strike price, until it reaches 1. Notice how Delta is zero when the option is deep OTM.

Gamma
Gamma (acceleration) is always positive with a long call, and it peaks when Delta is at its fastest (steepest) rate.

Theta
Theta is negative, illustrating that time decay hurts the long call position.

Vega
Vega is positive, illustrating that volatility is helpful to the position because higher volatility translates into higher option values.

Rho
Rho is positive, illustrating that higher interest rates would increase the value of the calls and therefore help the position.

1.1.5 Advantages and Disadvantages

Advantages

- Cheaper than buying the stock outright.
- Far greater leverage than simply owning the stock.
- Uncapped profit potential with capped risk.

Disadvantages

- Potential 100% loss if the strike price, expiration dates, and stock are badly chosen.
- High leverage can be dangerous if the stock price moves against you.

1.1.6 Exiting the Trade

Exiting the Position

- Sell the calls you bought!

Mitigating a Loss

- Use the underlying asset or stock to determine where your stop loss should be placed.

1.1.7 Example

ABCD is trading at $28.88 on February 19, 2004.

Buy the January 2005 $27.50 strike call for $4.38.

You Pay	Call premium **$4.38**
Maximum Risk	Call premium **$4.38** Maximum risk is 100% of our total cost here
Maximum Reward	Unlimited as the stock price rises
Breakeven	Strike price + call premium **$27.50 + $4.38 = $31.88**

1.2 Short (Naked) Call

Proficiency	Direction	Volatility	Asset Legs	Max Risk	Max Reward	Strategy Type
(icon)	(icon)	N/A	(icon)	(icon)	(icon)	(icon)
Advanced	Bearish		Short Call	Uncapped	Capped	Income

1.2.1 Description

Although simple to execute, shorting a call (without any form of cover) is a risky strategy, hence its categorization as an advanced strategy. A Short Call exposes us to uncapped risk if the stock rises meteorically, and brokers will only allow experienced options traders to trade the strategy in the first place.

A call is an option to buy, so it stands to reason that when you buy a call, you're hoping that the underlying share price will rise. If you're selling or shorting a call, it's therefore logical that you'd want the stock to do the opposite—fall.

Sell call

Steps to Trading a Short Call

1. Sell the call option with a strike price higher than the current stock price.

   - Remember that for option contracts in the U.S., one contract is for 100 shares. So when you see a price of $1.00 for a call, you will receive $100 for one contract.

   Steps In

   - Try to ensure that the trend is downward or rangebound and identify a clear area of resistance.

   Steps Out

   - Manage your position according to the rules defined in your Trading Plan.

   - Hopefully the stock will decline or remain static, allowing your sold option to expire worthless so you can keep the entire premium.

   - If the stock rises above your stop loss, then exit the position by buying back the calls.

   - Time decay will be eroding the value of your call every day, so all other things being equal, the call you sold will be declining in value every day, allowing you to buy it back for less than you bought it for, unless the underlying stock has risen of course.

1.2.2 Context

Outlook

- **Bearish**—You are expecting a **fall** in the stock price; you are certainly **not** expecting a rise in the stock.

Rationale

- To pick up short-term premium income as the stock develops price weakness.

Net Position

- This is a **net credit** transaction because you are receiving a premium for the call.

- Your maximum risk is uncapped.

- Your maximum reward is capped to the price you receive for the call.

Effect of Time Decay

- Time decay is helpful to your naked sold option, so take advantage of the maximum time erosion. Maximum time decay (or theta decay) occurs in the last month before the option's expiration, so it makes sense to sell one-month or less options only.

- Don't be fooled by the false economy that selling longer options would be more lucrative. Compare a one-month option to a 12-month option and multiply the shorter option price by 12. You will see that you are receiving far more per month for the one-month option. Also remember that you want the person on the long side of this trade to have as short a time as possible to be right.

- Give yourself as little time as possible to be wrong because your maximum risk is uncapped.

Appropriate Time Period to Trade

- One month or less.

Selecting the Stock

- Choose from stocks with adequate liquidity, preferably over 500,000 Average Daily Volume (ADV).

- Try to ensure that the trend is downward and identify a clear area of resistance.

Selecting the Option

- Choose options with adequate liquidity; open interest should be at least 100, preferably 500.

- **Strike**—Look for OTM strikes above the current stock price.

- **Expiration**—Give yourself as little time to be wrong. Remember that your short position exposes you to uncapped risk, and that time decay accelerates exponentially (in your favor when you're short) in the last month before expiration, so only short the option with a maximum of one month to expiration, preferably less.

1.2.3 Risk Profile

- **Maximum Risk**   [Uncapped]

- **Maximum Reward** [Call premium]

- **Breakeven**   [Call strike + call premium]

1.2.4 Greeks

Risk Profile
As the stock price rises, the short call loses money more and more quickly, particularly when the stock price is greater than the strike price.

Delta
Delta (speed) is negative and moves at its fastest (negative) rate around the strike price, until it reaches -1. Notice how Delta is zero when the option is deep.

Gamma
Gamma (acceleration) is always negative with a Short Call, and it peaks inversely when Delta is at its fastest (steepest) rate. Gamma is zero when the position is deep OTM or ITM (i.e., when Delta isn't moving).

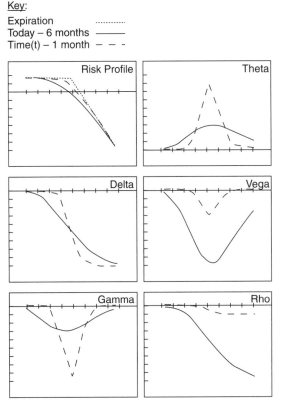

Key:
Expiration ....
Today – 6 months ———
Time(t) – 1 month – – -

Theta
Theta is positive, illustrating that time decay helps the short call position. As an option seller, this is of course completely logical.

Vega
Vega is negative, illustrating that volatility is unhelpful to the position because higher volatility translates into higher option values. As the seller of option premium, we'd rather the option value decreases.

Rho
Rho is negative, illustrating that higher interest rates would harm the Short Call position.

1.2.5 Advantages and Disadvantages

Advantages

- If done correctly, you can profit from falling or rangebound stocks in this way.
- This is another type of income strategy.

Disadvantages

- Uncapped risk potential if the stock rises.
- A risky strategy that is difficult to recommend on its own.

1.2.6 Exiting the Trade

Exiting the Position

- Buy back the options you sold or wait for the sold option to expire worthless (if the underlying stock falls and stays below the strike price) so that you can keep the entire premium.

Mitigating a Loss

- Use the underlying asset or stock to determine where your stop loss should be placed.

1.2.7 Example

ABCD is trading at $28.20 on February 19, 2004.

Sell the March 2004 $30.00 strike call for $0.90.

You Receive	Call premium $0.90
Maximum Risk	Uncapped
Maximum Reward	Call premium $0.90
Breakeven	Strike price + call premium $30.00 + $0.90 = $30.90

1.3 Long Put

Proficiency	Direction	Volatility	Asset Legs	Max Risk	Max Reward	Strategy Type
Novice	Bearish	N/A	Long Put	Capped	Uncapped	Capital Gain

1.3.1 Description

Buying a put is the opposite of buying a call. A put is an option to sell. When you buy a put, your outlook is bearish.

ITM	In the Money	stock < put strike price
ATM	At the Money	stock = put strike price
OTM	Out of the Money	stock > put strike price

Buy put

Steps to Trading a Long Put

1. Buy the put option.
   - Remember that for option contracts in the U.S., one contract is for 100 shares. So when you see a price of $1.00 for a put, you will have to pay $100 for one contract.
   - For S&P Futures options, one contract is exercisable into one futures contract. If the option price is $1.00, you will pay $250 for one futures contract upon exercise.

   Steps In

   - Try to ensure that the trend is downward and identify a clear area of resistance.

   Steps Out

   - Manage your position according to the rules defined in your Trading Plan.
   - Sell your long options before the final month before expiration if you want to avoid the effects of time decay.
   - If the stock rises above your stop loss, then exit by selling the puts.

1.3.2 Context

Outlook

- With a Long Put, your outlook is **bearish.** You expect a fall in the underlying asset price.

Rationale

- To make a better return than if you had simply sold short the stock itself. Do ensure that you give yourself enough time to be right; this means you should go at least six months out, if not one or two year LEAPs. If you think these are expensive, then simply divide the price by the number of months left to expiration and then compare that to shorter-term put prices. You will see that LEAPs and longer-term options are far better value per month, and they give you more time to be right, thus improving your chances of success. Another method is to buy only deep ITM options.

Net Position

■ This is a **net debit** transaction because you pay for the put option.

■ Your maximum risk is capped to the price you pay for the put.

■ Your maximum reward is uncapped until the stock falls to zero, whereupon the maximum profit is the strike price less what you paid for the put.

Effect of Time Decay

■ Time decay works against your bought option, so give yourself plenty of time to be right.

■ Don't be fooled by the false economy that shorter options are cheaper. Compare a one-month option to a 12-month option and divide the longer option price by 12. You will see that you are paying far less per month for the 12-month option.

Appropriate Time Period to Trade

■ At least three months, preferably longer depending on the particular circumstances.

Selecting the Stock

■ Choose from stocks with adequate liquidity, preferably over 500,000 Average Daily Volume (ADV).

■ Try to ensure that the trend is downward and identify a clear area of resistance.

Selecting the Option

■ Choose options with adequate liquidity; open interest should be at least 100, preferably 500.

■ **Strike**—Look for either the ATM or ITM (higher) strike above the current stock.

■ **Expiration**—Give yourself enough time to be right; remember that time decay accelerates exponentially in the last month before expiration, so give yourself a minimum of three months to be right, knowing you'll never hold into the last month. That gives you at least two months before you'll need to sell. Longer would be better, though.

1.3.3 Risk Profile

- **Maximum Risk**   [Put premium]

- **Maximum Reward** [Put strike − put premium]

- **Breakeven**   [Put strike − put premium]

1.3.4 Greeks

Key:
Expiration   ....
Today − 6 months ————
Time(t) − 1 month − − −

Risk Profile
As the stock price falls, the long put moves into profit more and more quickly, particularly when the stock price is lower than the strike price.

Delta
Delta (speed) is negative and moves at its fastest rate around the strike price, until it reaches -1. Notice how Delta is zero when the option is deep OTM.

Gamma
Gamma (acceleration) is always positive with a long put, and it peaks when Delta is at its fastest (steepest) rate.

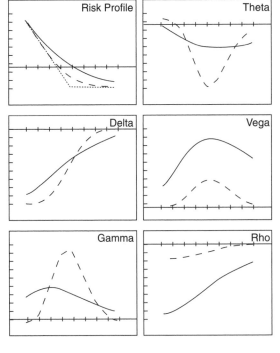

Theta
Theta is negative, illustrating that time decay hurts the long put position.

Vega
Vega is positive, illustrating that volatility is helpful to the position because higher volatility translates into higher option values.

Rho
Rho is negative, illustrating that higher interest rates would reduce the value of the puts and therefore hurt the position.

1.3.5 Advantages and Disadvantages

Advantages

- Profit from declining stock prices.

- Far greater leverage than simply shorting the stock.

- Uncapped profit potential with capped risk.

Disadvantages

- Potential 100% loss if the strike price, expiration dates, and stock are badly chosen.

- High leverage can be dangerous if the stock price moves against you.

1.3.6 Exiting the Trade

Exiting the Position

- Sell the puts you bought!

Mitigating a Loss

- Use the underlying asset or stock to determine where your stop loss should be placed.

1.3.7 Example

ABCD is trading at $28.88 on February 19, 2004.

Buy the January 2005 $30.00 strike put for $4.38.

You Pay	Put premium **$4.38**
Maximum Risk	Put premium **$4.38** Maximum risk is 100% of our total cost here
Maximum Reward	Strike price − put premium **$30.00 − $4.38 = $25.62**
Breakeven	Strike price − put premium **$30.00 − $4.38 = $25.62**

1.4 Short (Naked) Put

Proficiency	Direction	Volatility	Asset Legs	Max Risk	Max Reward	Strategy Type
Intermediate	Bullish	N/A	Short Put	Capped*	Capped	Income

*Risk uncapped until the stock falls to zero.

1.4.1 Description

Selling a put is a simple, short-term income strategy. A put is an option to sell. When you sell a put, you have sold someone the right to sell. As the stock falls, you may be obligated to buy the stock if you are exercised. Therefore, only sell puts Out of the

Money and on stocks you'd love to own at the strike price (which is lower than the current stock price).

The maximum risk of a naked put is the strike price less the premium you receive. Some people consider this to be an unlimited risk profile, and others consider it to be limited risk. A compromise is to consider it unlimited until the stock falls to zero—in other words, unlimited until the stock falls to zero.

Sell put

Steps to Trading a Naked Put

1. Sell the put option with a strike price lower than the current stock price.

   - Remember that for option contracts in the U.S., one contract is for 100 shares. So when you see a price of $1.00 for a put, you will receive $100 for one contract.

   - For S&P Futures options, one contract is exercisable into one futures contract. If the option price is $1.00, you will pay $250 for one futures contract upon exercise.

   Steps In

   - Try to ensure that the trend is upward (or sideways) and identify a clear area of support.

   Steps Out

   - Manage your position according to the rules defined in your Trading Plan.

   - Hopefully the stock will rise or remain static, allowing your sold option to expire worthless so that you can keep the entire premium.

   - If the stock falls below your stop loss, then exit the position by buying back the puts.

   - Time decay will be eroding the value of your put every day, so all other things being equal, the put you sold will be declining in price every day, allowing you to buy it back for less than you bought it for, unless the underlying stock has fallen of course.

1.4.2 Context

Outlook

- **Bullish**—You are expecting the stock to rise or stay sideways at a minimum.

Rationale

- To pick up short-term premium income as the share develops price strength.

- To lower the cost basis of buying a share (if the put is exercised).

Net Position

- This is a **net credit** transaction because you receive a premium for selling the put.

- Your maximum risk is the put strike price less the premium you receive for the put. This is considered a high-risk strategy.

- Your maximum reward is limited to the premium you receive for the option.

Effect of Time Decay

- Time decay works with your naked sold option. To take advantage of the maximum rate of time decay, sell the put in the last month before the option's expiration.

- Don't be fooled by the false economy that options with longer to expiration are more lucrative. Compare a one-month option to a 12-month option and multiply the shorter option price by 12. You will see that you are receiving far more per month for the one-month option.

Appropriate Time Period to Trade

- One month or less.

Selecting the Stock

- Choose from stocks with adequate liquidity, preferably over 500,000 Average Daily Volume (ADV).

- Try to ensure that the trend is upward and identify a clear area of support.

Selecting the Option

- Choose options with adequate liquidity; open interest should be at least 100, preferably 500.

- **Strike**—Look for OTM (lower strike) options, below the current stock price.

- **Expiration**—Give yourself as little time to be wrong; remember that your short position exposes you to uncapped risk (until the stock falls to zero) and that time decay accelerates exponentially (in your favor when you're short) in the last month before expiration, so only short the option with a maximum of one month to expiration, preferably less.

1.4.3 Risk Profile

- **Maximum Risk**   [Put strike − put premium]

- **Maximum Reward**   [Put premium]

- **Breakeven**   [Put strike − put premium]

1.4.4 Greeks

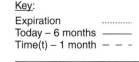

Key:
Expiration   ....
Today – 6 months ————
Time(t) – 1 month – – –

Risk Profile
As the stock price falls, the naked put moves into loss more and more quickly, particularly when the stock price is lower than the strike price.

Delta
Delta (speed) is positive and falls to zero after the position reaches its maximum profit potential after the stock has risen above the strike price.

Gamma
Gamma (acceleration) is always negative with a naked put (because you are net seller of options), and it peaks inversely when Delta is at its fastest (steepest) rate, which is when the position is ATM.

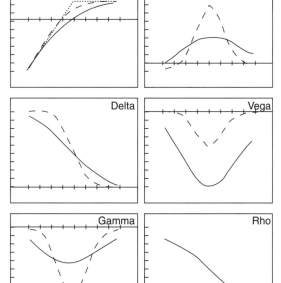

Theta
Theta is positive, illustrating that time decay helps the naked put position.

Vega
Vega is negative, illustrating that volatility is harmful to the position because higher volatility translates into higher option values.

Rho
Rho is positive, illustrating that higher interest rates would help the naked put position.

1.4.5 Advantages and Disadvantages

Advantages

■ If done correctly, you can use Naked Puts to gain a regular income from rising or rangebound stocks.

■ The Naked Put is an alternative way of buying a stock at a cheaper price than in the current market. This is because if you're exercised, you're obligated to buy stock at the low strike price, having already received a premium for selling the puts in the first place.

Disadvantages

■ Naked Puts expose you to uncapped risk (as the stock falls to zero) if the stock falls.

■ Not a strategy for the inexperienced. You must only use this strategy on stocks you'd love to own at the put strike price you're selling at. The problem is that if you were to be exercised, you'd be buying a stock that is falling. The way to avoid this is to position the put strike around an area of strong support within the context of a rising trend. A Fibonacci retracement point would be the type of area you'd use to position your naked put strike . . . well below the current stock price.

1.4.6 Exiting the Trade

Exiting the Position

- Buy back the options you sold or wait for the sold put to expire worthless so that you can keep the entire premium.

Mitigating a Loss

- Use the underlying asset or stock to determine where your stop loss should be placed.

1.4.7 Example

ABCD is trading at $27.35 on May 12, 2004.

Sell the June 2004 $25.00 strike put for $1.05.

You Receive	Put premium **$1.05**
Maximum Risk	Strike price − put premium **$25.00 − $1.05 = $23.95**
Maximum Reward	Put premium **$1.05**
Breakeven	Strike price − put premium **$25.00 − $1.05 = $23.95**
Return on Risk	4.38%
Cushion (from Breakeven)	$3.40 or 12.43%

2

Income Strategies

Introduction

Options uniquely enable us to enhance our returns by way of combining buy/sell legs so that we can generate income on a regular basis. Income strategies are characterized typically by being short-term strategies, whereby option premium is sold on a monthly basis. Many investors generate significant percentage returns in this way, even if the underlying stock hasn't moved. Imagine collecting income when your chosen stock hasn't even moved at all.

As with all aspects of trading, it's crucial to be level-headed and not to get greedy. A 3–4% return every month is very significant when compounded to an annual rate. Would you take a 30% return on your money every year? Of course you would . . . or at least you should! I know you aspire for more, and that's ok, but remember that fund managers would kill for such returns, though remember that they are fettered by all kinds of regulatory and compliance criteria that the private investor never has to worry about.

The basic income strategies outlined here can be employed by traders of all levels and experience. Don't get hung up on thinking that complex strategies must yield higher returns. That simply isn't the case. Higher returns are generated by good trading plans that are consistently executed time after time. Some of the greatest traders execute the same simple processes over and over again. The challenge they have is to keep their enthusiasm up year after year.

In short, there is nothing wrong with choosing a Covered Call as your staple strategy, and don't let "option snobs" tell you otherwise! Naked Puts are also incredibly simple, but unless you have sufficient experience (and collateral in your account!), a broker may not let you trade them because of the perceived risk. In such a case, you can create a Bull Put Spread by buying a lower strike put, which will have the effect of capping the risk of the Naked Put.

Income Strategies Staircase

This diagram shows how the various income strategies link together, highlighting their similarities and differences. You may want to complete the chapter first before coming back to this diagram so you can better appreciate the links.

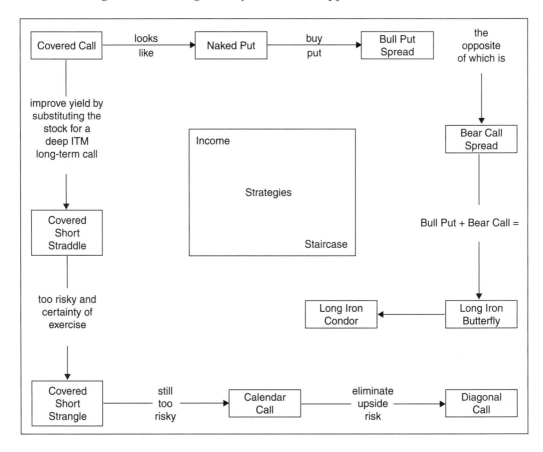

Combining Strategies

The opposite of a Bull Put spread is a Bear Call Spread, and the combination of the two forms a Long Iron Butterfly. There are several ways in which a Covered Call can be enhanced, but the best way is by substituting the stock with a Deep In the Money, long term call option, creating a Diagonal Call. This has the effect of increasing the yield and reducing the cost basis. However, there are nuances that must be understood before jumping into Diagonal Calls, and we'll cover these points in the Diagonal Call Guide.

We'll also add in another three strategies (the Calendar Put, Diagonal Put, and Covered Put), though we would rarely, if ever, seek to use them for reasons that we'll cover in those sections.

2.1 Covered Call

Proficiency	Direction	Volatility	Asset Legs	Max Risk	Max Reward	Strategy Type
		N/A				
Novice	Bullish		■ Long Stock ■ Short Call	Capped*	Capped	Income

*Risk uncapped until the stock falls to zero.

2.1.1 Description

The Covered Call is the most basic of income strategies, yet it is also highly effective and can be used by novices and experts alike.

The concept is that in owning the stock, you then sell an Out of the Money call option on a monthly basis as a means of collecting rent (or a dividend) while you own the stock.

If the stock rises above the call strike, you'll be exercised, and the stock will be sold . . . but you make a profit anyway. (You're covered because you own the stock in the first place.) If the stock remains static, then you're better off because you collected the call premium. If the stock falls, you have the cushion of the call premium you collected.

On occasion, it's attractive to sell an In the Money or At the Money call while you already own the stock. In such cases, the premium you collect will be higher, as will the likelihood of exercise, meaning you'll end up delivering the stock at the strike price of the sold call.

Buy stock	+	Sell OTM call	=	Covered Call

Steps to Trading a Covered Call

1. Buy (or own) the stock.

2. Sell calls one or two strike prices out of the money [OTM] (i.e., calls with strike prices one or two strikes price higher than the stock).

   ■ If the stock is purchased simultaneously with writing the call contract, the strategy is commonly referred to as a "buy-write."

   ■ Generally, only sell the calls on a monthly basis. In this way you will capture more in premiums over several months, provided you are not exercised. Selling premium every month will net you more over a period of time than selling premium a long way out. Remember that whenever you are selling options premium, time decay works in your favor. Time decay is at its fastest rate in the last 20 trading days (i.e., the last month), so when you sell option premiums, it is best to sell them with a month left, and do it again the following month.

■ Remember that your maximum gain is capped when the stock reaches the level of the call's strike price.

■ If trading U.S. stocks and options, you will be required to buy (or be long in) 100 shares for every options contract that you sell.

Steps In

■ Some traders prefer to select stocks between $10.00 and $50.00, considering that above $50.00, it would be expensive to buy the stock. Ultimately it's what you feel comfortable with.

■ Try to ensure that the trend is upward or rangebound and identify a clear area of support.

Steps Out

■ Manage your position according to the rules defined in your Trading Plan.

■ If the stock closes above the strike at expiration, you will be exercised. You will deliver the stock at the strike price, whilst having profited from both the option premium you received and the uplift in stock price to reach the strike price. Exercise is automatic.

■ If the stock remains below the strike but above your stop loss, let the call expire worthless and keep the entire premium. If you like, you can then write another call for the following month.

■ If the stock falls below your stop loss, then either sell the stock (if you're approved for naked call writing) or reverse the entire position (the call will be cheap to buy back).

2.1.2 Context

Outlook

■ With a Covered Call, your outlook is **neutral to bullish.** You expect a steady rise.

Rationale

■ To buy (or own) a stock for the medium or long term with the aim of capturing monthly **income** by selling calls every month. This is like collecting rent for holding the stock and will have the effect of lowering your cost basis of holding the stock.

- If the stock rises, your short call may be exercised, in which case you will make some profit. If you are exercised, then your shares will be sold.

- If the stock falls, your sold call will expire worthless, and you will keep the premium, thus enabling you to have bought the stock cheaper (because you offset the received premium against the price you paid for the stock).

Net Position

- This is a **net debit** transaction because you are paying for the stock and only taking in a small premium for the sold call options. You can increase your yield by purchasing the stock on margin, thereby doubling your yield if you use 50% margin.

- Your maximum risk is the price you paid for the stock less the premium you received for the call.

Effect of Time Decay

- Time decay is helpful to your trade here because it should erode the value of the call you sold. Provided that the stock does not hit the strike price at expiration, you will be able to retain the entire option premium for the trade, thus reducing your original cost of buying the share.

Appropriate Time Period to Trade

- Sell the calls on a monthly basis.

Selecting the Stock

- Choose from stocks with adequate liquidity, preferably over 500,000 Average Daily Volume (ADV).

- Select a stock price range you feel comfortable with. Some traders prefer lower priced stocks; others don't have a preference. Ultimately the direction of the stock is more important.

- Try to ensure that the trend is upward or rangebound and identify a clear area of support.

Selecting the Option

- Choose options with adequate liquidity; open interest should be at least 100, preferably 500.

- **Strike**—Look for either the ATM or just OTM (higher) strike above the current stock. If you're bullish, then choose a higher strike; if neutral, choose the ATM strike.

- **Expiration**—Look at either of the next two expirations and compare monthly yields. Look for over 3% monthly initial cash yield.

2.1.3 Risk Profile

- **Maximum Risk**   [Stock price paid − call premium]

- **Maximum Reward**   [Call strike − stock price paid] + call premium

- **Breakeven**   [Stock price paid − call premium]

2.1.4 Greeks

Key:
Expiration   ....
Today − 2 months ───────
Time(t) − 10 days − − −

Risk Profile
As the stock price rises, the covered call moves into profit but slows down as it approaches the strike price and maximum profit.

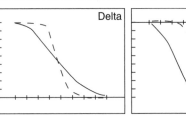

Theta
Theta is positive, illustrating that time decay is helpful to the position.

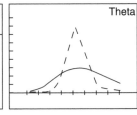

Delta
Delta (speed) is positive and falls to zero as the asset price rises above the strike price and the maximum profit is achieved.

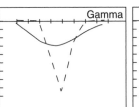

Vega
Vega is negative, illustrating that volatility is harmful to the position.

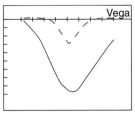

Gamma
Gamma (acceleration) is always negative with this position because you are a net seller of calls.

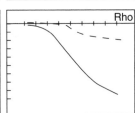

Rho
Rho is negative, illustrating that higher interest rates would be harmful to the position.

2.1.5 Advantages and Disadvantages

Advantages

- Generate monthly income.

- Lower risk than simply owning the stock.

- Can profit from rangebound stocks.

Disadvantages

- Some traders consider this to be an expensive strategy in terms of cash outlay. For regular stock traders, this is not true. For traders who only trade options, then it is true but is not particularly relevant.

- Capped upside if the stock rises.

- Uncapped downside if the stock falls, cushioned only by the call premium received.

2.1.6 Exiting the Trade

Exiting the Position

- If the share price rises above the strike price, you will be exercised and therefore make a profit.

- If the share stays below the strike price, you will have successfully reduced your cost of entry because the premium you took in will offset the price you paid for the stock. You will retain the entire option premium you received because it will expire worthless.

- If the shares plummet, then your exit depends on what type of account you have:

  - If your account permits you to sell naked options, then you will be able to sell the shares and let the option expire worthless. Because the option will have declined in value so much, you may consider buying it back to avoid any contingent losses that could occur if the share price suddenly bounced back up after you sold it. You should take extreme care if holding an uncovered Short Call position because you will be exposed to uncapped risk potential.

  - If your account does not permit you to sell naked options and you're not sufficiently experienced, then you should buy back the options you sold and consider selling the stock, too. This is the safest way to exit a losing covered call trade.

Mitigating a Loss

- Either sell the shares, or sell the shares and buy back the option you sold.

- Another tactic could be to buy a put option as well, which would then cover your downside risk. Your yield would be reduced, but so would your maximum risk. See *Collar*.

2.1.7 Example

ABCD is trading at $28.20 on February 25, 2004.

Buy the stock for $28.20.

Sell the March 30, 2004 strike call for $0.90.

You Pay	Stock price – call premium 28.20 – 0.90 = 27.30
Maximum Risk	Stock price – call premium 28.20 – 0.90 = 27.30 Maximum risk of $27.30 is 100% of your total cost here
Maximum Reward	Limited to the call premium received plus the call strike less the stock price paid 0.90 + 30.00 – 28.20 = 2.70
Breakeven	Stock price – call premium received 28.20 – 0.90 = 27.30
Initial Cash Yield (Also Cushion)	3.19%
Maximum Yield if Exercised	9.57% (if the stock reaches $30.00 at expiration).

2.2 Naked Put

We know from Chapter 1, "The Four Basic Options Strategies," that a Covered Call looks like a Naked Put. We won't repeat an entire section on the Naked Put (Section 1.4), but this is the natural place for the Naked Put to reside, so please refer to it now so you can compare it with the Covered Call. These are the two basic income strategies, although those without Level 3 account status won't be able to trade naked options strategies.

After you've reviewed the Naked Put again, please move on to the Bull Put Spread.

2.3 Bull Put Spread

Proficiency	Direction	Volatility	Asset Legs	Max Risk	Max Reward	Strategy Type
Intermediate	Bullish	N/A	▦ Long Put ▦ Short Put	Capped	Capped	Income

2.3.1 Description

The Bull Put spread is an intermediate strategy that can be profitable for stocks that are either rangebound or rising.

The concept is to protect the downside of a Naked Put by buying a lower strike put to insure the one you sold. Both put strikes should be lower than the current stock price so as to ensure a profit even if the stock doesn't move at all.

The lower strike put that you buy is further OTM than the higher strike put that you sell. Therefore you receive a net credit because you buy a cheaper option than the one you sell, thereby highlighting that options are cheaper the further OTM you go.

If the stock rises, both puts will expire worthless, and you simply retain the net credit.

If the stock falls, then your breakeven is the higher strike less the net credit you receive. Provided the stock remains above that level, then you'll make a profit. Otherwise you could make a loss. Your maximum loss is the difference in strikes less the net credit received.

| Buy lower strike put | + | Sell OTM put | = | Bull Put Spread |

Steps to Trading a Bull Put Spread

1. Buy lower strike puts.
2. Sell the same number of higher strike puts with the same expiration date.

   - Both strikes should be lower than the current stock price.

   Steps In

   - Try to ensure that the trend is upward or rangebound and identify a clear area of support.

   Steps Out

   - Manage your position according to the rules defined in your Trading Plan.

   - If the stock falls below your stop loss, then buy back the short put or unravel the entire position.

   - If the stock remains above the higher strike put, the options will expire worthless, and you'll retain the net credit.

2.3.2 Context

Outlook

   - With bull puts, your outlook is **bullish** or neutral to bullish.

Rationale

   - To execute a bullish **income** trade for a net credit whilst reducing your maximum risk. The bought puts will have the effect of limiting your downside, whilst the sold puts produce the income element.

Net Position

   - This is a **net credit** trade because your bought puts will be cheaper than your sold puts, which are further out of the money. (Remember that calls and puts work in the opposite way to each other—an OTM call is an ITM put and vice versa.)

■ Your maximum reward on the trade itself is limited to the net credit of the sold puts less the bought puts. Your maximum risk on the trade is the difference between the strike prices less your net credit.

Effect of Time Decay

■ Time decay is helpful to this position when it is profitable and harmful when it is loss-making. Remember, if you're buying and selling OTM options to make a net credit, you'll make a profit if the stock doesn't move. Therefore, you want to trade this type of strategy in short time periods only. If the position becomes unprofitable, time decay will start to work against you because the nearer you are to expiration, the nearer you'll be to making your maximum loss.

Appropriate Time Period to Trade

■ It's safest to trade this strategy on a short-term basis, preferably with one month or less to expiration.

Selecting the Stock

■ Choose from stocks with adequate liquidity, preferably over 500,000 Average Daily Volume (ADV).

■ Try to ensure that the trend is upward or rangebound and identify a clear area of support well above the higher strike price.

Selecting the Options

■ Choose options with adequate liquidity; open interest should be at least 100, preferably 500.

■ **Lower Strike**—Typically $5.00 below the higher strike, but it can be $2.50 below or more. The key is to try to find a decent cushion for downside protection while also securing a decent yield, preferably over 10%, which typically means around $0.50 net credit for a $5.00 spread between the strikes.

■ **Higher Strike**—Try to give yourself at least a 10% cushion below the current stock price; the level of cushion will depend on how close you are to the relevant expiration date.

■ **Expiration**—One month or less. Use the same expiration date for both legs.

2.3.3 Risk Profile

■ **Maximum Risk**   [Difference in strikes − net credit]

■ **Maximum Reward**   [Net credit received]

■ **Breakeven**   [Higher strike − net credit]

2.3.4 Greeks

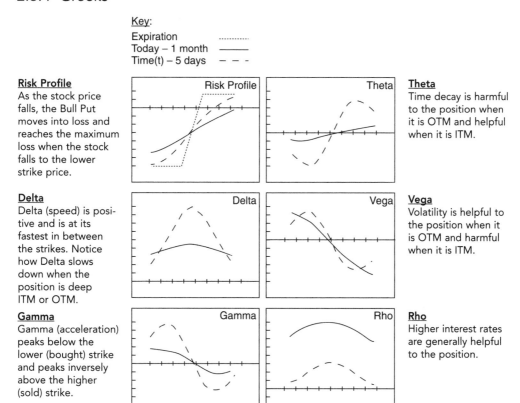

Key:
Expiration ....
Today – 1 month ————
Time(t) – 5 days – – -

Risk Profile
As the stock price falls, the Bull Put moves into loss and reaches the maximum loss when the stock falls to the lower strike price.

Delta
Delta (speed) is positive and is at its fastest in between the strikes. Notice how Delta slows down when the position is deep ITM or OTM.

Gamma
Gamma (acceleration) peaks below the lower (bought) strike and peaks inversely above the higher (sold) strike.

Theta
Time decay is harmful to the position when it is OTM and helpful when it is ITM.

Vega
Volatility is helpful to the position when it is OTM and harmful when it is ITM.

Rho
Higher interest rates are generally helpful to the position.

2.3.5 Advantages and Disadvantages

Advantages

- Short-term income strategy not necessarily requiring any movement of the stock.

- Capped downside protection compared to a Naked Put.

Disadvantages

- Maximum loss is typically greater than the maximum gain, despite the capped downside.

- High yielding trades tend to mean less protective cushion and are therefore riskier.

- Capped upside if the stock rises.

2.3.6 Exiting the Trade

Exiting the Position

- With this strategy, you can simply unravel the spread by buying back the puts you sold and selling the puts you bought in the first place.

Mitigating a Loss

- Unravel the trade as described previously.

- Advanced traders may choose to only partially unravel the spread leg-by-leg. In this way, they leave one leg of the spread exposed in order to attempt to profit from it.

2.3.7 Example

ABCD is trading at $27.00 on May 12, 2004.

Buy the June 2004 20 strike put for $0.50.

Sell the June 2004 25 strike put for $1.00.

Net Credit	Premium sold − premium bought **1.00 − 0.50 = 0.50**
Maximum Risk	Difference in strikes − net credit **5.00 − 0.50 = 4.50** Maximum risk is greater than your net credit
Maximum Reward	Net credit **0.50**
Breakeven	Higher strike − net credit **25.00 − 0.50 = 24.50**
Max ROI	11.11%
Cushion	$2.50 or 9.26% from breakeven

2.4 Bear Call Spread

Proficiency	Direction	Volatility	Asset Legs	Max Risk	Max Reward	Strategy Type
Intermediate	Bearish	N/A	▦ Short Call ▦ Long Call	Capped	Capped	Income

2.4.1 Description

The Bear Call Spread is an intermediate strategy that can be profitable for stocks that are either rangebound or falling.

The concept is to protect the downside of a Naked Call by buying a higher strike call to insure the one you sold. Both call strikes should be higher than the current stock price so as to ensure a profit even if the stock doesn't move at all.

The higher strike call that you buy is further OTM than the lower strike call that you sell. Therefore, you receive a net credit because you buy a cheaper option than the one you sell, thereby highlighting that options are cheaper the further OTM you go.

If the stock falls, both calls will expire worthless, and you simply retain the net credit.

If the stock rises, then your breakeven is the lower strike plus the net credit you receive. Provided the stock remains below that level, then you'll make a profit. Otherwise you could make a loss. Your maximum loss is the difference in strikes less the net credit received.

Sell lower strike call   Buy OTM call   Bear Call Spread

Steps to Trading a Bear Call Spread

1. Sell lower strike calls.

2. Buy the same number of higher strike calls with the same expiration date.

   ■ Both strikes should be higher than the current stock price.

   Steps In

   ■ Try to ensure that the trend is downward or rangebound and identify a clear area of resistance.

   Steps Out

   ■ Manage your position according to the rules defined in your Trading Plan.

   ■ If the stock rises above your stop loss, then buy back the short call or unravel the entire position.

   ■ If the stock remains below the lower strike call, the options will expire worthless, and you'll retain the net credit.

2.4.2 Context

Outlook

■ With bear calls, your outlook is **bearish** or neutral to bearish.

Rationale

■ To execute a bearish **income** trade for a net credit while reducing your maximum risk. The bought calls will have the effect of limiting your risk, while the sold calls produce the income element.

Net Position

■ This is a **net credit** trade because your bought calls will be cheaper than your sold calls, which are further out of the money.

■ Your maximum reward on the trade itself is limited to the net credit of the sold calls less the bought calls. Your maximum risk on the trade is the difference between the strike prices less the net credit received.

Effect of Time Decay

■ Time decay is helpful to this position when it is profitable and harmful when it is loss-making. Remember, if you're buying and selling OTM options to make a net credit, you'll make a profit if the stock doesn't move. Therefore, you want to trade this type of strategy in short time periods only. If the position becomes unprofitable, time decay will start to work against you because the nearer you are to expiration, the nearer you'll be to making your maximum loss.

Appropriate Time Period to Trade

■ It's safest to trade this strategy on a short-term basis, preferably with one month or less to expiration.

Selecting the Stock

■ Choose from stocks with adequate liquidity, preferably over 500,000 Average Daily Volume (ADV).

■ Try to ensure that the trend is downward or rangebound and identify a clear area of resistance well below the lower strike price.

Selecting the Options

■ Choose options with adequate liquidity; open interest should be at least 100, preferably 500.

■ **Lower Strike**—Try to give yourself at least 10% cushion above the current stock price; the level of cushion will depend on how close you are to the relevant expiration date.

■ **Higher Strike**—Typically $5.00 above the lower strike, but it can be $2.50 above or more. The key is to try to find a decent cushion for protection while also securing a decent yield, preferably over 10%, which typically means around $0.50 net credit for a $5.00 spread between the strikes.

■ **Expiration**—One month or less. Use the same expiration date for both legs.

2.4.3 Risk Profile

■ **Maximum Risk**   [Difference in strikes − net credit]

■ **Maximum Reward**   [Net credit received]

■ **Breakeven**   [Lower strike + net credit]

2.4.4 Greeks

Key:
Expiration   ....
Today – 1 month ————
Time(t) – 5 days   – – –

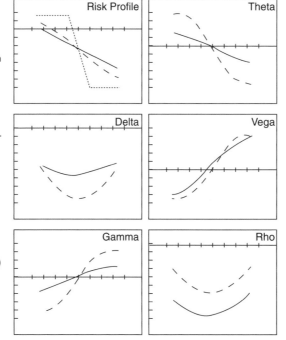

Risk Profile
As the stock price rises, the Bear Call moves into loss and reaches the maximum loss when the stock rises to the higher strike price.

Theta
Time decay is harmful to the position when it is profitable and helpful when it is unprofitable.

Delta
Delta (speed) is negative and is at its fastest in between the strikes. Notice how Delta slows down when the position is deep ITM or OTM.

Vega
Volatility is helpful to the position when it is unprofitable and harmful when it is profitable.

Gamma
Gamma (acceleration) peaks above the upper (bought) strike and peaks inversely below the lower (sold) strike.

Rho
Higher interest rates are generally unhelpful to the position.

2.4.5 Advantages and Disadvantages

Advantages

- Short-term income strategy not necessarily requiring any movement of the stock.

- Capped downside protection compared to a Naked Call.

Disadvantages

- Maximum loss is typically greater than the maximum gain, despite the capped downside.

- High yielding trades tend to mean less protective cushion and are therefore riskier.

- Capped upside if the stock falls.

2.4.6 Exiting the Trade

Exiting the Position

- With this strategy, you can simply unravel the spread by buying back the calls you sold and selling the calls you bought in the first place.

Mitigating a Loss

- Unravel the trade as described previously.

- Advanced traders may choose to only partially unravel the spread leg-by-leg. In this way, they will leave one leg of the spread exposed in order to attempt to profit from it.

2.4.7 Example

ABCD is trading at $28.00 on May 12, 2004.

Sell the June 2004 30 strike call for 1.00.

Buy the June 2004 35 strike call for 0.50.

Net Credit	Premium sold − premium bought **1.00 − 0.50 = 0.50**
Maximum Risk	Difference in strikes − net credit **5.00 − 0.50 = 4.50** Maximum risk is greater than your net credit
Maximum Reward	Net credit **0.50**
Breakeven	Lower strike + net credit **30.00 + 0.50 = 30.50**
Max ROI	11.11%
Cushion	$2.50 or 8.93% from breakeven

2.5 Long Iron Butterfly

Proficiency	Direction	Volatility	Asset Legs	Max Risk	Max Reward	Strategy Type
Intermediate	Neutral	Low	■ Long Put ■ Short Put ■ Short Call ■ Long Call	Capped	Capped	Income

2.5.1 Description

The Long Iron Butterfly is an intermediate strategy that can be profitable for stocks that are rangebound. It is, in fact, the combination of a Bull Put Spread and a Bear Call Spread. The higher strike put shares the same strike as the lower strike call to create the butterfly shape. The combination of two income strategies also makes this an income strategy. Often, traders will leg into the Long Iron Butterfly, first trading a Bull Put Spread just below support and then as the stock rebounds off resistance adding a Bear Call Spread, thereby creating the Long Iron Butterfly.

Ideally the stock will remain between the lower and higher strikes, with the maximum profit occurring if the options expire when the stock is priced at the central strike price. In this ideal scenario, effectively all the options expire worthless, and you just keep the combined net credit. The combined net credit serves to widen the area of your breakevens—in other words, the Bull Put element helps the Bear Call element, and vice versa.

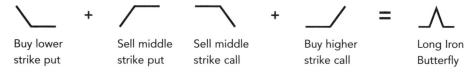

| Buy lower strike put | Sell middle strike put | Sell middle strike call | Buy higher strike call | Long Iron Butterfly |

Steps to Trading a Long Iron Butterfly

1. Buy one lower strike (OTM) put.

2. Sell one middle strike (ATM) put.

3. Sell one middle strike (ATM) call.

4. Buy one higher strike (OTM) call.

   ■ All options share the same expiration date for this strategy.

   ■ For this strategy, you must use both calls and puts. A Long Iron Butterfly is the combination of a Bull Put Spread and a Bear Call Spread.

   ■ The short put and the short call share the same middle (ATM) strike price.

   ■ Remember that there should be equal distance between each strike price, while the stock price should generally be as close as possible to the middle strike price.

Steps In

   ■ Try to ensure that the trend is rangebound and identify clear areas of support and resistance.

Steps Out

   ■ Manage your position according to the rules defined in your Trading Plan.

   ■ Remember that the Long Iron Butterfly is a combination of other strategies, so it can be unraveled in two-leg chunks.

   ■ You can unravel the position just before expiration—remember to include all the commissions in your calculations.

2.5.2 Context

Outlook

- With Long Iron Butterflies, your outlook is **direction neutral.** You expect little movement in the stock price.

Rationale

- With Long Iron Butterflies, you are looking to execute a potentially high yielding trade at a net credit whereby your maximum profits occur where the stock finishes around the middle strike price at expiration.

- You are anticipating low volatility with the stock price, which will lead you to profit.

- If you examine what you've done here, you have simply combined a Bull Put Spread with a Bear Call Spread, both of which are net credit spreads. It can also be seen as a narrow Short Straddle, combined with a wider Long Strangle.

Net Position

- This is a **net credit** trade.

- Your maximum risk is the difference between any two strikes less your net credit. (Remember that all the different strike prices are equidistant to each other.) Your maximum reward is the net credit you receive.

Effect of Time Decay

- Time decay is helpful to this position when it is profitable and harmful when the position is unprofitable. When you enter the trade, typically the stock price will be in the profitable area of the risk profile, so from that perspective, time decay harms the position.

Appropriate Time Period to Trade

- It's safest to trade this strategy on a short-term basis, preferably with one month or less to expiration.

Selecting the Stock

- Choose from stocks with adequate liquidity, preferably over 500,000 Average Daily Volume (ADV).

- Try to ensure that the trend is rangebound and identify clear areas of support and resistance.

Selecting the Options

- Choose options with adequate liquidity; open interest should be at least 100, preferably 500.

■ **Lower Strike**—Below the current stock price (or below where you think the stock will be at expiration).

■ **Middle Strike**—As close to ATM (or where you think the stock will be at expiration) as possible.

■ **Higher Strike**—The same distance above the middle strike as the lower is below it; use online tools to find the optimum yields and breakeven points at and before expiration.

■ **Expiration**—One month or less. Use the same expiration date for all legs.

2.5.3 Risk Profile

■ **Maximum Risk**   [Difference in adjacent strikes − net credit]

■ **Maximum Reward**   [Net credit received]

■ **Breakeven Down**   [Middle strike − net credit]

■ **Breakeven Up**   [Middle strike + net credit]

2.5.4 Greeks

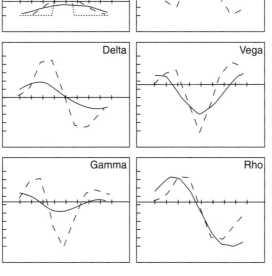

Key:
Expiration   ....
Today – 3 months ———
Time(t) – 1 month – – -

Risk Profile
As the stock price remains rangebound, the position is profitable, with maximum profit occurring at the middle strike price.

Delta
Delta (speed) is at its greatest the outer strikes and is zero around the middle strike.

Gamma
Gamma (acceleration) peaks positively outside the outer strikes and peaks inversely around the middle strike, highlighting the position's major turning point and middle Delta neutral point.

Theta
Time decay is helpful to the position when it is profitable and unhelpful when it is unprofitable.

Vega
Volatility is generally unhelpful to the position unless the stock moves outside the outer strikes.

Rho
Higher interest rates are generally helpful to the position when the stock price is lower and vice versa.

2.5.5 Advantages and Disadvantages

Advantages

- ■ Profit from a rangebound stock for no cost and low downside risk.

- ■ Capped and low risk compared with potential reward.

- ■ Comparatively high profit potential if the stock remains rangebound.

Disadvantages

- ■ The higher profit potential comes with a narrower range between the wing strikes.

- ■ The higher profit potential only comes nearer expiration.

- ■ Bid/Ask Spread can adversely affect the quality of the trade.

2.5.6 Exiting the Trade

Exiting the Position

- ■ With this strategy, you can simply unravel the spread by buying back the options you sold and selling the options you bought in the first place.

- ■ Advanced traders may leg up and down or only partially unravel the spread as the underlying asset fluctuates up and down. In this way the trader will be taking smaller incremental profits before the expiration of the trade.

Mitigating a Loss

- ■ Unravel the trade as described previously.

- ■ Advanced traders may choose to only partially unravel the spread leg-by-leg and create alternative risk profiles.

2.5.7 Example

ABCD is trading at $25.00 on April 12, 2004.

Buy the May 2004 20 strike put for $0.30.

Sell the May 2004 25 strike put for $1.50.

Sell the May 2004 25 strike call for $2.00.

Buy the May 2004 30 strike call for $0.50.

Net Credit	Premiums sold − premiums bought **2.70**
Maximum Risk	Difference in adjacent strikes − net credit **5.00 − 2.70 = 2.30**
Maximum Reward	Net credit **2.70**
Breakeven Down	Middle strike − net credit **25.00 − 2.70 = 22.30**
Breakeven Up	Middle strike + net credit **25.00 + 2.70 = 27.70**
Max RO	117.39% if the stock is at the middle strike at expiration

2.6 Long Iron Condor

Proficiency	Direction	Volatility	Asset Legs	Max Risk	Max Reward	Strategy Type
Intermediate	Neutral	Low	■ Long Put ■ Short Put ■ Short Call ■ Long Call	Capped	Capped	Income

2.6.1 Description

The Long Iron Condor is an intermediate strategy that can be profitable for stocks that are rangebound. A variation of the Long Iron Butterfly, it is in fact the combination of a Bull Put Spread and a Bear Call Spread. The higher strike put is lower than the lower strike call in order to create the condor shape. The combination of two income strategies also makes this an income strategy. Traders often will leg into the Long Iron Condor, first trading a Bull Put Spread just below support and then as the stock rebounds off resistance adding a Bear Call Spread, thereby creating the Long Iron Condor.

Ideally the stock will remain between the two middle strikes, with the maximum profit occurring if the options expire between these. In this ideal scenario, effectively all the options expire worthless, and you just keep the combined net credit. The combined net credit serves to widen the area of your breakevens—in other words, the Bull Put element helps the Bear Call element, and vice versa.

| Buy lower strike put | + | Sell middle lower strike put | + | Sell middle higher strike call | + | Buy higher strike call | = | Long Iron Condor |

Steps to Trading a Long Iron Condor

1. Buy one lower strike (OTM) put.

2. Sell one lower middle strike (OTM) put.

3. Sell one higher middle strike (OTM) call.

4. Buy one higher strike (OTM) call.

- All options share the same expiration date for this strategy.

- For this strategy, you must use both calls and puts. A Long Iron Condor is the combination of a Bull Put Spread and a Bear Call Spread.

- The short put strike is lower than the short call strike.

- Remember that there should be equal distance between each strike price, while the stock price should generally be between the two middle strikes.

Steps In

- Try to ensure that the trend is rangebound and identify clear areas of support and resistance.

Steps Out

- Manage your position according to the rules defined in your Trading Plan.

- Remember the Long Iron Condor is a combination of other strategies, so it can be unraveled in two-leg chunks.

- You can unravel the position just before expiration—remember to include all the commissions in your calculations.

2.6.2 Context

Outlook

- With Long Iron Condors, your outlook is **direction neutral.** You expect little movement in the stock price.

Rationale

- With Long Iron Condors, you are looking to execute a potentially high-yielding trade at a net credit, whereby your maximum profits occur where the stock finishes between the middle strikes at expiration.

■ You are anticipating low volatility with the stock price, which will lead you to profit.

■ If you examine what you've done here, you have simply combined a Bull Put Spread with a Bear Call Spread, both of which are net credit spreads. It can also be seen as a narrow Short Strangle combined with a wider Long Strangle.

Net Position

■ This is a **net credit** trade.

■ Your maximum risk is the difference between any two strikes less your net credit. (Remember that the all the different strike prices are equidistant to each other.) Your maximum reward is the net credit you receive.

Effect of Time Decay

■ Time decay is helpful to this position when it is profitable and harmful when the position is unprofitable. When you enter the trade, typically the stock price will be in the profitable area of the risk profile, so from that perspective, time decay harms the position.

Appropriate Time Period to Trade

■ It's safest to trade this strategy on a short-term basis, preferably with one month or less to expiration.

Selecting the Stock

■ Choose from stocks with adequate liquidity, preferably over 500,000 Average Daily Volume (ADV).

■ Try to ensure that the trend is rangebound and identify clear areas of support and resistance.

Selecting the Options

■ Choose options with adequate liquidity; open interest should be at least 100, preferably 500.

■ **Lower (put) Strikes**—Below the current stock price (or below where you think the stock will be at expiration).

■ **Higher (call) Strikes**—Above the current stock price (or above where you think the stock will be at expiration).

■ **Expiration**—One month or less. Use the same expiration date for all legs.

2.6.3 Risk Profile

- **Maximum Risk**   [Difference in adjacent strikes − net credit]

- **Maximum Reward**   [Net credit received]

- **Breakeven Down**   [Middle short put strike − net credit]

- **Breakeven Up**   [Middle short call strike + net credit]

2.6.4 Greeks

Key:
Expiration   ············
Today – 3 months   ——————
Time(t) – 1 month   – – – –

Risk Profile
As the stock price remains rangebound, the position is profitable, with maximum profit occurring between the middle strikes.

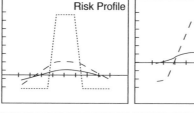

Theta
Time decay is helpful to the position when it is profitable and unhelpful when it is unprofitable.

Delta
Delta (speed) is at its greatest the outer strikes and is zero between the middle strikes.

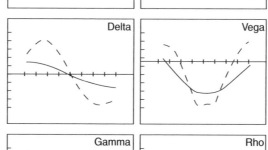

Vega
Volatility is generally unhelpful to the position unless the stock moves outside the outer strikes.

Gamma
Gamma (acceleration) peaks positively outside the outer strikes and peaks inversely around the middle strikes, highlighting the position's major turning point and middle Delta neutral point.

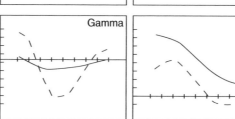

Rho
Higher interest rates are generally helpful to the position when the stock price is lower and vice versa.

2.6.5 Advantages and Disadvantages

Advantages

- Profit from a rangebound stock for no cost and low downside risk.

- Capped and low risk compared with potential reward.

- Comparatively high profit potential if the stock remains rangebound.

Disadvantages

- The higher profit potential comes with a narrower range between the wing strikes.

- The higher profit potential only comes nearer expiration.

- Bid/Ask Spread can adversely affect the quality of the trade.

2.6.6 Exiting the Trade

Exiting the Position

- With this strategy, you can simply unravel the spread by buying back the options you sold and selling the options you bought in the first place.

- Advanced traders may leg up and down or only partially unravel the spread as the underlying asset fluctuates up and down. In this way, the trader will be taking smaller incremental profits before the expiration of the trade.

Mitigating a Loss

- Unravel the trade as described previously.

- Advanced traders may choose to only partially unravel the spread leg-by-leg and create alternative risk profiles.

2.6.7 Example

ABCD is trading at $27.50 on April 12, 2004.

Buy the May 2004 20 strike put for $0.25.

Sell the May 2004 25 strike put for $1.25.

Sell the May 2004 30 strike call for $1.30.

Buy the May 2004 35 strike call for $0.35.

Net Credit	Premiums sold − premiums bought **1.95**
Maximum Risk	Difference in adjacent strikes − net credit **5.00 − 1.95 = 3.05**
Maximum Reward	Net credit **1.95**
Breakeven Down	Lower middle strike − net credit **25.00 − 1.95 = 23.05**
Breakeven Up	Upper middle strike + net credit **30.00 + 1.95 = 31.95**
Max ROI	63.93% if the stock is between the middle strikes at expiration

2.7 Covered Short Straddle

Proficiency	Direction	Volatility	Asset Legs	Max Risk	Max Reward	Strategy Type
(icon)	(icon)	N/A	(icon) + (icon)	(icon)	(icon)	(icon)
			+ (icon)			
Advanced	Bullish		■ Long Stock	Uncapped	Capped	Income
			■ Short Put			
			■ Short Call			

2.7.1 Description

The Covered Short Straddle is the most risky type of income strategy and is not recommended!

The concept is to increase the yield of the Covered Call by selling a put at the same strike as the sold call. In this way, we take in the additional income from the sold put; however, there is a significant price to pay in terms of risk.

First, the sold put adds significant extra risk to the trade. The amount of potential risk added is the put strike less the put premium received. Say if we trade a Covered Call on a $24.00 stock, taking in $1.00 for the call, our risk and breakeven is $23.00. If we sold a put for another $1.00, our initial yield on cash would be doubled . . . but our risk would have increased by another $24.00 ($25.00 − $1.00), making our total risk $47.00 if the stock falls to zero. Although this is unlikely to occur in just one month, the position can become loss-making at approximately double the speed as a simple Covered Call position, so if the stock starts to fall, we're in trouble much more quickly.

Second, with a Covered Short Straddle, we are almost certain to be exercised because we have shorted both the put and the call at the same strike price. So unless the stock is at the strike price at expiration, we face a certain exercise, which many people are uncomfortable with. If the stock is above the strike at expiration, then we're quite happy because our sold put expires worthless, our sold call is exercised, and we simply deliver the stock we already own. However, if the stock is below the strike at expiration, then our call expires worthless, our sold put is exercised, and we are required to purchase more stock at the strike price. With a falling stock, this can be pricey and undesirable.

I've seen this taught as a viable strategy . . . *don't* do it! There are better ways to enhance the income of a Covered Call, which we'll go through later in this chapter!

| Buy stock | Sell put | Sell call | Covered Short Straddle |

Steps to Trading a Covered Short Straddle

1. Buy (or own) the stock.

2. Sell puts with a strike price lower than where you think the stock will be at expiration.

3. Sell calls with the same strike and expiration.

   ▪ Generally, only sell the straddle element on a monthly basis. In this way you will capture more in premiums over several months, provided you are not exercised. Selling premium every month will net you more over a period of time than selling premium a long way out. Remember that whenever you are selling options premium, time decay works in your favor. Time decay is at its fastest rate in the last 20 trading days (i.e., the last month), so when you sell option premiums, it is best to sell them with a month left, and do it again the following month.

   ▪ Remember that your maximum gain is capped when the stock reaches the level of the (call) strike price.

   ▪ You need to ensure that the strike price is below the level at which you think the stock will be at expiration; otherwise the sold put will be exercised, and you'll have to buy more stock.

   ▪ If trading U.S. stocks and options, you will be required to buy (or be long in) 100 shares for every options contract that you sell.

Steps In

▪ Preferably between $10.00 and $50.00. Above $50.00, it would be expensive.

▪ Try to ensure that the trend is upward or rangebound and identify a clear area of support.

Steps Out

▪ Manage your position according to the rules defined in your Trading Plan.

▪ If the stock closes above the strike at expiration, your call will be exercised. You will deliver the stock at the strike price, and you will have profited from both the option premiums you received and the uplift (if any) in stock price to reach the strike price. Exercise is automatic.

▪ If the stock remains or falls below the strike, your put will be exercised, forcing you to buy more shares at the strike price. This could become expensive.

▪ If the stock is resting at the strike price at expiration, then you'll make a profit—but this is a highly risky strategy, and it's unlikely that the stock will close precisely on the strike price anyway.

2.7.2 Context

Outlook

■ With covered short straddles, your outlook is **bullish.** You expect a steady rise.

Rationale

■ With covered short straddles, you are enhancing the yield of a covered call by introducing the sale of puts in addition to the calls you have sold against the stock you have bought. This has the effect of increasing your yield.

■ The hope is that if the stock rises, your sold puts will expire worthless, and you will keep the premium, whereas if your calls are exercised, you already own the stock to deliver. The biggest problem is if the stock plummets—your sold calls will expire worthless, enabling you to keep the premium, but you will be exercised on your sold puts, in which case you will have to buy more stock. Therefore, only use this strategy on stocks that you want to continue holding and adding to your position. This is a high-risk strategy.

Net Position

■ This is a **net debit** transaction because you are paying for the stock and are only taking in small premiums for the sold put and call options. You can increase your yield by purchasing the stock on margin, thereby doubling your yield if you use 50% margin—this is even more risky, however, if the stock falls below the strike price.

■ Your maximum risk is the price you pay for the stock, plus the (put) strike price, less the premiums you receive for the sold call and put. This is high-risk.

Effect of Time Decay

■ Time decay is helpful to your trade here because it should erode the value of the options you sold.

Appropriate Time Period to Trade

■ Sell the options on a monthly basis.

Selecting the Stock

■ Choose from stocks with adequate liquidity, preferably over 500,000 Average Daily Volume (ADV).

■ Preferably between $10.00 and $50.00. Above $50.00, it would be expensive to buy the stock.

■ Try to ensure that the trend is upward or rangebound and identify a clear area of support.

Selecting the Option

- Choose options with adequate liquidity; open interest should be at least 100, preferably 500.

- **Strike**—Choose a strike that you feel is lower than where the stock will be at expiration. You do not want the put to be exercised because it means you'll have to buy more stock, which could be very expensive.

- **Expiration**—Look at either of the next two expirations and compare monthly yields. Use the same expiration date for both put and call. Look for over 5% monthly initial cash yield.

2.7.3 Risk Profile

- **Maximum Risk**   [Stock price paid + strike price − put premium − call premium]

- **Maximum Reward**   Limited to the premiums received for the sold calls and puts plus [the strike price] less [the purchase price of the stock]

- **Breakeven**   The [strike price] less [half of the options premiums received] plus [half of the difference between the stock price and the strike price]

2.7.4 Greeks

Key:
Expiration   ....
Today − 1 month   ————
Time(t) − 5 days   − − -

Risk Profile
As the stock price rises above the strike price, the position reaches its maximum profit potential. As the stock falls below the strike, the position falls at twice the speed because of the sold puts.

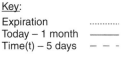
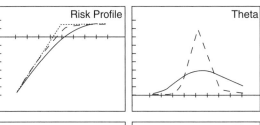

Theta
Theta is positive, illustrating that time decay is helpful to the position.

Delta
Delta (speed) is positive and falls to zero as the asset price rises above the strike price where the maximum profit is achieved and the position speed slows down.

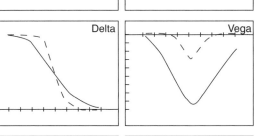

Vega
Vega is negative, illustrating that volatility is harmful to the position.

Gamma
Gamma (acceleration) is always negative with this position because you are a net seller of options.

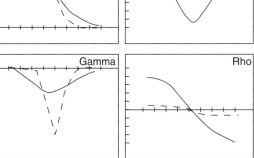

Rho
Higher interest rates are harmful to the position when it is profitable and helpful when the position is unprofitable.

2.7.5 Advantages and Disadvantages

Advantages

- Generate monthly income.

- Greater income potential than a Covered Call.

Disadvantages

- Very risky if the stock falls. The sold put means that the risk is effectively doubled, and the rate at which you lose money in the event of the stock declining is also doubled.

- Unless the stock price is at the strike price at expiration, you face certain exercise of either the put or call. If the stock falls and the put is exercised, you'll have to buy more stock at the strike price.

- Expensive strategy in terms of cash outlay.

- Capped upside if the stock rises.

- Uncapped downside potential. This is *not* a recommended strategy.

2.7.6 Exiting the Trade

Exiting the Position

- If the share rises above the (call) strike price, you will be exercised at expiration (or before) and therefore make a profit.

- If the share falls below the (put) strike price, you will be exercised at expiration (or before) and will have to buy more stock at the put exercise price. Your sold calls will expire worthless, and you will keep the premium.

- If the share is at the strike price at expiration, you will have successfully reduced your cost of entry because the premiums you took in will offset the price you paid for the stock. You will retain the option premiums you sold because they will both expire worthless.

Mitigating a Loss

- Either sell the share or sell the share and buy back the call option you sold. If the put is exercised, then you will be required to buy the stock at the put strike price.

- Please note that Covered Short Straddles are highly risky, and you should ensure that you have enough cash in your account to fulfill the exercise obligations you may have on the downside.

2.7.7 Example

ABCD is trading at $28.20 on February 25, 2004.

Buy the stock for $28.20.

Sell the March 2004 30 strike put for $2.60.

Sell the March 2004 30 strike call for $0.90.

You Pay	Stock price − option premiums **28.20 − 2.60 − 0.90 = 24.70**
Maximum Risk	Stock price + put strike − put premium − call premium **28.20 + 30.00 − 2.60 − 0.90 = 54.70** Maximum risk of 54.70 is more than double your net debit here!
Maximum Reward	Limited to the options premiums received + the strike price − the stock price paid **0.90 + 2.60 + 30.00 − 28.20 = 5.30**
Breakeven	Strike price − half the premiums received + half the difference between stock price and strike price **29.15**
Initial Cash Yield	12.41%
Maximum Yield on Risk	6.40%

2.8 Covered Short Strangle

Proficiency	Direction	Volatility	Asset Legs	Max Risk	Max Reward	Strategy Type
		N/A	⊘ + ⌒	☠		ⓢ
			+ ⌒			
Advanced	Bullish		■ Long Stock	Uncapped	Capped	Income
			■ Short Put			
			■ Short Call			

2.8.1 Description

The Covered Short Strangle is another risky income strategy, though it is certainly an improvement on the Covered Short Straddle.

The concept is to increase the yield of the Covered Call by selling an OTM (lower strike) put. In this way we take in the additional income from the sold put; however, if the stock price falls below the put strike, there is a significant price to pay in terms of risk.

The sold put adds significant extra risk to the trade. The amount of potential risk added is the put strike less the put premium received. Say if we trade a Covered Call on a $24.00 stock, taking in $1.00 for the $25 strike call, our risk and breakeven is $23.00. If we sold a $22.50 strike put for another $1.00, our initial yield on cash would be doubled . . . but our risk would have increased by another $21.50 ($22.50 − $1.00), making our total risk $44.50 if the stock falls to zero. Although this is unlikely to occur in just one month, the position can become loss-making at approximately double the speed as a simple Covered Call position, so if the stock starts to fall, we can be in trouble much more quickly.

If the stock falls below the put strike at expiration, the call will expire worthless (so we keep the premium), the put will be exercised, and we'll have to buy more stock at the put strike price. With a falling stock, this can be pricey and undesirable. If the stock is above the call strike at expiration, then we're happy because our sold put expires worthless, our sold call is exercised, and we simply deliver the stock we already own.

I've seen Wall Street traders use this strategy for their own devices without realizing the downside risk to which they were exposing themselves. Although this is far preferable to the Covered Short Straddle, there are still better ways to enhance the income of a Covered Call, which we'll go through later in this chapter.

Buy stock   Sell OTM put   Sell OTM call   Covered Short Strangle

Steps to Trading a Covered Short Strangle

1. Buy (or own) the stock.

2. Sell OTM (lower strike) puts with a strike price lower than where you think the stock will be at expiration.

3. Sell OTM (higher strike) calls with the same expiration date.

   ■ Generally, only sell the strangle element on a monthly basis. In this way you will capture more in premiums over several months, provided you are not exercised. Selling premium every month will net you more over a period of time than selling premium a long way out. Remember that whenever you are selling options premium, time decay works in your favor. Time decay is at its fastest rate in the last 20 trading days (i.e., the last month), so when you sell option premiums, it is best to sell it with a month left, and do it again the following month.

   ■ Remember that your maximum gain is capped when the stock reaches the level of the call's strike price.

   ■ You need to ensure that the put strike price is OTM and below the level at which you think the stock will be at expiration; otherwise the sold put will be exercised, and you'll have to buy more stock at the put strike price.

   ■ If trading U.S. stocks and options, you will be required to buy (or be long in) 100 shares for every options contract that you sell.

Steps In

■ Preferably between $10.00 and $50.00. Above $50.00, it would be expensive to buy the stock.

■ Try to ensure that the trend is upward or rangebound and identify a clear area of support.

Steps Out

■ Manage your position according to the rules defined in your Trading Plan.

■ If the stock closes above the call strike at expiration, your call will be exercised. You will deliver the stock at the strike price and will have profited from both the option premiums you received and the uplift (if any) in stock price to reach the strike price. Exercise is automatic.

■ If the stock falls below the put strike, your put will be exercised, forcing you to buy more shares at the put strike price. This could become expensive.

■ If the stock is resting between the strike prices at expiration, then you'll keep the premiums, but this is a dangerous strategy and is not recommended because of the downside risk.

2.8.2 Context

Outlook

■ With covered short strangles, your outlook is **bullish.** You expect a steady rise.

Rationale

■ With covered short strangles, you are enhancing the yield of a covered call by introducing the sale of OTM puts in addition to the calls you have sold against the stock you have bought. This has the effect of increasing your (monthly) yield.

■ The hope is that if the stock rises, your sold puts will expire worthless, and you will keep the premium, whereas if your calls are exercised, you already own the stock to deliver. The biggest problem is that if the stock plummets, your sold calls will expire worthless, enabling you to keep the premium, but you could be exercised on your sold puts, in which case you will have to buy more stock. Therefore, only use this strategy on stocks that you want to continue holding and adding to your position.

Net Position

■ With stocks, this is a **net debit** transaction because you are paying for the stock and only taking in small premiums for the sold put and call options. You can increase your yield by purchasing the stock on margin, thereby doubling your yield if you use 50% margin.

■ Your maximum risk is the price you pay for the stock, plus the put strike price, less the premiums you receive for the sold call and put. This is a high-risk strategy.

Effect of Time Decay

■ Time decay is helpful to your trade here because it will erode the value of the options you sold. Provided that the stock remains between the strikes at expiration, you will be able to retain both premiums, thus reducing your original cost of buying the share.

Appropriate Time Period to Trade

■ Sell the options on a monthly basis.

Selecting the Stock

■ Choose from stocks with adequate liquidity, preferably over 500,000 Average Daily Volume (ADV).

■ Preferably between $10.00 and $50.00. Above $50.00, it would be expensive to buy the stock.

■ Try to ensure that the trend is upward or rangebound and identify a clear area of support.

Selecting the Option

■ Choose options with adequate liquidity; open interest should be at least 100, preferably 500.

■ **Put Strike**—Look for OTM strike below the current stock price.

■ **Call Strike**—Look for OTM strike above the current stock price.

■ **Expiration**—Look for either of the next two expirations and compare monthly yields. Use the same expiration date for both put and call. Look for over 5% monthly initial cash yield.

2.8.3 Risk Profile

■ **Maximum Risk**	[Stock price paid + put strike price − put premium − call premium]
■ **Maximum Reward**	Limited to the premiums received for the sold calls and puts + call strike price − the purchase price of the stock
■ **Breakeven**	Varies depending on the relationship between the stock price, premiums received, and the strikes

2.8.4 Greeks

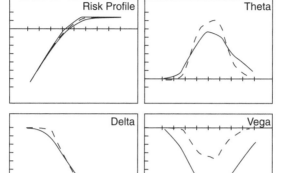

Key:
Expiration   ....
Today – 1 month   ——————
Time(t) – 2 weeks   – – -

Risk Profile
As the stock price rises above the call strike, the position reaches its maximum profit potential. As the stock falls below the put strike, the position falls at twice the speed because of the sold puts.

Delta
Delta (speed) is positive and falls to zero as the asset price rises above the call strike where the maximum profit is achieved and the position speed slows down.

Gamma
Gamma (acceleration) is always negative with this position because you are a net seller of options.

Theta
Theta is positive, illustrating that time decay is helpful to the position.

Vega
Vega is negative, illustrating that volatility is harmful to the position.

Rho
Higher interest rates are harmful to the position when it is profitable and helpful when the position is unprofitable.

2.8.5 Advantages and Disadvantages

Advantages

- Generate monthly income.
- Greater income potential than a Covered Call.
- Less risky than a Covered Short Straddle.

Disadvantages

- Risky if the stock falls. The sold put means that the risk is effectively doubled, and the rate at which you lose money in the event of the stock declining is also doubled.
- Unless the stock price is between the strike prices at expiration, you face exercise of either the put or call. If the stock falls and the put is exercised, you'll have to buy more stock at the strike price.

- Expensive strategy in terms of cash outlay.

- Capped upside if the stock rises.

- Uncapped downside potential. This is not a recommended strategy.

2.8.6 Exiting the Trade

Exiting the Position

- If the share rises above the call strike price, you will be exercised at expiration (or before) and therefore make a profit.

- If the share falls below the put strike price, you will be exercised at expiration (or before) and will have to buy more stock at the put exercise price. Your sold calls will expire worthless, and you will keep the premium.

- If the share stays between the strike prices, you will have successfully reduced your cost of entry because the premiums you took in will offset the price you paid for the stock. You will retain the entire option premiums you sold because they will expire worthless.

Mitigating a Loss

- Either sell the share or sell the share and buy back the call option you sold. If the put is exercised, then you will be required to buy the stock at the put strike price.

- Please note that covered short strangles are risky, and you should ensure that you have enough cash in your account to fulfill the exercise obligations you may have on the downside.

2.8.7 Example

ABCD is trading at $28.20 on February 25, 2004.

Buy the stock for $28.20.

Sell the March 2004 27.50 strike put for $1.20.

Sell the March 2004 30 strike call for $0.90.

You Pay	Stock price − option premiums **28.20 − 1.20 − 0.90 = 26.10**
Maximum Risk	Stock price + put strike − put premium − call premium **28.20 + 27.50 − 1.20 − 0.90 = 53.60** Maximum risk of 53.60 is more than double your net debit here!
Maximum Reward	Limited to the options premiums received + the call strike price less − the stock price paid **0.90 + 1.20 + 30.00 − 28.20 = 3.90**
Breakeven	**26.80**
Initial Cash Yield	7.45%
Maximum Yield on Risk	3.92%

2.9 Calendar Call

Proficiency	Direction	Volatility	Asset Legs	Max Risk	Max Reward	Strategy Type
Intermediate	Bullish	N/A	■ Long Call ■ Short Call	Capped	Capped	Income

2.9.1 Description

Calendar spreads are known as *horizontal spreads*, and the Calendar Call is a variation of a Covered Call, where you substitute the long stock with a long-term long call option instead. This has the effect of radically reducing the investment, thereby increasing the initial yield. However, this initial yield is not necessarily reflective of the maximum yield at the expiration of the short-term short call. The maximum yield will depend on both the stock price and the residual value of the long unexpired call.

The problem with a Calendar Call is in the very essence of the *shape* of the risk profile (see the following). What we'd like to do is create something similar to a Covered Call, but with a better yield and without the expense. The Calendar Call certainly requires less investment; however, the shape is different. If the stock rises too far too soon, then the Calendar Call can become loss-making. So even though you got the direction of the trade right, you could still lose money! This happens because the long call, being near the money, only moves at around half the speed as the underlying stock as the stock price rises. This means that in the event of exercise, if the stock has risen by, say, $10.00 from $30.00, and your option has only risen by $5.00, you may be exercised on the short call; therefore you buy the stock at $40.00 and sell it at $30.00 (if that was the strike), yet your long call has only risen by $5.00, giving you a $5.00 loss. If you only received $2.00 for the short call, you're looking at a $3.00 loss on the trade.

Both options share the same strike, so if the stock rises above the strike, your short call will be exercised. You'll then have to sell the long call (hopefully for a profit), use the proceeds to buy the stock at the market price, and then sell it back at the strike price. Therefore, the best thing that can happen is that the stock is at the strike price at the first expiration. This will enable you to write another call for the following month if you like.

Buy call   Sell call   Calendar Call

Steps to Trading a Calendar Call

1. Buy a long-term expiration call with a near the money strike price.

2. Sell a short-term call (say monthly) with the same strike price.

Steps In

■ Try to ensure that the trend is upward or rangebound and identify clear areas of support and resistance.

Steps Out

■ Manage your position according to the rules defined in your Trading Plan.

■ If the stock closes above the strike at expiration, you will be exercised. You will sell your long call, buy the stock at the market price, and deliver it at the strike price, having profited from both the short option premium you received and the uplift in the long option premium. Exercise of the short option is automatic. Do not exercise the long option or you will forfeit its time value.

■ If the stock remains below the strike but above your higher stop loss, let the short call expire worthless and keep the entire premium. You can then write another call for the following month.

■ If the stock falls below your lower stop loss, then either sell the long option (if you're approved for naked call writing) or reverse the entire position.

2.9.2 Context

Outlook

■ With a Calendar Call, your outlook is **neutral to bullish.** You expect a steady rise.

Rationale

■ To generate income against your longer term long position by selling calls and receiving the premium.

Net Position

■ This is a **net debit** transaction because your bought calls will be more expensive than your sold calls, which have less time value.

■ Your maximum risk on the trade itself is limited to the net debit of the bought calls less the sold calls. Your maximum reward is limited to the residual call value when the stock is at the strike price at the first expiration, less the net debit.

Effect of Time Decay

■ Time decay affects your Calendar Call trade in a mixed fashion. It erodes the value of the long call but helps you with your income strategy by eroding the value faster on the short call.

Appropriate Time Period to Trade

■ You will be safest to choose a long time to expiration with the long call and a short time (one month) for the short call.

Selecting the Stock

■ Choose from stocks with adequate liquidity, preferably over 500,000 Average Daily Volume (ADV).

■ Try to ensure that the trend is upward or rangebound and identify clear areas of support and resistance.

Selecting the Option

■ Choose options with adequate liquidity; open interest should be at least 100, preferably 500.

■ **Strike**—Look for either the ATM or just OTM (higher) strike above the current stock. If you're bullish, then choose a higher strike; if neutral, choose the ATM strike.

■ **Expiration**—Look at either of the next two expirations for the short option and compare monthly yields. Look for over six months for the long option.

2.9.3 Risk Profile

■ **Maximum Risk**	Limited to the net debit paid
■ **Maximum Reward**	[Long call value at the time of the short call expiration, when the stock price is at the strike price] − [net debit]
■ **Breakeven Down**	Depends on the value of the long call option at the time of the short call expiration
■ **Breakeven Up**	Depends on the value of the long call option at the time of the short call expiration

2.9.4 Greeks

Key:
Expiration ....
Today – 1 month ——
Time(t) – 5 days – – -

Risk Profile
Maximum profit is achieved when the stock is at the strike price at the time of the short call expiration date. Any substantial move up or down is dangerous for the position.

Delta
Delta (speed) is at its fastest either side of the strike price, indicating the increasing speed of the position in one direction and then the other.

Gamma
Gamma (acceleration) peaks inversely around the strike price, showing where the Delta line is steepest.

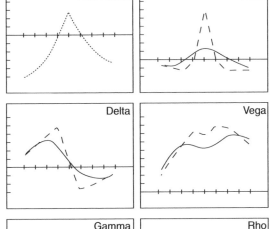

Theta
Theta is positive, illustrating that time decay is helpful to the position around the strike price, where the position is profitable. Time decay is not so helpful when the position is unprofitable.

Vega
Increasing volatility is helpful because it will mean the long call's residual value should be higher.

Rho
Higher interest rates become more helpful as the underlying asset price rises.

2.9.5 Advantages and Disadvantages

Advantages

■ Generate monthly income.

■ Can profit from rangebound stocks and make a higher yield than with a Covered Call.

Disadvantages

■ Capped upside if the stock rises.

■ Can lose on the upside if the stock rises significantly.

■ High yield does not necessarily mean a profitable or high probability profitable trade.

2.9.6 Exiting the Trade

Exiting the Position

- With this strategy, you can simply unravel the spread by buying back the calls you sold and selling the calls you bought in the first place.

- Advanced traders may leg up and down as the underlying asset fluctuates up and down. In this way, you can take incremental profits before the expiration of the trade.

Mitigating a Loss

- Unravel the trade as described previously.

- Advanced traders may choose to only partially unravel the spread leg-by-leg. In this way, they will leave one leg of the spread exposed in order to attempt to profit from it.

2.9.7 Example

ABCD is trading at $65.00 on May 5, 2004, with Historical Volatility at 30%.

- Buy January 2006 65 strike calls at $12.50.

- Sell June 2004 65 strike calls at $2.70.

At June Expiration

1. Scenario: stock falls to $60.00

Long calls worth approximately 8.40; loss so far = 4.10
Short calls expire worthless; profit 2.70

No exercise

Total position = 12.50 + 2.70 − 4.10 = 11.10 = loss of 1.40

2. Scenario: stock falls to $62.50

Long calls worth approximately 9.80; loss so far = 2.70
Short calls expire worthless; profit 2.70

No exercise

Total position = 12.50 + 2.70 − 2.70 = 0.00 = breakeven

3. Scenario: stock stays at $65.00

Long calls worth approximately 11.40; loss so far = 1.10
Short calls expire worthless; profit 2.70

No exercise

Total position = 12.50 + 2.70 − 1.10 = 14.10 = profit of 1.60

4. Scenario: stock rises to $70.00

Long calls worth approximately 14.80; profit so far = 2.30
Short calls expire $5.00 ITM

Procedure: sell bought calls; buy stock at current price and sell at strike price

Exercised at $65.00

Buy stock at 70.00
Sell stock at 65.00
Loss = 5.00

Sell long call for a profit = 2.30
Keep short call premium = 2.70
Loss on Exercise = 5.00

Total position = 0.00 breakeven

5. Scenario: stock rises to $75.00

Long calls worth approximately 18.35; profit so far = 5.85
Short calls expire $10.00 In the Money

Procedure: sell bought calls; buy stock at current price and sell at strike price

Exercised at $65.00

Buy stock at 75.00
Sell stock at 65.00
Loss = 10.00

Sell long call for a profit = 5.85
Keep short call premium = 2.70
Loss on Exercise = 10.00

Total position = 1.45 loss

If you tried to exercise the bought call:

Procedure: exercise bought calls at $65.00; deliver stock at $65.00 for exercised sold call

Buy call at 12.50
Sell call at 2.70
Net cost = 9.80

Buy stock at 65.00
Sell stock at 65.00
Net profit at 0.00

Total = 9.80 − $0.00 = loss of 9.80

Lesson: Never exercise a long-term option because you'll miss out on Time Value!

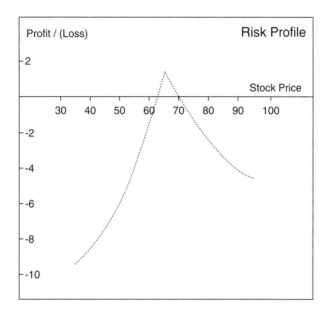

2.10 Diagonal Call

Proficiency	Direction	Volatility	Asset Legs	Max Risk	Max Reward	Strategy Type
		N/A	+			
Intermediate	Bullish		■ Long Call ■ Short Call	Capped	Capped	Income

2.10.1 Description

The Diagonal Call is a variation of a Covered Call where you substitute the long stock with a long-term deep In the Money long call option instead. This has the effect of reducing the investment, thereby increasing the initial yield. As with the Calendar Call, this initial yield is not necessarily reflective of the maximum yield at the expiration of the short-term short call. The maximum yield will depend on both the stock price and the residual value of the long unexpired call.

The Diagonal Call solves the problems experienced with the Calendar Call, in that the *shape* of the risk profile (see the following) is more akin to the Covered Call, which is what we want. Yet the Diagonal Call is going to be a far cheaper investment! If the stock rises explosively, then unlike the Calendar Call, the Diagonal Call done correctly won't become loss-making. The key is not to get too greedy!

Let's say we're looking to do a Diagonal Call on a $25.00 stock. The two-year $20.00 call is say, $7.50, and we sell next month's $27.50 call for $0.75, giving us an initial cash yield of 10%. If the share rises to $40.00, within the next month, our long call will be worth at least $22.00 ($20.00 intrinsic value alone!). We'll have to buy the stock for $40.00 and sell it at $20.00 (making a $20.00 loss), but we'll retain the $0.75 from the selling the short-term OTM option. Total position is still profitable by around $2.75.

At the end of this section, we'll go through a real example, but the main point is this: Because we're buying deep ITM calls, the long option will have a higher delta and will move more in step (dollar for dollar) with the stock as it rises. This means that the stock rising explosively won't damage our position, unlike with the Calendar Call.

The bought option is long-term and deep ITM, and the short option is short-term and OTM. If the stock rises above the higher (short) strike, your short call will be exercised. You'll then have to sell the long call (for a profit), use the proceeds to buy the stock at the market price, and then sell it back at the strike price. The maximum profit occurs where the stock is at the short call (higher) strike price at the first expiration.

Buy call   Sell call   Diagonal Call

Steps to Trading a Diagonal Call

1. Buy a deep ITM (lower strike) long-term expiration call.

2. Sell a higher strike short-term call (say monthly).

   Steps In

   ■ Try to ensure that the trend is upward or rangebound and identify a clear area of support.

   Steps Out

   ■ Manage your position according to the rules defined in your Trading Plan.

   ■ If the stock closes above the higher strike at expiration, you will be exercised. You will sell your long call, buy the stock at the market price, and deliver it at the higher strike price, having profited from both the option premium you received and the uplift in the long option premium. Exercise of the short option is automatic. Do not exercise the long option or you will forfeit its time value.

   ■ If the stock remains below the higher strike but above your stop loss, let the short call expire worthless and keep the entire premium. If you like, you can then write another call for the following month.

   ■ If the stock falls below your stop loss, then either sell the long option (if you're approved for Naked Call writing) or reverse the entire position.

2.10.2 Context

Outlook

■ With a Diagonal Call, your outlook is **bullish.**

Rationale

■ To generate income against your longer term long position by selling calls and receiving the premium.

Net Position

■ This is a **net debit** transaction because your bought calls will be more expensive than your sold calls, which are OTM and have less time value.

■ Your maximum risk on the trade itself is limited to the net debit of the bought calls less the sold calls. Your maximum reward occurs when the stock price is at the sold call (higher) strike price at the expiration of the sold call.

Effect of Time Decay

■ Time decay affects your Diagonal Call trade in a mixed fashion. It erodes the value of the long call but helps you with your income strategy by eroding the value faster on the short call.

Appropriate Time Period to Trade

■ You will be safest to choose a long time to expiration with the long call and a short time (one month) for the short call.

Selecting the Stock

■ Choose from stocks with adequate liquidity, preferably over 500,000 Average Daily Volume (ADV).

■ Try to ensure that the trend is upward or rangebound and identify a clear area of support.

Selecting the Option

■ Choose options with adequate liquidity; open interest should be at least 100, preferably 500.

■ **Lower Strike**—Look for either the ATM or ITM (ideally about 10–20% ITM preferred) strike below the current stock price. If you're bullish, then choose a lower strike; if neutral, choose the ATM strike in anticipation of writing more calls in the future.

- **Higher Strike**—Look for OTM by more than one strike to enable the long call to rise in value if you get exercised on the short call.

- **Expirations**—Look at either of the next two expirations for the short option and compare monthly yields. Look for over six months for the long option.

2.10.3 Risk Profile

- **Maximum Risk**   Limited to the net debit paid

- **Maximum Reward**   [Long call value at the time of the short call expiration, when the stock price is at the higher strike price] − [net debit]

- **Breakeven Down**   Depends on the value of the long call option at the time of the short call expiration

- **Breakeven Up**   Depends on the value of the long call option at the time of the short call expiration

2.10.4 Greeks

Key:
Expiration   ....
Today – 1 month   ————
Time(t) – 5 days   – – –

Risk Profile
Maximum profit is achieved when the stock is at the higher strike price at the time of the short call expiration date.

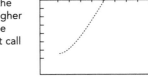

Theta
Theta is positive, illustrating that time decay is most helpful to the position around the higher strike price, where the position is most profitable.

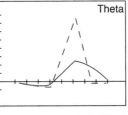

Delta
Delta (speed) is at its fastest either side of the strike price, indicating the increasing speed of the position in one direction and then the other.

Vega
Increasing volatility is helpful because it will mean the long call's residual value should be higher.

Gamma
Gamma (acceleration) peaks inversely around the higher strike price, showing where the Delta line is steepest.

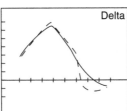
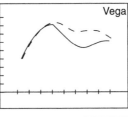
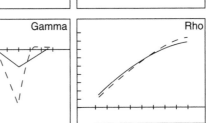

Rho
Higher interest rates become more helpful as the underlying asset price rises.

2.10.5 Advantages and Disadvantages

Advantages

- Generate monthly income.
- Can profit from rangebound stocks and make a higher yield than with a Covered Call.

Disadvantages

- Capped upside if the stock rises.
- Can lose on the upside if the stock rises significantly.
- High yield does not necessarily mean a profitable or high probability profitable trade.

2.10.6 Exiting the Trade

Exiting the Position

- With this strategy, you can simply unravel the spread by buying back the calls you sold and selling the calls you bought in the first place.
- Advanced traders may leg up and down as the underlying asset fluctuates up and down. In this way, you can take incremental profits before the expiration of the trade.

Mitigating a Loss

- Unravel the trade as described previously.
- Advanced traders may choose to only partially unravel the spread leg-by-leg. In this way, they will leave one leg of the spread exposed in order to attempt to profit from it.

2.10.7 Example

ABCD is trading at $26.00 on March 19, 2003, with Historical Volatility at 40%.

- Buy January 2005 25 calls at $6.60
- Sell April 2003 27.50 calls at $0.55

At April Expiration

1. Scenario: stock falls to $23.00

Long calls worth approximately 4.28; loss so far = 2.32
Short calls expire worthless; profit 0.55

No exercise

Total position = 6.60 + 0.55 − 2.32 = 4.83 = loss of 1.77

2. Scenario: stock falls to $25.00

Long calls worth approximately 5.46; loss so far = 1.14
Short calls expire worthless; profit 0.55

No exercise

Total position = 6.60 + 0.55 − 1.14 = 6.01 = loss of 0.59

3. Scenario: stock stays at $26.00

Long calls worth approximately 6.09; loss so far = 0.51
Short calls expire worthless; profit 0.55

No exercise

Total position = 6.60 + 0.55 − 0.51 = 6.64 = profit of 0.04

4. Scenario: stock rises to $27.50

Long calls worth approximately 7.09; profit so far = 0.49
Short calls expire worthless; profit 0.55

No exercise

Total position = 6.60 + 0.55 + 0.49 = 7.64 = profit of 1.04

5. Scenario: stock rises to $30.00

Long calls worth approximately 8.82; profit so far = 2.22
Short calls expire $2.50 ITM

Procedure: sell bought calls; buy stock at current price and sell at strike price

Exercised at $27.50

Buy stock at 30.00
Sell stock at 27.50
Loss = 2.50

Sell long call for a profit = 2.22
Keep short call premium = 0.55
Loss on Exercise = 2.50

Total position = 0.27 profit

If you tried to exercise the bought call:

Procedure: exercise bought calls at $25.00; deliver stock at $27.50 for exercised sold call

Buy call at 6.60
Sell call at 0.55
Net cost = 6.05

Buy stock at 25.00
Sell stock at 27.50
Net profit at 2.50

Total = 2.50 − 6.05 = loss of 3.55

Lesson: Never exercise a long-term option because you'll miss out on Time Value!

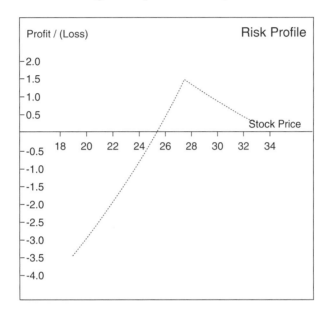

Before we wrap up this chapter, we're going to introduce two additional strategies. They're variations of the Calendar Call and Diagonal Call. They're simply the equivalent strategies using puts; hence they're called a Calendar Put and Diagonal Put. We put them at the end of this section in order to be thorough.

2.11 Calendar Put

Proficiency	Direction	Volatility	Asset Legs	Max Risk	Max Reward	Strategy Type
Advanced	Bearish	N/A	■ Short Put ■ Long Put	Capped	Capped	Income

2.11.1 Description

The Calendar Put is the put version of the Calendar Call. Instead of buying longer term calls you buy longer term puts. Instead of selling calls with less time to expiration, you sell puts with less time to expiration. Ultimately the strategy is virtually identical but in the exact reverse. You make an income out of a stock that is falling or rangebound.

Like the Calendar Call, the problem with a Calendar Put is in the very essence of the shape of the risk profile (see below). What we'd like to do is create something similar to a Covered Put, but with a better yield and without the hassle of margin. The Calendar Put certainly achieves both, however, the shape is different. If the stock falls too far too soon, then the Calendar Put can become loss making. So even though you got the direction of the trade right, you could still lose money!

Both options share the same strike, so if the stock rises above the strike, your short put will expire worthless while your long put will be less valuable because it's now OTM. If the stock falls, the short put will be exercised, you'll then have to sell the long put (typically for a profit), use the proceeds to sell the stock at the market price, and then buy it back at the strike price. Therefore, the best thing that can happen is that the stock is at the strike price at the expiration of the short put. This will enable you to write another put for the following month if you like.

| Sell put | + | Buy put | = | Calendar Put |

Steps to Trading a Calendar Put

1. Buy a long-term expiration put with a Near-the-Money strike price

2. Sell a short term put (say monthly) with the same strike price.

   Steps In

   ■ Try to ensure that the trend is downward or rangebound and identify clear areas of support and resistance.

   Steps Out

   ■ Manage your position according to the rules defined in your Trading Plan.

   ■ If the stock closes below the shared strike at expiration, your short put will be exercised. You will sell your long put, buy the stock at the shared strike price, deliver it at the lower market price, while having profited from both the option premium you received and the uplift in the long put option premium. Exercise of the short option is automatic. Do not exercise the long option or you will forfeit its time value. If you're going to be exercised then it's best to simply reverse the entire position and close the trade the day before expiration.

   ■ If the stock remains above the shared strike but below your stop loss, let the short put expire worthless and keep the entire premium. If you like you can then write another put for the following month if you're still neutral to bearish on the stock.

   ■ If the stock rises above your stop loss, then either sell the long option (if you're approved for naked put writing), or reverse the entire position.

2.11.2 Context

Outlook

- With a Calendar Put, your outlook is **neutral** to **bearish**.

Rationale

- To generate income against your longer term long put position by selling puts and receiving the premium.

Net Position

- This is a net debit transaction because your longer term bought puts will be more expensive than your shorter term sold puts which have less time value.

- Your maximum risk on the trade itself is limited to the net debit of the bought puts less the sold puts. Your maximum reward occurs when the stock price is at the strike price at the expiration of the sold put.

Effect of Time Decay

- Time decay affects your Calendar Put trade in a mixed fashion. It erodes the value of the long put but can help you with your income strategy by eroding the value faster on the short put.

Appropriate Time Period to Trade

- You will be safest to choose a long time to expiration with the long put and a shorter time (say 1 month) for the short put.

Selecting the Stock

- Choose from stocks with adequate liquidity, preferably over 500,000 Average Daily Volume (ADV).

- Try to ensure that the trend is downward or rangebound and identify clear areas of support and resistance.

Selecting the Option

- Choose options with adequate liquidity, open interest should be at least 100, preferably 500.

- **Strike**—Look for either the ATM or just ITM (higher) strike above the current stock price. If you're bearish, then choose a lower strike, if neutral choose the ATM strike in anticipation of writing more puts in the future.

- **Expirations**—Look at either of the next two expirations for the short option and compare monthly yields. Look for over six months for the long option.

2.11.3 Risk Profile

- **Maximum Risk**   Typically the net debit paid

- **Maximum Reward**   [long put value at strike price at first expiration] – [net debit]

- **Breakeven Down**   Depends on the value of the long put option at the time of the short put expiration

- **Breakeven Up**   Depends on the value of the long put option at the time of the short put expiration

2.11.4 Greeks

Risk Profile
Maximum profit is achieved when the stock is at the strike price at the time of the short put expiration date. Any substantial move up or down is dangerous for the position.

Delta
Delta (speed) is at its fastest either side of the strike price, indicating the increasing speed of the position in one direction and then the other.

Gamma
Gamma (acceleration) peaks inversely around the higher strike price, showing where the Delta line is steepest.

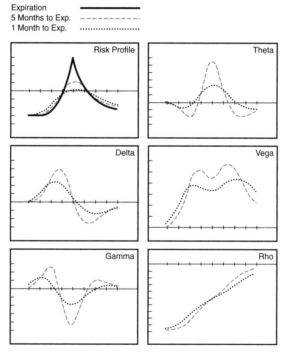

Theta
Theta is positive, when the position is profitable and negative when the position is making a loss. In other words, time decay is helpful when we're in profit and unhelpful when we're making a loss.

Vega
Increasing volatility is helpful because it will mean the long put's residual value should be higher.

Rho
Lower interest rates become more unhelpful as the underlying asset price falls.

2.11.5 Advantages and Disadvantages

Advantages

- Generate (monthly) income.

- Can profit from rangebound stocks and make a higher yield than with a Covered Put or Naked Call.

Disadvantages

- Capped profits if the stock falls.

- Can lose if the stock falls significantly and you haven't either bought deep enough ITM, or sold far enough OTM away.

- High yield does not necessarily mean a profitable or high probability profitable trade.

2.11.6 Exiting the Trade

Exiting the Position

- With this strategy you can simply unravel the spread by buying back the puts you sold and selling the puts you bought in the first place.

- Advanced traders may leg up and down as the underlying asset fluctuates up and down. In this way you can take incremental profits before the expiration of the trade.

Mitigating a Loss

- Unravel the trade as above.

- Advanced traders may choose to only partially unravel the spread leg by leg. In this way they will leave one leg of the spread exposed in order to attempt to profit from it.

2.11.7 Example

ABCD is trading at $81.60 on January 2, 2008, with Historical Volatility at 40%.

- Sell March 2008 $80.00 puts @ $5.00

- Buy June 2008 $80.00 puts @ $7.30

At the March Expiration

Net Debit	Higher strike put premium – lower strike put premium **$7.30 – $5.00** **$2.30**
Maximum Risk	Higher strike put premium – lower strike put premium **$7.30 – $5.00** **$2.30**
Maximum Reward	[long put value at the time of the short put expiration, when the stock price is at the strike price] less [net debit] Assuming implied volatility remains at 40%, here the maximum reward = **$3.70**

Breakevens	Depends on the value of the long put option at the time of the short put expiration.
	Assuming implied volatility remains at 40%, here the breakevens are **71.80** and **91.90** respectively.
	Note there are two breakevens with calendar spread trades. This means you can be right in terms of direction, yet still lose money if the stock falls too far too quickly.

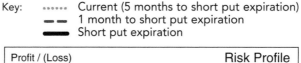

Key: ⋯⋯   Current (5 months to short put expiration)
        ▬ ▬   1 month to short put expiration
        ▬▬▬   Short put expiration

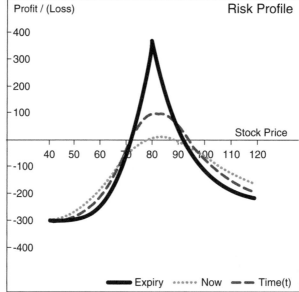

Let's look at a few scenarios of this strategy:

At the March Expiration

1. Scenario: stock rises to $150.00

Assuming no change in implied volatility, the long puts are now approximately zero; loss so far = 7.30
Short puts expire worthless: profit = 5.00

No exercise

Total position = (7.30) + 5.00 = loss so far of 2.30

2. Scenario: stock rises to $95.00

Assuming no change in implied volatility, the long puts are now worth approximately 1.75; loss so far = 5.55
Short puts expire worthless: profit = 5.00

No exercise

Total position = (5.55) + 5.00 = loss so far of 0.55

3. Scenario: stock rises to $92.00

Assuming no change in implied volatility, the long puts are now worth approximately 2.30; loss so far = 5.00
Short puts expire worthless: profit = 5.00

No exercise

Total position = (5.00) + 5.00 = breakeven

4. Scenario: stock falls to $80.00

Assuming no change in implied volatility, the long puts are now worth approximately 6.00; loss so far = 1.30
Short puts expire worthless: profit = 5.00

No exercise

Total position = (1.30) + 5.00 = profit so far of 3.70

5. Scenario: stock falls to $75.00

Assuming no change in implied volatility, the long puts are now worth approximately 8.55; profit so far = 1.25
Short puts exercised at $80.00:

Buy stock @ 80.00
Sell stock @ 75.00
Loss = 5.00

Sell long put for a profit = 1.25
Keep short put premium = 5.00
Loss on Exercise = 5.00

Total position = 1.25 profit

If you tried to exercise the bought put:

Procedure: exercise bought puts @ $80.00; sell stock @ $80.00.

Buy put @ 7.30
Sell put @ 5.00
Net cost = 2.30

Buy stock @ 80.00
Sell stock @ 80.00
Net = 0.00

Total = (2.30) + 0.00 = loss of 2.30 (less than the 1.25 profit above)

Lesson: Never exercise a long term option because you'll miss out on Time Value!

As we can see, by exercising our long put, we would forego the time value portion of the option and the trade would become a loss.

2.12 Diagonal Put

Proficiency	Direction	Volatility	Asset Legs	Max Risk	Max Reward	Strategy Type
Advanced	Bearish	N/A	▪ Short Put ▪ Long Put	Capped	Capped	Income

2.12.1 Description

The Diagonal Put is the put equivalent of the Diagonal Call. Instead of buying lower strike calls you buy *higher* strike *puts*. Instead of selling higher strike calls with less time to expiration, you sell *lower strike puts* with less time to expiration. Ultimately the strategy is the exact reverse. Here you derive income from a stock that is falling or rangebound.

The Diagonal Put solves the problems experienced with the Calendar Put, in that the *shape* of the risk profile (see below) is more akin to the Covered Put, which is preferable. The Diagonal Put is going to be easier to trade than a Covered Put because we don't margin as we're not shorting the stock here. If the stock declines rapidly, then unlike the Calendar Put, the Diagonal Put (done correctly) won't become loss making. The key is not to get too greedy with your yields.

The bought option is ITM and has longer to expiration, and the short option is OTM and short term. If the stock remains above the lower (short) strike, your short put will expire worthless, meaning you keep the premium. If the stock price doesn't move the long put will decrease in value through time decay, though this should be minimal because the long put should be deep ITM, meaning the premium contained minimal time value. If the stock falls below the lower (short) put strike, it will be exercised by or at expiration, meaning you will be "put" the stock at that lower strike price—this means you'd have to buy the stock at the lower strike price. In the meantime, the stock may fall further buty your long put will have increased in value.

Sell put   +   Buy put   =   Diagonal Put

Steps to Trading a Diagonal Put

1. Sell a lower strike short term expiration put (say monthly).

2. Buy a higher strike longer term put.

    Steps In

    ▪ Try to ensure that the trend is downward or rangebound and identify a clear area of resistance.

Steps Out

- Manage your position according to the rules defined in your Trading Plan.

- If the stock closes below the lower strike at expiration, you will be exercised. You will sell your long put, buy the stock at the short put strike price, deliver it at the lower market price, while having profited from both the option premium you received and the uplift in the long put option premium. Exercise of the short option is automatic. Do not exercise the long option or you will forfeit its time value. If you're going to be exercised then it's best to simply reverse the entire position and close the trade the day before expiration.

- If the stock remains above the lower strike but below your stop loss, let the short put expire worthless and keep the entire premium. If you like you can then write another put for the following month if you're still neutral to bearish on the stock.

- If the stock rises above your stop loss, then either sell the long option (if you're approved for naked put writing), or reverse the entire position.

2.12.2 Context

Outlook

- With a Diagonal Put, your outlook is **bearish**.

Rationale

- To generate income against your longer term long put position by selling puts and receiving the premium.

Net Position

- This is a net debit transaction because your bought puts will be more expensive than your sold puts which are OTM and have less time value.

- Your maximum risk on the trade itself is limited to the net debit of the bought puts less the sold puts. Your maximum reward occurs when the stock price is at the sold put (lower) strike price at the expiration of the sold put.

Effect of Time Decay

- Time decay affects your Diagonal Put trade in a mixed fashion. It erodes the value of the long put but can help you with your income strategy by eroding the value faster on the short put.

Appropriate Time Period to Trade

- You will be safest to choose a long time to expiration with the long put and a shorter time (say 1 month) for the short put.

Selecting the Stock

■ Choose from stocks with adequate liquidity, preferably over 500,000 Average Daily Volume (ADV).

■ Try to ensure that the trend is downward or rangebound and identify a clear area of resistance.

Selecting the Option

■ Choose options with adequate liquidity, open interest should be at least 100, preferably 500.

■ **Lower Strike**—Look for OTM by more than one strike below the current stock price to enable the long put to rise in value if you get exercised on the short put.

■ **Higher Strike**—Look for either the ATM or ITM (ideally about 10-20% ITM preferred) strike above the current stock price. If you're bearish, then choose a higher strike, if neutral choose the ATM strike in anticipation of writing more puts in the future.

■ **Expirations**—Look at either of the next two expirations for the short option and compare monthly yields. Look for over six months for the long option.

2.12.3 Risk Profile

■ **Maximum Risk**   Limited to the net debit paid

■ **Maximum Reward**   [long put value at the time of the short put expiration, when the stock price is at the lower strike price] less [net debit]

■ **Breakeven Down**   Depends on the value of the long put option at the time of the short put expiration.

■ **Breakeven Up**   Depends on the value of the long put option at the time of the short put expiration.

2.12.4 Greeks

Key:
Expiration ————
5 Months to Exp. – – – – – – –
1 Month to Exp. ·················

Risk Profile
Maximum profit is achieved when the stock is at the lower strike price at the time of the short put expiration date.

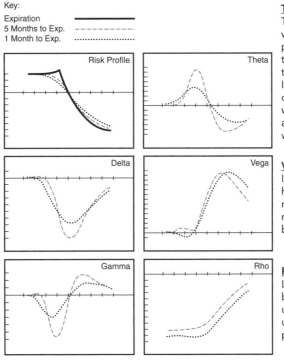

Theta
Theta is positive when the position is profitable and negative when the position is making a loss. In other words, time decay is most helpful when we're in profit and unhelpful when we're making a loss.

Delta
Delta (speed) is at its fastest either side of the strike price, indicating the increasing speed of the position in one direction and then the other.

Vega
Increasing volatility is helpful because it will mean the long put's residual value should be higher.

Gamma
Gamma (acceleration) peaks inversely around the higher strike price, showing where the Delta line is steepest.

Rho
Lower interest rates become more unhelpful as the underlying asset price falls.

2.12.5 Advantages and Disadvantages

Advantages

- Generate (monthly) income.

- Can profit from rangebound stocks and make a higher yield than with a Covered Put or Naked Call.

Disadvantages

- Capped profits if the stock falls.

- If poorly constructed, the Diagonal Put can lose if the stock falls significantly and you haven't either bought deep enough ITM, or sold far enough OTM away.

- High yield does not necessarily mean a profitable or high probability profitable trade.

2.12.6 Exiting the Trade

Exiting the Position

- With this strategy you can simply unravel the spread by buying back the puts you sold and selling the puts you bought in the first place.

■ Advanced traders may leg up and down as the underlying asset fluctuates up and down. In this way you can take incremental profits before the expiration of the trade.

Mitigating a Loss

■ Unravel the trade as above.

■ Advanced traders may choose to only partially unravel the spread leg by leg. In this way they will leave one leg of the spread exposed in order to attempt to profit from it.

2.12.7 Example

ABCD is trading at $81.60 on January 2, 2008, with Historical Volatility at 40%.

■ Sell March 2008 $75.00 puts @ $3.40

■ Buy June 2008 $95.00 puts @ $16.70

This is a well placed trade where the bought put is deep ITM meaning a high inverse delta, so the put will gain $1.00 as the stock falls by $1.00. The short put is some way OTM but still gives a decent premium. Both of these legs are exactly how you want them to be, and therefore the trade will be uncomplicated.

At the March Expiration

Net Debit	Higher strike put premium – lower strike put premium **$16.70 – $3.40** **$13.30**
Maximum Risk	Higher strike put premium – lower strike put premium **$16.70 – $3.40** **$13.30**
Maximum Reward	[long put value at the time of the short put expiration, when the stock price is at the lower strike price] less [net debit] Assuming implied volatility remains at 40%, here the maximum reward = **$6.94**
Breakeven	Depends on the value of the long put option at the time of the short put expiration. Assuming implied volatility remains at 40%, here the breakeven = **84.04**. Because the long put is deep ITM and the short put is OTM enough, we only have a single breakeven point with this trade. This is good news and the sign of a well place diagonal spread trade. It also means that no matter how far the stock price falls we'll still make a profit with this trade. If our long put wasn't deep enough ITM then this may not have been the case.

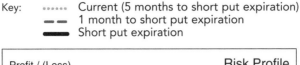

Key: •••••• Current (5 months to short put expiration)
        — —   1 month to short put expiration
        ▬▬▬   Short put expiration

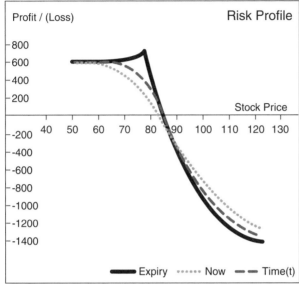

Let's look at a few scenarios of this strategy:

At the March Expiration

1. Scenario: stock rises to $150.00
Assuming no change in implied volatility, the long puts are now worth approximately zero; loss so far = 16.70
Short puts expire worthless: profit = 3.40

No exercise

Total position = (16.70) + 3.40 = loss so far of 13.30

2. Scenario: stock rises to $90.00
Assuming no change in implied volatility, the long puts are now worth approximately 9.63; loss so far = 7.07
Short puts expire worthless: profit = 3.40

No exercise

Total position = (7.07) + 3.40 = loss so far of 3.67

3. Scenario: stock rises to $84.00
Assuming no change in implied volatility, the long puts are now worth approximately 13.33; loss so far = 3.40
Short puts expire worthless: profit = 3.40

No exercise

Total position = (3.40) + 3.40 = breakeven

4.   Scenario: stock falls to $75.00

Assuming implied volatility rises to 60%, the long puts are now worth approximately 22.40; profit so far = 5.70
Short puts expire worthless: profit = 3.40

No exercise

Total position = 5.70 + 3.40 = profit so far of 9.10

5.   Scenario: stock falls to $60.00

Assuming implied volatility rises to 70%, the long puts are now worth approximately 35.40; profit so far = 18.70
Short puts exercised at $75.00:

Buy stock @ 75.00
Sell stock @ 60.00
Loss = 15.00

Sell long put for a profit = 18.70
Keep short put premium = 3.40
Loss on Exercise = 15.00

Total position = 7.10 profit

If you tried to exercise the bought put:

Procedure: exercise bought puts @ $95.00; sell stock @ $95.00.

Buy put @ 16.70
Sell put @ 3.40
Net cost = 13.30

Buy stock @ 75.00
Sell stock @ 95.00
Net profit = 20.00

Total = (13.30) + 20.00 = profit of 6.70 (less than the 7.10 profit above)

Lesson: Never exercise a long term option because you'll miss out on Time Value!

In this situation, even though implied volatility had risen significantly the puts were only worth a small amount over their intrinsic value. It's likely that such a precipitous drop in share price would be accompanied with a sharp rise in implied volatility, perhaps to more than 70%, in which case the long puts would be worth more.

As mentioned above, this example is a particularly well constructed diagonal spread, because the long side is deep ITM and the short side is sufficiently OTM. This means that even as the stock drops lower and lower, this particular Diagonal Put will continue to make virtually the same amount of profit.

Let's take the example to even more extreme levels:

6.   Scenario: stock falls to $30.00

Assuming implied volatility has risen to 150%, the long puts are now worth approximately 65.20; profit so far = 48.50
Short puts exercised at $75.00:

Buy stock @ 75.00
Sell stock @ 30.00
Loss = 45.00

Sell long put for a profit = 48.50
Keep short put premium = 3.40
Loss on Exercise = 45.00

Total position = 6.90 profit

As we can see, the profit level is similar to when the stock dropped to $60.00. It's important to understand that if you had bought a Near-the-Money put instead, then the profits would have dwindled as the stock fell. This seems counter intuitive because the strategy is bearish and thrives on the stock falling. Well, this is only the case if you buy a deep ITM put in the first place.

If you had bought a Near-the-Money put then the strategy would benefit from rangebound stock price action. However, if the stock price plummeted, the strategy, despite being bearish in nature, could start to make losses even though you were right in terms of your market direction.

A similar concept applies in terms of the short leg. Your short put should be near enough to generate a decent income yield but not so close that the stock won't have a chance to move and make the long side profitable.

When trading diagonal spreads I prefer not to be greedy and will buy a deep ITM option for my long leg, and will never sell an option with a strike too close to the current stock price. This way I won't get punished for being "too" right.

Just so you can see how this works, let's adjust the above example as follows:

■   Instead of buying the 95 strike put for 16.70 we're going to buy the 85 strike put for 10.70.

■   Instead of selling the 75 strike put for 3.40 we're going to sell the 80 strike put for 5.00.

Now, initially this looks better as our yield is almost 50% instead of 20%. However, look at the risk profile on the following page and compare it to the original one above.

Do you see the difference? With these tighter strikes, the strategy will actually make a loss as the stock falls below $70. With our wider strikes we kept on making money, no matter how far the stock fell. We sacrificed the initial yield in order to keep making a profit in the event of a real surprise to the downside. Ultimately the Diagonal Put is a bearish strategy. We don't want to be punished for getting it right.

In real world trading I would strongly advise you to virtual trade the diagonals and see for yourself what happens in all scenarios. I'm cautious by nature and can't bear to lose when I'm right, let alone when I'm wrong! By being conservative with my diagonals, I'm never exposed to a nasty surprise.

Key: .... Current (5 months to short put expiration)
        ― ― 1 month to short put expiration
        ▬▬▬ Short put expiration

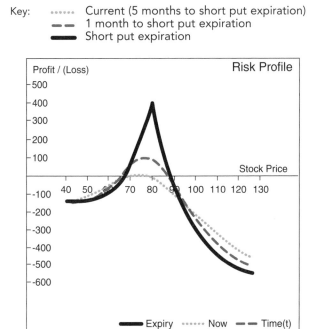

2.13 Covered Put (Also Known as a *Married Put*)

Proficiency	Direction	Volatility	Asset Legs	Max Risk	Max Reward	Strategy Type
🚶	🔽	N/A	🔲 + 🔲	☠️	🔒	💰
Advanced	Bearish		■ Short Stock	Uncapped	Capped	Income
			■ Short Put			

2.13.1 Description

The Covered Put is the opposite process to a Covered Call, and it achieves the opposite risk profile. Whereas the Covered Call is bullish, the Covered Put is a bearish income strategy, where you receive a substantial net credit for shorting both the put and the stock simultaneously to create the spread.

The concept is that in shorting the stock, you then sell an Out of the Money put option on a monthly basis as a means of collecting rent (or a dividend) while you are short the stock.

The trade-off is that an OTM Covered Put will give a higher potential yield but less cushion, whereas an ITM Covered Put will give a lower yield but much more cushion. This is not a recommended strategy (partly because it's a little confusing!), but "you pays your money, you takes your chances" on this one!

If the stock falls below the put strike, you'll be exercised and will have to buy the stock at the strike price . . . but you make a profit because you've already shorted it, so the purchase simply closes your stock position, and you retain the premium for the sold put. (You're covered because you shorted the stock in the first place.) If the stock remains static, then you simply collect the put premium. If the stock rises, you have the cushion of the put premium you collected.

| Short stock | + | Sell OTM put | = | Covered Put |

Steps to Trading a Covered Put

1. Short sell the stock.

2. Sell puts one strike price out of the money [OTM] (i.e., puts with a strike price lower than the stock).

   ■ If the stock is purchased simultaneously with writing the call contract, the strategy is commonly referred to as a "buy-write."

   ■ Generally, only sell the puts on a monthly basis. In this way you will capture more in premiums over several months, provided you are not exercised. Selling premium every month will net you more over a period of time than selling premium a long way out. Remember that whenever you are selling options premium, time decay works in your favor. Time decay is at its fastest rate in the last 20 trading days (i.e., the last month), so when you sell option premiums, it is best to sell it with a month left, and do it again the following month.

   ■ Remember that your maximum gain is capped when the stock falls to the level of the put strike price.

   ■ If trading U.S. stocks and options, you will be required to sell (or be short in) 100 shares for every put contract that you sell.

Steps In

   ■ Try to ensure that the trend is downward or rangebound and identify a clear area of resistance.

Steps Out

   ■ Manage your position according to the rules defined in your Trading Plan.

   ■ If the stock closes below the strike at expiration, you will be exercised. You will have to buy back the stock at the strike price, having profited from both the option premium you received and the fall in stock price to reach the lower strike price.

- If the stock remains above the strike but below your stop loss, let the put expire worthless and keep the entire premium. If you like, you can then write another put for the following month.

- If the stock rises above your stop loss, then either buy back the stock (if you're approved for naked put writing) or reverse the entire position (the put will be cheap to buy back).

2.13.2 Context

Outlook

- With a Covered Put, your outlook is **neutral to bearish.** You expect a steady decline.

Rationale

- To sell (short) a stock for the medium or long term with the aim of capturing monthly income by selling puts every month. This is like collecting rent after selling the stock.

- If the stock rises, you will lose money because you have shorted the stock.

- If the stock falls, you will make money because of your short position on the stock; however, you will only make limited profit because if the stock declines down to the sold put strike price, you will be exercised at that strike price. This means that you will have to buy the stock at the sold put strike price if the stock declines to that level at expiration.

Net Position

- This is a **net credit** transaction because you are selling the stock and taking in a premium for the sold put options.

- Your maximum risk is unlimited if the stock price rises.

Effect of Time Decay

- Time decay is helpful to your trade here because it should erode the value of the put you sold. Provided that the stock does not hit the strike price at expiration, you will be able to retain the entire option premium for the trade.

Appropriate Time Period to Trade

- Sell the puts on a monthly basis.

Selecting the Stock

- Choose from stocks with adequate liquidity, preferably over 500,000 Average Daily Volume (ADV).

- Try to ensure that the trend is downward or rangebound and identify a clear area of resistance.

Selecting the Option

■ Choose options with adequate liquidity; open interest should be at least 100, preferably 500.

■ **Strike**—Look for either the ATM or just OTM (lower) strike below the current stock. If you're confident of the stock falling, then choose a lower strike; if neutral, choose the ATM strike.

■ **Expiration**—Look at either of the next two expirations and compare monthly yields.

2.13.3 Risk Profile

■ **Maximum Risk**   Uncapped

■ **Maximum Reward**   [Shorted stock price − strike price] + put premium

■ **Breakeven**   [Shorted stock price + put premium]

2.13.4 Greeks

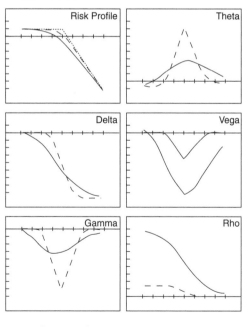

Key:
Expiration   ············
Today – 2 months   ————
Time(t) – 10 days   – – –

Risk Profile
As the stock price falls, the covered put moves into profit but slows down as it approaches the strike price and maximum profit.

Delta
Delta (speed) is negative and rises to zero as the asset price falls below the strike price and the maximum profit is achieved.

Gamma
Gamma (acceleration) is always negative with this position because you are a net seller of puts.

Theta
Theta is positive, illustrating that time decay is helpful to the position.

Vega
Vega is negative, illustrating that volatility is harmful to the position.

Rho
Rho is positive, illustrating that higher interest rates would be helpful to the position.

2.13.5 Advantages and Disadvantages

Advantages

■ Generate monthly income.

■ Can profit from rangebound or bearish stocks with no capital outlay.

Disadvantages

- Capped upside if the stock falls.
- Uncapped downside if the stock rises.

2.13.6 Exiting the Trade

Exiting the Position

- If the share falls below the strike price, you will be exercised and therefore make a limited profit.
- If the share rises above the strike price (plus premium you received), you will be losing money.
- If the share rises in this way, then your exit depends on what type of account you have:
  - If your account permits you to sell naked options, then you will be able to buy back the share and let the sold put option expire worthless. Because the put option will have declined in value so much, you may consider buying it back to avoid any contingent losses that could occur if the share suddenly bounced back down after you sold it!
  - If your account does not permit you to sell naked options, then you should buy back the options you sold and consider buying back the stock, too. This is the safest way to exit a losing covered put trade.

Mitigating a Loss

- Either buy back the share or buy back both the share and the put option you sold.

2.13.7 Example

ABCD is trading at $50.00 on February 25, 2004.

Sell short the stock for $49.75.

Sell the March 2004 45 strike put for $1.50.

You Receive	Stock price + put premium **49.75 + 1.50 = 51.25**
Maximum Risk	Uncapped
Maximum Reward	[Shorted stock price − strike price] + put premium received **49.75 − 45.00 + 1.50 = 6.25**
Breakeven	Shorted stock price + put premium received **49.75 + 1.50 = 51.25**
Maximum ROI	13.89%
Cushion (from Breakeven)	$1.50 or 3.02%

3

Vertical Spreads

Introduction

Vertical spreads are typically defined as two-legged option strategies with different strike prices but the same expiration date.

Whereas Calendar spreads are two-legged option strategies where both legs share the strike but not expiration (hence known as *horizontal spreads*), vertical spreads are the complete opposite.

Diagonal spreads are so called because both the strikes and the expiration dates are different for both legs.

Vertical spreads can be categorized into two types: *net debit* spreads and *net credit* spreads. A net debit spread is where you pay a net debit for the trade, thereby making you net long in options. Because you are net long in options, you're better off giving yourself plenty of time in terms of the expiration date you choose so that you're not hurt too much by time decay.

A net credit spread is where you receive a net credit for the trade, thereby making you net short in options. Because you're net short in options, you're better off doing a short-term trade in terms of the expiration date and allowing time decay to do its work for you.

We've actually already covered two vertical spread strategies in Chapter 2, "Income Strategies"—the *Bull Put* and *Bear Call* spreads. These are net credit vertical spread trades that produce a short-term income. In this chapter, we're going to cover the two net debit vertical spreads, and to ensure that the chapter isn't too short, we'll also run through the Ladder strategies, which simply contain an extra leg. So, there are a total of four vertical spread strategies plus four Ladder strategies.

The ladders are not popular strategies, and they can be a little confusing, so by all means skip those sections if you're purely looking for the most practical strategies to use.

3.1 Bull Call Spread

Proficiency	Direction	Volatility	Asset Legs	Max Risk	Max Reward	Strategy Type
Intermediate	Bullish	N/A	■ Long Call ■ Short Call	Capped	Capped	Capital Gain

3.1.1 Description

The Bull Call is a *vertical* spread strategy that creates a net debit in your account. You buy a near the money long-term (typically over six months to expiration) call and sell a higher strike (typically OTM) call with the same expiration.

The net effect of the strategy is to bring down the cost and breakeven on the trade compared to simply buying the long call. The bought leg is closer to the money than the sold leg, so it is more expensive and also has a higher Delta than the OTM sold call leg. Therefore you don't want to be over-exposed to time decay, which is at its most profound in the last month. When you add the fact that your stock must move upwards in order for you to reach your breakeven point, bull calls tend to be more suited to longer-term trades where you need time to be right.

The Bull Call Spread requires a bullish outlook because you will make a profit only when the stock price rises. However, the returns possible on this strategy can be spectacular if you get it right and everything goes in your favor. The bought leg gives you the leverage, but the sold leg reduces your cost and increases your leverage, though at the expense of capping your upside.

Many so-called options instructors advocate the Bull Call Spread because it's easy to show spectacular potential returns. The key word here is *potential*. It's all very well demonstrating a trade where you can make 400% more than your initial stake, but if the stock has to rise by 50% for us to get there, then I'm more likely to look at the odds of that happening, rather than being suckered in by the attractive *potential* yield. Personally, when I do these, I always look first at where my breakeven point is. If it's not too far away, then I'll see if the yield is attractive enough.

So, in summary, if the stock falls below the lower (bought) strike, you make your maximum loss; if the stock rises to the higher (sold) strike, you make your maximum profit. In between these points, your breakeven point lies at the lower strike plus the net debit.

| Buy lower strike call | Sell OTM call | Bull Call Spread |

Steps to Trading a Bull Call Spread

1. Buy lower strike calls.

2. Sell the same number of higher strike calls with the same expiration date.

   Steps In

   ■ Try to ensure that the trend is upward and identify a clear area of support.

   Steps Out

   ■ Manage your position according to the rules defined in your Trading Plan.

   ■ If the stock falls below your stop loss, then sell the Long Call, and if you're not permitted to trade Naked Calls, then unravel the entire position.

   ■ In any event, look to unravel the trade at least one month before expiration, either to capture your profit or to contain your losses.

3.1.2 Context

Outlook

■ With a Bull Call, your outlook is **bullish.** You need a rise in the stock price.

Rationale

■ To execute a bullish trade for a capital gain while reducing your maximum risk. The sold calls will have the effect of capping your upside but also reducing your cost basis, risk, and breakeven points.

Net Position

■ This is a **net debit** transaction because your bought calls will be more expensive than your sold calls, which are further out of the money.

■ Your maximum risk on the trade itself is limited to the net debit of the bought calls less the sold calls. Your maximum reward on the trade is limited to the difference between the strike prices less your net debit.

Effect of Time Decay

■ Time decay is helpful to this position when it is profitable and harmful when it is loss-making. With this trade, you're incurring a net debit, and the stock must move upwards to at least break even. Therefore, you want to trade this type of strategy in longer time periods to give yourself enough time to be right. If the position remains unprofitable, time decay will work against you because the nearer you are to expiration, the nearer you'll be to making your maximum loss. When the position moves into profit, then time decay will help because you'll be getting closer to achieving your maximum profit, which happens at the expiration date.

Appropriate Time Period to Trade

- It's safest to trade this strategy on a longer-term basis, preferably with at least six months to expiration.

Selecting the Stock

- Choose from stocks with adequate liquidity, preferably over 500,000 Average Daily Volume (ADV).

- Try to ensure that the trend is upward and identify a clear area of support.

Selecting the Options

- Choose options with adequate liquidity; open interest should be at least 100, preferably 500.

- **Lower Strike**—Either ATM or slightly OTM (remember, you're bullish here!).

- **Higher Strike**—Higher than the bought strike—use online tools to find the optimum yields and breakeven points at and before expiration.

- **Expiration**—Preferably over six months. Use the same expiration date for both legs.

3.1.3 Risk Profile

- **Maximum Risk**   [Net debit paid]

- **Maximum Reward**   [Difference in strikes − net debit]

- **Breakeven**   [Lower strike + net debit]

3.1.4 Greeks

Key:
Expiration   ....
Today – 6 months ———
Time(t) – 1 month – – –

Risk Profile
As the stock price rises, the Bull Call moves into profit and reaches the maximum profit when the stock rises to the higher strike price.

Delta
Delta (speed) is positive and is at its fastest in between the strikes. Notice how Delta slows down when the position is deep ITM or OTM.

Gamma
Gamma (acceleration) peaks below the lower (bought) strike and peaks inversely above the higher (sold) strike.

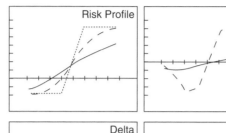
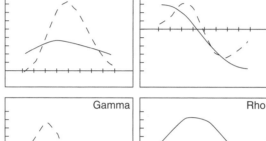
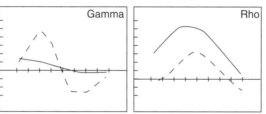

Theta
Time decay is harmful to the position when it is OTM and helpful when it is ITM.

Vega
Volatility is helpful to the position when it is OTM and harmful when it is ITM.

Rho
Higher interest rates are generally helpful to the position.

3.1.5 Advantages and Disadvantages

Advantages

■ Reduced risk, cost, and breakeven point for a medium- to long-term bullish trade as compared to buying a call alone.

■ Capped downside (although still 100% of the outlay).

■ The farther away from expiration you are, the more downside protection you have in the event of the stock declining rapidly.

Disadvantages

■ The higher yields only arise if you select significantly higher strikes and the underlying stock price rises up to the higher of those two strikes.

■ Capped upside if the stock rises.

■ The farther away from expiration you are, the slower you make your maximum returns; this is the price you pay for the downside protection.

3.1.6 Exiting the Trade

Exiting the Position

- With this strategy, you can simply unravel the spread by buying back the calls you sold and selling the calls you bought in the first place.

- Advanced traders may leg up and down as the underlying asset fluctuates up and down. In this way, the trader will be taking smaller incremental profits before the expiration of the trade.

Mitigating a Loss

- Unravel the trade as described previously.

- Advanced traders may choose to only partially unravel the spread leg-by-leg. In this way, they will leave one leg of the spread exposed in order to attempt to profit from it.

3.1.7 Example

ABCD is trading at $26.00 on May 13, 2004.

Buy the January 2005 $27.50 strike call for $1.40.

Sell the January 2005 $32.50 strike call for $0.25.

Net Debit	Premium bought − premium sold **$1.40 − $0.25 = $1.15**
Maximum Risk	Net debit **$1.15**
Maximum Reward	Difference in strikes − net debit **$5.00 − $1.15 = $3.85** Maximum reward is greater than your net debit
Breakeven	Lower strike + net debit **$27.50 + $1.15 = $28.65**
Max ROI	334.78%

Notice how high our maximum reward is (334.78%), but the stock needs to rise to $32.50 within the next seven to eight months in order for this to happen. Normally we wouldn't hold on to expiration, so we'd close the position with around one month to go or earlier.

3.2 Bear Put Spread

Proficiency	Direction	Volatility	Asset Legs	Max Risk	Max Reward	Strategy Type
Intermediate	Bearish	N/A	■ Short Put ■ Long Put	Capped	Capped	Capital Gain

3.2.1 Description

The Bear Put is a *vertical* spread strategy that creates a net debit in your account. You buy a near the money long-term (typically over six months to expiration) put and sell a lower strike (typically OTM) put with the same expiration.

The net effect of the strategy is to bring down the cost and raise the breakeven on the trade compared to simply buying the long put. The bought leg is closer to the money than the sold leg, so it is more expensive. Therefore, you don't want to be over-exposed to time decay, which is at its most profound in the last month. When you add the fact that your stock must move downwards in order for you to reach your breakeven point, Bear Puts tend to be more suited to longer-term trades where you need time to be right.

The Bear Put Spread requires a bearish outlook because you will make a profit only when the stock price falls. However, the possible returns on this strategy can be spectacular if you get it right and everything goes in your favor. The bought leg gives you the leverage, but the sold leg reduces your cost and increases your leverage, though at the expense of capping your upside.

The Bear Put Spread appears attractive because it can show spectacular potential returns. Again, the key word here is *potential*. It's all very well demonstrating a trade where you can make 400% more than your initial stake, but if the stock must fall by 50% for us to get there, then I'm more likely to look at the odds of that happening, rather than being suckered in by the attractive *potential* yield.

So, in summary, if the stock rises above the higher (bought) strike, you make your maximum loss; if the stock falls to the lower (sold) strike, you make your maximum profit. In between these points, your breakeven point lies at the higher strike less the net debit.

Sell lower strike put   Buy OTM put   Bear Put Spread

Steps to Trading a Bear Put Spread

1. Sell lower strike puts.

2. Buy the same number of higher strike puts with the same expiration date.

   Steps In

   ■ Try to ensure that the trend is downward and identify a clear area of resistance.

   Steps Out

   ■ Manage your position according to the rules defined in your Trading Plan.

   ■ If the stock rises above your stop loss, then sell the Long Put, and if you're not permitted to trade Naked Puts, then unravel the entire position.

   ■ In any event, look to unravel the trade at least one month before expiration, either to capture your profit or to contain your losses.

3.2.2 Context

Outlook

- With a Bear Put, your outlook is **bearish.** You need a fall in the stock price.

Rationale

- To execute a bearish trade for a capital gain while reducing your maximum risk. The bought puts will have the effect of capping your downside, while the sold puts will reduce your cost basis, risk, and breakeven points.

Net Position

- This is a **net debit** transaction because your bought puts will be more expensive than your sold puts, which are further out of the money. (Remember that calls and puts work in the opposite way to each other.)

- Your maximum risk on the trade itself is limited to the net debit of the bought puts less the sold puts. Your maximum reward on the trade is limited to the difference between the strike prices less your net debit.

Effect of Time Decay

- Time decay is helpful to this position when it is profitable and harmful when it is loss-making. With this trade, you're incurring a net debit, and the stock must move downwards to at least achieve the breakeven. Therefore, you want to trade this type of strategy in longer time periods to give yourself enough time to be right. If the position remains unprofitable, time decay will work against you because the nearer you are to expiration, the nearer you'll be to making your maximum loss. When the position moves into profit, then time decay will help because you'll be getting closer to achieving your maximum profit, which happens at the expiration date.

Appropriate Time Period to Trade

- It's safest to trade this strategy on a longer-term basis, preferably with at least six months to expiration.

Selecting the Stock

- Choose from stocks with adequate liquidity, preferably over 500,000 Average Daily Volume (ADV).

- Try to ensure that the trend is downward and identify a clear area of resistance.

Selecting the Options

- Choose options with adequate liquidity; open interest should be at least 100, preferably 500.

- **Lower Strike**—Lower than the bought strike; use online tools to find the optimum yields and breakeven points at and before expiration.

- **Higher Strike**—Either ATM or slightly OTM (remember, you're bearish here!).

- **Expiration**—Preferably over six months. Use the same expiration date for both legs.

3.2.3 Risk Profile

- **Maximum Risk**   [Net debit paid]

- **Maximum Reward**   [Difference in strikes − net debit]

- **Breakeven**   [Higher strike − net debit]

3.2.4 Greeks

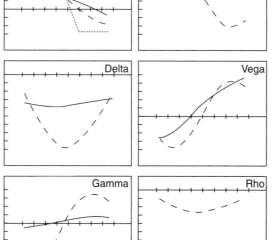

Key:
Expiration   ....
Today – 6 months ————
Time(t) – 1 month − − −

Risk Profile
As the stock price falls, the Bear Put moves into profit and reaches the maximum profit when the stock falls to the lower strike price.

Delta
Delta (speed) is negative and is at its fastest in between the strikes. Notice how Delta slows down when the position is deep ITM or OTM.

Gamma
Gamma (acceleration) peaks inversely below the lower (sold) strike and peaks above the higher (bought) strike.

Theta
Time decay is harmful to the position when it is loss-making and helpful when it is ITM.

Vega
Volatility is helpful to the position when it is loss-making and harmful when it is profitable.

Rho
Higher interest rates are generally unhelpful to the position.

3.2.5 Advantages and Disadvantages

Advantages

- Reduced risk, cost, and breakeven point for a medium- to long-term bearish trade as compared to buying a put alone.

- Capped risk (although still 100% of the outlay).

- The farther away from expiration you are, the more downside protection you have in the event of the stock rising rapidly.

Disadvantages

- The higher yields only arise if you select significantly lower strikes and the underlying stock price declines down to the lower of those two strikes.

- Capped upside if the stock falls.

- The farther away from expiration you are, the slower you make your maximum returns; this is the price you pay for the risk protection.

3.2.6 Exiting the Trade

Exiting the Position

- With this strategy, you can simply unravel the spread by buying back the puts you sold and selling the puts you bought in the first place.

- Advanced traders may leg up and down as the underlying asset fluctuates up and down. In this way, the trader will be taking smaller incremental profits before the expiration of the trade.

Mitigating a Loss

- Unravel the trade as described previously.

- Advanced traders may choose to only partially unravel the spread leg-by-leg. In this way, they will leave one leg of the spread exposed in order to attempt to profit from it.

3.2.7 Example

ABCD is trading at $26.00 on May 13, 2004.

Sell the January 2005 20 strike put for $0.35.

Buy the January 2005 25 strike put for $1.80.

Net Debit	Premium bought − premium sold **$1.80 − $0.35 = $1.45**
Maximum Risk	Net debit **$1.45**
Maximum Reward	Difference in strikes − net debit **$5.00 − $1.45 = $3.55** Maximum reward is greater than your net debit
Breakeven	Higher strike − net debit **$25.00 − $1.45 = $23.55**
Max ROI	244.83%

Notice how high our maximum reward is (244.83%), but the stock needs to fall to $20.00 within the next seven to eight months in order for this to happen. Normally we wouldn't hold on to expiration, so we'd close the position with around one month to go or earlier.

3.3 Bull Put Spread

We covered the Bull Put Spread in Chapter 2 in Section 2.3 on the basis that it is an income strategy.

It's also a net credit vertical spread. There's no need to repeat the entire text here, but the strategy could be placed in either chapter.

3.4 Bear Call Spread

We covered the Bear Call Spread in Section 2.4 on the basis that it is an income strategy.

It's also a net credit vertical spread. There's no need to repeat the entire text here, but the strategy could be placed in either chapter.

3.5 Bull Call Ladder

Proficiency	Direction	Volatility	Asset Legs	Max Risk	Max Reward	Strategy Type
Advanced	Neutral	Low Volatility	■ Long Call ■ Short Call ■ Short Call	Uncapped	Capped	Income

3.5.1 Description

The Bull Call Ladder is an extension to the Bull Call Spread. By shorting another call at a higher strike price, the position assumes uncapped risk potential if the stock soars upwards. The problem is that now it's not totally clear if we have a bullish or bearish strategy, so we have to designate it as a direction neutral strategy! We'd love the stock to rise to the middle strike price (the first Short Call) but not above the higher short call strike price. Anywhere in between the middle and higher strike is ideal.

Because of the dangers of uncapped risk, this strategy becomes more appropriate for a short-term income trade. The net effect of the higher short strike is to reduce the cost and breakeven of the Bull Call Spread and adjust the directional nature of the trade. The higher call strike prices are further OTM and will therefore have lower premiums than the lower strike bought call.

So, in summary, if the stock falls below the lower (buy) strike, you can make a loss; if the stock rises to anywhere between the middle and upper (short) strikes, you make your maximum profit; if the stock rises above the highest strike, then you can make unlimited losses. The extra leg also ensures that you may have two breakeven points.

| Buy call | Sell call | Sell call | Bull Call Ladder |

Steps to Trading a Bull Call Ladder

1. Buy lower strike calls.

2. Sell the same number of middle strike calls with the same expiration date.

3. Sell the same number of higher strike calls with same expiration date.

   Steps In

   ■ Try to ensure that the trend is upward but identify a clear area of support and resistance.

   Steps Out

   ■ Manage your position according to the rules defined in your Trading Plan.

   ■ If the stock falls below your stop loss, then sell the long call, and if you're not permitted to trade naked calls, then unravel the entire position.

3.5.2 Context

Outlook

■ A Bull Call Ladder is a Bull Call Spread financed by selling an additional call further OTM. Although this strategy has an uncapped risk potential as the underlying asset rises significantly, with Bull Call Ladders, your outlook is dependent on the relationship between the stock price and the first strike price. If we look at the strategy as an extension of a Bull Call Spread, then our outlook becomes conservatively bullish. However, for our purposes, we're going to call this a direction-neutral strategy.

Rationale

■ To execute a direction neutral/conservatively bullish trade for enhanced **income.** The lower strike sold calls will have the effect of capping your upside, and the higher strike sold calls will reduce the cost basis and breakeven further, but at the expense of an uncapped downside.

Net Position

■ This can be a net debit or net credit trade because while your bought calls will be more expensive than your sold calls, you're selling more calls that you're buying. Most of the time this is likely to be a **net debit** trade.

■ Your maximum risk on the trade is uncapped because you are selling more calls than you're buying. Your maximum reward on the trade is limited to the difference between the middle and lower strike prices less your net debit or plus your net credit.

Effect of Time Decay

■ Time decay is harmful to the position around the lower strike price and becomes more helpful around the highest strike price.

Appropriate Time Period to Trade

■ It's safest to choose a shorter term to expiration in order to reduce the possibility of uncapped risk if the underlying asset rises too much.

Selecting the Stock

■ Choose from stocks with adequate liquidity, preferably over 500,000 Average Daily Volume (ADV).

■ Try to ensure that the trend is upward but identify a clear area of support and resistance.

Selecting the Options

■ Choose options with adequate liquidity; open interest should be at least 100, preferably 500.

■ The selection of your option legs really depends on whether you're using the strategy as a repair to the Bull Call Spread or as a Bull Call Ladder in its own right. You really need to use online tools to evaluate the optimum trade in your chosen context.

■ **Lower Strike**—Either ATM or slightly OTM.

■ **Middle Strike**—Higher (further OTM) than the lower strike.

■ **Higher Strike**—Even further OTM—use online tools to find the optimum yields and breakeven points at and before expiration.

■ **Expiration**—Because this started as a Bull Call Spread, you'd preferably have over six months; however, this can become dangerous with a Bull Call Ladder because you are now a net seller of options, which typically dictates that a shorter time to expiration is preferable. Use same expiration date for all legs.

3.5.3 Risk Profile

- **Maximum Risk**   [Uncapped]
- **Interim Risk**   [Net debit]
- **Maximum Reward** [Middle strike − lower strike − net debit]
- **Breakeven Down** [Lower strike + net debit]
- **Breakeven Up**   [Higher strike + middle strike − lower strike] − net debit

3.5.4 Greeks

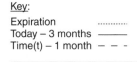

Key:
Expiration   ············
Today – 3 months ————
Time(t) – 1 month – – –

Risk Profile
As the stock price rises toward the middle strike, the position moves into profit. Maximum profit is achieved between then middle and higher strikes. The position then falls as the stock rises above the higher strike.

Delta
Delta (speed) is positive at lower levels and turns negative as the position changes direction.

Gamma
Gamma (acceleration) peaks around the lower strike, and then inversely around the higher strike, indicating how fast the position is moving at those points.

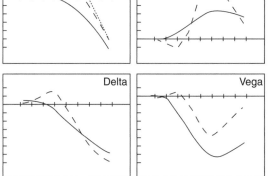

Theta
Time decay is helpful to the position when it is profitable.

Vega
Volatility is unhelpful to the position when it is profitable.

Rho
Higher interest rates are generally unhelpful to the position particularly when the stock reaches higher levels.

3.5.5 Advantages and Disadvantages

Advantages

- Lower cost and breakeven than a Bull Call Spread.

Disadvantages

- Confusing as to whether this is a bullish or bearish strategy.

- Uncapped downside if the stock rises.

- Typically used as a repair to a Bull Call Spread; therefore, this is only for more advanced traders.

3.5.6 Exiting the Trade

Exiting the Position

- With this strategy, you can simply unravel the spread by buying back the calls you sold and selling the calls you bought in the first place.

- Advanced traders may leg up and down as the underlying asset fluctuates up and down. In this way, the trader will be taking smaller incremental profits before the expiration of the trade.

Mitigating a Loss

- Unravel the trade as described previously.

- Advanced traders may choose to only partially unravel the spread leg-by-leg. In this way, they will leave one leg of the spread exposed in order to attempt to profit from it.

3.5.7 Example

ABCD is trading at $26.10 on May 14, 2004.

Buy the June 2004 25 strike call for $1.60.

Sell the June 2004 $27.50 strike call for $0.20.

Sell the June 2004 30 strike call for $0.10.

Net Debit	Premium bought − premiums sold **$1.60 − $0.20 − $0.10 = $1.30**
Interim Risk	Net debit **$1.30**
Maximum Risk	Unlimited
Maximum Reward	Middle strike − lower strike − net debit **$27.50 − $25.00 − $1.30 = $1.20**
Breakeven (Downside)	Lower strike + net debit **$25.00 + $1.30 = $26.30**
Breakeven (Upside)	Higher strike + middle strike − lower strike − net debit **$30.00 + $27.50 − $25.00 − $1.30 = $31.20**
Max ROI	92.31%

3.6 Bull Put Ladder

Proficiency	Direction	Volatility	Asset Legs	Max Risk	Max Reward	Strategy Type
(symbol)	(symbol)	(symbol)	(symbol) + (symbol) + (symbol)	(symbol)	(symbol)	(symbol)
Advanced	Bearish	High Volatility	■ Long Put ■ Long Put ■ Short Put	Capped	Uncapped	Income

3.6.1 Description

Can you see now why Ladders are so confusing? Here we have a *"Bull* Put Ladder," yet looking at it suggests that it has to be a *bearish* strategy!

The Bull Put Ladder is an extension to the Bull Put Spread. By buying another put at a lower strike, the position assumes uncapped reward potential if the stock plummets.

The problem is that now it's not totally clear if we have a bullish or bearish strategy, but because we are net long puts and we have uncapped profit potential if the stock falls, do we have to call this a bearish strategy? The answer lies in the reason for the trade and the position of the stock relative to the strikes.

Because we're net long options (and particularly OTM options), we're better off trading this as a longer-term strategy in order to counter the effects of time decay.

So, in summary, if the stock falls below the lower (buy) strike, we make potentially uncapped profit until the stock reaches zero; if the stock rises to anywhere between the middle and upper (short) strikes, we make our maximum loss. The extra leg also ensures that we may have two breakeven points.

Buy put   +   Buy put   +   Sell put   =   Bull Put Ladder

Steps to Trading a Bull Put Ladder

1. Buy lower strike puts.

2. Buy the same number of middle strike puts with the same expiration date.

3. Sell the same number of higher strike puts with same expiration date.

Steps In

■ Try to ensure you understand the direction of the trend and identify a clear area of both support and resistance.

Steps Out

- Manage your position according to the rules defined in your Trading Plan.

- In any event, look to unravel the position at least one month before expiration, either to capture your profit or to contain your losses.

3.6.2 Context

Outlook

- A Bull Put Ladder is a Bull Put Spread with an additional lower bought put further OTM. Although this strategy has an uncapped reward as the underlying asset declines significantly, with Bull Put Ladders, your outlook is dependent on the relationship between the stock price and the higher strike price. Because we are buying an additional put leg, we can categorize our outlook here as being **bearish.** Typically a Bull Put Ladder arises when a Bull Put Spread has gone wrong and the trader adjusts the position to become bearish.

Rationale

- To execute a bearish trade for a capital gain. The lower strike bought puts will have the effect of uncapping your profit potential; the higher strike sold puts will reduce the cost basis.

Net Position

- This can be a net debit or net credit transaction because while your sold puts will be more valuable than your bought puts, you're buying more puts that you're selling.

- Your maximum reward on the trade is uncapped because you are buying more puts than you're selling. Your total risk on the trade is limited to the difference between the lower and middle strike prices less your interim risk.

Effect of Time Decay

- Time decay is generally harmful when the position is losing money, particularly around the middle strike.

Appropriate Time Period to Trade

- Depending on the reasons for the trade, you will be safest to choose a medium to long term to expiration, enough time to allow the underlying asset to move and make the position profitable without time decay destroying the long options.

Selecting the Stock

■ Choose from stocks with adequate liquidity, preferably over 500,000 Average Daily Volume (ADV).

■ Try to ensure you understand the direction of the trend and identify a clear area of both support and resistance.

Selecting the Options

■ Choose options with adequate liquidity; open interest should be at least 100, preferably 500.

■ The selection of your option legs really depends on whether you're using the strategy as a repair to the Bull Put Spread or as a Bull Put Ladder in its own right. You really need to use online tools to evaluate the optimum trade in your chosen context, but here we'll assume the intent is to repair the Bull Put Spread.

■ **Lower Strike**—One or two strikes below the middle strike.

■ **Middle Strike**—One or two strikes below the higher strike because you started with a Bull Put Spread.

■ **Higher Strike**—Below support, preferably OTM.

■ **Expiration**—Typically, a Bull Put Spread is a short-term income strategy, so if you're adding the lowest buy leg to repair the original Bull Put, then by definition it will have been short-term (one month) trade. However, if trading the Bull Put Ladder in its own right, you are long two puts, so a medium term to expiration will be safer. Use the same expiration date for all legs.

3.6.3 Risk Profile

■ **Maximum Risk**	Limited to the difference between the middle and higher strikes plus the net debit.
■ **Interim Risk**	[Net debit]
■ **Maximum Reward**	[Lower strike − maximum risk]
■ **Breakeven Down**	[Lower strike − maximum risk]
■ **Breakeven Up**	[Higher strike + net debit] (or − net credit)

3.6.4 Greeks

Risk Profile

The position makes its maximum profit if the stock plummets. However, as an adjustment to the Bull Put Spread, the position can be profitable if the stock remains higher than the highest strike.

Delta

Delta (speed) is negative at lower levels and turns positive as the position changes direction.

Gamma

Gamma (acceleration) peaks around the lower strike.

Key:
Expiration   ···········
Today – 3 months ————
Time(t) – 1 month – – -

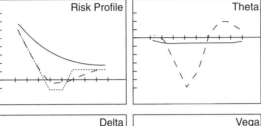

Theta

Time decay is helpful to the position when it is profitable and unhelpful when it is unprofitable.

Vega

Volatility is unhelpful to the position when it is profitable.

Rho

Higher interest rates are generally unhelpful to the position particularly when the stock reaches lower levels.

3.6.5 Advantages and Disadvantages

Advantages

■ Uncapped profit potential.

■ Capped risk.

Disadvantages

■ Confusing as to whether this is a bullish or bearish strategy.

■ The trade may be a net debit, whereas the standard Bull Put Spread is a net credit.

■ Typically used as a repair to a Bull Put Spread; therefore, this is only for more advanced traders.

3.6.6 Exiting the Trade

Exiting the Position

- With this strategy, you can simply unravel the spread by buying back the puts you sold and selling the puts you bought in the first place.

- Advanced traders may leg up and down as the underlying asset fluctuates up and down. In this way, the trader will be taking smaller incremental profits before the expiration of the trade.

Mitigating a Loss

- Unravel the trade as described previously.

- Advanced traders may choose to only partially unravel the spread leg-by-leg. In this way, they will leave one leg of the spread exposed in order to attempt to profit from it.

3.6.7 Example

ABCD is trading at $52.00 on May 15, 2004.

Buy the August 2004 40 strike put for $1.20.

Buy the August 2004 45 strike put for $2.40.

Sell the August 2004 50 strike put for $4.60.

Net Credit	Premium sold − premiums bought **$4.60 − $1.20 − $2.40 = $1.00**
Interim Risk	Net debit
	Here there is a net credit, so interim risk doesn't apply.
Maximum Risk	Higher strike − middle strike + net debit (or − net credit) **$50.00 − $45.00 − $1.00 = $4.00**
Maximum Reward	Lower strike − maximum risk **$40.00 − $4.00 = $36.00**
Breakeven (Downside)	Lower strike − maximum risk **$40.00 − $1.00 = $39.00**
Breakeven (Upside)	Higher strike + net debit (or − net credit) **$50.00 − $1.00 = $49.00**
Max ROI (If Stock Falls to Zero)	900.00%
Interim ROI (If Stock Rises Above Higher Strike)	25.00%

3.7 Bear Call Ladder

Proficiency	Direction	Volatility	Asset Legs	Max Risk	Max Reward	Strategy Type
Advanced	Bullish	High Volatility	■ Short Call ■ Long Call ■ Long Call	Capped	Uncapped	Capital Gain

3.7.1 Description

Again, can you see why Ladders are so confusing? Here we have a *"Bear* Call Ladder," yet looking at it would suggest that it has to be a *bullish* strategy!

The Bear Call Ladder is an extension to the Bear Call Spread. By buying another call at a higher strike, the position assumes uncapped reward potential if the stock soars.

The problem is that now it's not totally clear if we have a bullish or bearish strategy, but because we are net long calls and we have uncapped profit potential if the stock rises, do we have to call this a bearish strategy? The answer lies in the reason for the trade and the position of the stock relative to the strikes.

Because we're net long options (and particularly OTM options), we're better off trading this as a longer-term strategy in order to counter the effects of time decay.

So, in summary, if the stock rises above the higher (buy) strike, we make potentially uncapped profit; if the stock falls to anywhere between the middle and lower strikes, we make our maximum loss. The extra leg also ensures that we may have two breakeven points.

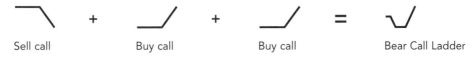

| Sell call | Buy call | Buy call | Bear Call Ladder |

Steps to Trading a Bear Call Ladder

1. Sell lower strike calls.

2. Buy the same number of middle strike calls with the same expiration date.

3. Buy the same number of higher strike calls with same expiration date.

   Steps In

   ■ The selection of your option legs really depends on whether you're using the strategy as a repair to the Bear Call Spread or as a Bear Call Ladder in its own right.

- Try to ensure that you understand the direction of the trend and identify a clear area of both support and resistance

Steps Out

- Manage your position according to the rules defined in your Trading Plan.

- In any event, look to unravel the position at least one month before expiration, either to capture your profit or to contain your losses.

3.7.2 Context

Outlook

- A Bear Call Ladder is a Bear Call Spread with an additional bought call leg further OTM. Although this strategy has an uncapped reward profile as the underlying asset rises significantly, with Bear Call Ladders, your outlook is dependent on the relationship between the stock price and the lower strike price. Because we are buying an additional call leg, we can categorize our outlook here as being **bullish.** Typically a Bear Call Ladder arises when a Bear Call Spread has gone wrong and the trader adjusts the position to become bullish.

Rationale

- To execute a bullish trade for a capital gain while reducing your maximum risk. The higher strike bought calls will have the effect of uncapping your upside potential.

Net Position

- This can be a net debit or net credit trade because while your sold call will be more valuable than your bought calls, you're buying more calls than you're selling.

- Your maximum risk on the trade is capped because you are buying more calls than you're selling. Your maximum reward on the trade is unlimited to the upside.

Effect of Time Decay

- Time decay is generally harmful when the position is losing money and helpful when the position is profitable.

Appropriate Time Period to Trade

- ■ Depending on the reasons for the trade, it's safest to choose a medium to long term to expiration, enough time to allow the underlying asset to move and make the position profitable without time decay destroying the long options.

Selecting the Stock

- ■ Choose from stocks with adequate liquidity, preferably over 500,000 Average Daily Volume (ADV).

- ■ Try to ensure you understand the direction of the trend and identify a clear area of both support and resistance

Selecting the Options

- ■ Choose options with adequate liquidity; open interest should be at least 100, preferably 500.

- ■ The selection of your option legs really depends on whether you're using the strategy as a repair to the Bear Call Spread or as a Bear Call Ladder in its own right. You really need to use online tools to evaluate the optimum trade in your chosen context, but here we'll assume the intent is to repair the Bear Call Spread.

- ■ **Lower Strike**—Slightly OTM, just above resistance for the stock.

- ■ **Middle Strike**—One or two strikes above the lower strike, i.e., further OTM.

- ■ **Higher Strike**—Above the middle strike, i.e., even further OTM.

- ■ **Expiration**—Typically, a Bear Call Spread is a short-term income strategy, so if you're adding the lowest buy leg to repair the original Bear Call, then by defi-nition it will have been short-term (one month) trade. However, with the Bear Call Ladder, you are long two calls, so a medium term to expiration (say around six months) would be safer. Use same expiration date for all legs.

3.7.3 Risk Profile

- ■ **Maximum Risk**   Limited to the difference between the lower and middle strikes plus the interim risk.

- ■ **Interim Risk**   [Net debit]

- ■ **Maximum Reward**   Uncapped

- ■ **Breakeven Down**   Lower strike − net debit (or + net credit)

- ■ **Breakeven Up**   [Higher strike + maximum risk]

3.7.4 Greeks

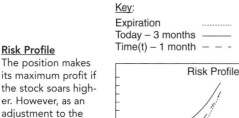

Key:
Expiration ....
Today – 3 months ———
Time(t) – 1 month – – –

Risk Profile
The position makes its maximum profit if the stock soars higher. However, as an adjustment to the Bear Call Spread, the position can be profitable if the stock remains lower than the lowest strike.

Delta
Delta (speed) is negative at lower levels and turns positive as the position changes direction.

Gamma
Gamma (acceleration) peaks around the higher strike.

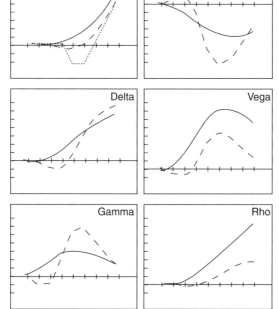

Theta
Time decay is helpful to the position at lower levels and becomes harmful at higher levels.

Vega
Volatility is helpful to the position at higher levels.

Rho
Higher interest rates are generally helpful to the position particularly when the stock reaches higher levels.

3.7.5 Advantages and Disadvantages

Advantages

- Uncapped profit potential.
- Capped risk.

Disadvantages

- Confusing as to whether this is a bullish or bearish strategy.
- The trade may be a net debit, whereas the standard Bear Call Spread is a net credit.
- Typically used as a repair to a Bear Call Spread; therefore, this is only for more advanced traders.

3.7.6 Exiting the Trade

Exiting the Position

- With this strategy, you can simply unravel the spread by buying back the calls you sold and selling the calls you bought in the first place.

- Advanced traders may leg up and down as the underlying asset fluctuates up and down. In this way, the trader will be taking smaller incremental profits before the expiration of the trade.

Mitigating a Loss

- Unravel the trade as described previously.

- Advanced traders may choose to only partially unravel the spread leg-by-leg. In this way, they will leave one leg of the spread exposed in order to attempt to profit from it.

3.7.7 Example

ABCD is trading at $48.00 on May 15, 2004.

Sell the August 2004 50 strike call for $4.20.

Buy the August 2004 55 strike call for $2.40.

Buy the August 2004 60 strike call for $0.80.

Net Credit	Premium sold − premiums bought **$4.20 − $2.40 − $0.80 = $1.00**
Interim Risk	Net debit Here there is a net credit, so interim risk doesn't apply.
Maximum Risk	Middle strike − lower strike + net debit (or − net credit) **$55.00 − $50.00 − $1.00 = $4.00**
Maximum Reward	Uncapped
Breakeven (Downside)	Lower strike − net debit (or + net credit) **$50.00 + $1.00 = $51.00**
Breakeven (Upside)	Higher strike + maximum risk **$60.00 − $4.00 = $64.00**
Interim ROI (If Stock Falls Below Lower Strike)	25.00%

3.8 Bear Put Ladder

Proficiency	Direction	Volatility	Asset Legs	Max Risk	Max Reward	Strategy Type
ⓘ	〰	⌇	⌒ + ⌒ + ◡	☠	⌐	💰
Advanced	Neutral	Low Volatility	■ Short Put ■ Short Put ■ Long Put	Uncapped	Capped	Income

3.8.1 Description

The Bear Put Ladder is an extension to the Bear Put Spread. By shorting another put at a lower strike price, the position assumes uncapped risk potential if the stock plummets downwards. Again, the problem is that now it's not totally clear if we have a bullish or bearish strategy, so we have to designate it as a direction neutral strategy! We'd love the stock to fall to the middle strike price but not below the lower short put strike price. Anywhere in between the middle and higher strike is ideal.

Because of the dangers of uncapped risk, this strategy becomes more appropriate for a short-term income trade. The net effect of the lower short strike is to reduce the cost and breakeven of the Bear Put Spread and adjust the directional nature of the trade. The lower put strike prices are further OTM and will therefore have lower premiums than the higher strike bought put.

So, in summary, if the stock rises above the higher (buy) strike, you can make a loss; if the stock falls to anywhere between the middle and lower (short) strikes, you make your maximum profit; if the stock falls below the lowest strike, then you can make unlimited losses. The extra leg also ensures that you may have two breakeven points.

╱‾	+	╱‾	+	╲_	=	╱╲
Sell put		Sell put		Buy put		Bear Put Ladder

Steps to Trading a Bear Put Ladder

1. Sell lower strike puts.

2. Sell the same number of middle strike puts with the same expiration date.

3. Buy the same number of higher strike puts with the same expiration date.

   Steps In

   ■ Try to ensure that the trend is downward but identify a clear area of support and resistance.

Steps Out

- Manage your position according to the rules defined in your Trading Plan.

- If the stock rises above your stop loss, then sell the Long Put, and if you're not permitted to trade Naked Puts, then unravel the entire position.

3.8.2 Context

Outlook

- A Bear Put Ladder is a Bear Put Spread financed by selling an additional put further OTM. Although this strategy has an uncapped risk potential if the underlying asset falls significantly, with Bear Put Ladders, your outlook is dependent on the relationship between the stock price and the higher strike price. If we look at the strategy as an extension of a Bear Put Spread, then our outlook becomes conservatively bearish. However, for our purposes we're going to call this a **direction neutral** strategy.

Rationale

- To execute a direction neutral/conservatively bearish trade for enhanced **income.** The lower strike sold puts will have the effect of uncapping your potential risk.

Net Position

- This can be a net debit or net credit trade because while your bought puts will be more expensive than your sold puts, you're selling more puts that you're buying. Most of the time this is likely to be a **net debit** trade.

- Your maximum risk on the trade is uncapped to the downside because you are selling more puts than you're buying. Your maximum reward on the trade is limited to the difference between the middle and higher strike prices less your net debit or plus your net credit.

Effect of Time Decay

- Time decay is generally helpful when the position is profitable, particularly around the middle strike.

Appropriate Time Period to Trade

- You will be safest to choose a shorter term to expiration in order to avoid the possibility of an uncapped loss scenario if the underlying asset falls too much.

Selecting the Stock

- Choose from stocks with adequate liquidity, preferably over 500,000 Average Daily Volume (ADV).

- Try to ensure that the trend is downward but identify a clear area of support and resistance.

Selecting the Options

- Choose options with adequate liquidity; open interest should be at least 100, preferably 500.

- The selection of your option legs really depends on whether you're using the strategy as a repair to the Bear Put Spread or as a Bear Put Ladder in its own right. You really need to use online tools to evaluate the optimum trade in your chosen context.

- **Lower Strike**—One or two strikes below the middle strike, depending on the amount of premium you can get.

- **Middle Strike**—One or two strikes below the higher strike.

- **Higher Strike**—Around ATM—use online tools to find the optimum yields and breakeven points at and before expiration.

- **Expiration**—Because this started as a Bear Put Spread, you'd preferably have over six months; however, this can become dangerous with a Bear Put Ladder because you are now a net seller of options, which typically dictates that a shorter time to expiration is preferable. Use the same expiration date for all legs.

3.8.3 Risk Profile

- **Maximum Risk**   Lower strike − [higher strike − middle strike] + net debit

- **Interim Risk**   Net debit.

- **Maximum Reward**   [Higher strike − middle strike − net debit]

- **Breakeven Down**   [Lower strike − maximum reward]

- **Breakeven Up**   [Higher strike + net debit]

3.8.4 Greeks

Key:
Expiration   ....
Today – 3 months ————
Time(t) – 1 month – – –

Risk Profile
As the stock price falls toward the middle strike, the position moves into profit. Maximum profit is achieved between then lower and middle strikes. The position then falls as the stock falls below the lower strike.

Delta
Delta (speed) is positive at lower levels and turns negative as the position changes direction.

Gamma
Gamma (acceleration) peaks inversely around the lower strike, and then positively around the higher strike.

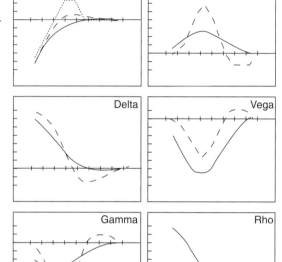

Theta
Time decay is helpful to the position when it is profitable.

Vega
Volatility is unhelpful to the position when it is profitable.

Rho
Higher interest rates are generally helpful to the position, particularly when the stock reaches lower levels.

3.8.5 Advantages and Disadvantages

Advantages

- Lower cost and better breakeven scenario than a Bear Put Spread.

- The farther away from expiration you are, the more downside protection you have in the event of the stock declining rapidly.

Disadvantages

- Confusing as to whether this is a bullish or bearish strategy.

- Capped upside if the stock rises.

- Uncapped downside if the stock falls.

- Typically used as a repair to a Bear Put Spread; therefore, this is only for more advanced traders.

3.8.6 Exiting the Trade

Exiting the Position

- With this strategy, you can simply unravel the spread by buying back the puts you sold and selling the puts you bought in the first place.

- Advanced traders may leg up and down as the underlying asset fluctuates up and down. In this way, the trader will be taking smaller incremental profits before the expiration of the trade.

Mitigating a Loss

- Unravel the trade as described previously.

- Advanced traders may choose to only partially unravel the spread leg-by-leg. In this way, they will leave one leg of the spread exposed in order to attempt to profit from it.

3.8.7 Example

ABCD is trading at $26.10 on May 14, 2004.

Sell the June 2004 $22.50 strike put for $0.30.

Sell the June 2004 25 strike put for $1.00.

Buy the June 2004 $27.50 strike put for $2.40.

Net Debit	Premium bought − premiums sold **$2.40 − $1.00 − $0.30 = $1.10**
Interim Risk	Net debit **$1.10**
Maximum Risk	Lower strike − [higher strike − middle strike] + net debit **$22.50 − ($27.50 − $25.00) + $1.10 = $21.10**
Maximum Reward	Higher strike − middle strike − net debit **$27.50 − $25.00 − $1.10 = $1.40**
Breakeven (Downside)	Lower strike − maximum reward **$22.50 − $1.40 = $21.10**
Breakeven (Upside)	Higher strike + net debit **$27.50 + $1.10 = $28.60**
Max ROI	6.64%
Interim ROI	Interim reward/maximum risk **N/A (there is no interim reward here, there is interim risk; therefore, there is no interim ROI).**

4

Volatility Strategies

Introduction

Volatility strategies are defined as those in which you can make a profit whether the stock moves up or down. The point is that you don't care which direction it moves, as long as it moves explosively in one direction or the other. The trick, of course, is spotting something that's about to make that move and then determining how to take advantage of it!

In my workshops, I always ask my delegates who's ever taken a stock tip before. Typically a number of sheepish faces look around the room at each other before the hands start to rise, and then I usher them all upwards! So, how about you? Have you ever taken a red-hot stock tip? I bet you have ... or will some time in the future!

So, if you took a tip, what happened? Did you win, or did you lose? Here's where most people admit that most of the tips went the wrong way. Very rarely does nothing happen—occasionally it goes your way, but in many cases, the precise opposite happens, time and time again!

The reality is that, as human beings, most of us will listen to a persuasive voice whose owner appears convinced as to the authenticity of the information he or she is now imparting to you. I tell most people that when evaluating a company, the last person you should ever listen to is the CEO, with the exception of the incomparable Warren Buffett! Typically, CEOs are rewarded on the strength of the performance of their companies in terms of profitability and share price. Has a CEO ever confided in you that his company is junk and you should run away from it? Of course not! So it's unlikely that you're going to get an objective analysis from a CEO.

So the question is this—what do we do if we get a stock tip and we're tempted to follow it? Well, I'm not so aloof as to completely look the other way, so I'm not going to preach that you should either! Instead, here's what to do. Typically a stock tip is a precursor to a big move in a stock. The rumors are flying around, and there's pent-up activity in the trading of the stock. The only things you don't know are the timing of such a move and the direction it's going to turn. Typically the incident won't be too far away, especially if the tip is concerning an announcement or news event. From here, one of three things is most likely to happen:

1. The news event happens as you were told it would, and the stock moves accordingly.

2. The news event happens in precisely the opposite way, and the stock accordingly explodes the other way!

3. The news event doesn't happen . . . and the stock moves the opposite way.

Occasionally the stock won't budge, but it's pretty rare. Why? Well, because people were expecting at least *something* to happen, and when nothing happens, there's either mass disappointment or mass relief. The point is that there will be a reaction to nothing, just as much as there would have been a reaction to something!

There are two great strategies for handling stock tips. The first is the Straddle, which we're going to cover in this section, and the second is the Synthetic Call, which we're going to cover in Chapter 7, "Synthetic Strategies." The Straddle involves buying and selling calls and puts with the same strike and expiration, which ensures that you can profit either way, provided that the stock moves explosively; the Synthetic Call ensures that you're insured if the stock falls, counter to your bullish expectations.

The Straddle can be made less expensive by adjusting the call and put strikes out of the money to create a Strangle. Because strangles are cheaper and your cost basis is lower, you stand to make bigger percentage returns if the stock moves explosively.

The other strategies in this section are "nice-to-haves," but they rarely form part of my trading arsenal, so don't worry unduly about them.

Volatility Strategies Staircase

This diagram shows how the various volatility strategies link together, highlighting their similarities and differences. You may want to complete the chapter first before coming back to this diagram so that you can better appreciate the links.

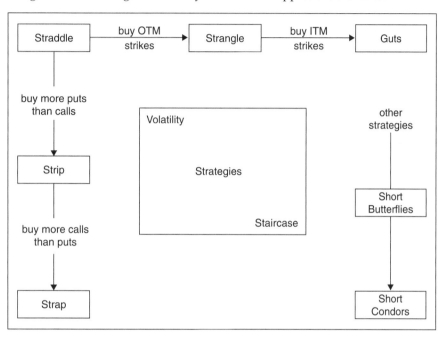

4.1 Straddle

Proficiency	Direction	Volatility	Asset Legs	Max Risk	Max Reward	Strategy Type
Intermediate	Neutral	High	▪ Long Put ▪ Long Call	Capped	Uncapped	Capital Gain

4.1.1 Description

The Straddle is the most popular volatility strategy and the easiest to understand. We simply buy puts and calls with the same strike price and expiration date so that we can profit from a stock soaring up or plummeting down. Each leg of the trade has limited downside (i.e., the call or put premium) but uncapped upside. Assuming that the movement of the stock is enough to cover the cost of the trade, we should be profitable.

However, we also need to apply various rules when trading straddles. The problem with buying options includes time decay and the Bid/Ask Spread. Time decay hurts long options positions because options are like wasting assets. The closer we get to expiration, the less time value there is in the option. Time decay accelerates exponentially during the last month before expiration, so we don't want to hold onto OTM or ATM options into the last month. We also do not want to be buying and selling the same Straddle too frequently because typically the Bid/Ask Spread is quite wide, and if we continually buy at the Ask and sell at the Bid when the stock hasn't moved for us, then the spread will cause us to lose.

So we must have a number of reasons for getting in, staying in, and then getting out. We also need to know that the price that we're paying for the Straddle is reasonable in comparison to the propensity the stock has to making a significant move. In other words, the cheaper the cost of the Straddle, the better, provided that the stock is one that can and will move explosively.

Here are the rules for trading straddles:

1. My personal preference is to choose stocks over $20.00, preferably no more than $60.00. That's not to say that you can't make profits from stocks outside of that range; it's simply my own comfort zone.

2. Only do a Straddle on a stock that is close to making an announcement, such as the week before an earnings report.

3. Buy ATM calls and puts with the expiration at least two months away, preferably three. You can get away with four months if nothing else is available.

4. The cost of the Straddle should be less than half of the stock's recent high less its recent low. By recent, we mean the last 40 trading days for a two-month straddle, the last 60 trading days for a three-month straddle, or the last 80 days for a four-month straddle. The point here is that the cost of the Straddle should be low in comparison with the potential of the stock to move.

5. Exit within two weeks after the news event occurs. Try to avoid holding the position during the final month before expiration. In the final month, options suffer from accelerating time decay, which would therefore erode our position.

6. Try to find a stock that is forming a consolidation pattern, such as a flag or pennant, or in other words, where the stock price action has become tighter and where volatility has shrunk in advance of a big move in either direction. You should familiarize yourself with the basics of technical analysis at the very least.

It's important to follow the entry and exit rules for straddles, and psychologically speaking, the Straddle is a tough strategy to play after you're in. It's very easy to find reasons to exit, even though it's in breach of your trading plan. But you must remember that you got in for a certain reason (or reasons), and you must stay in until one of your other reasons compels you to exit.

Buy ATM put   +   Buy ATM call   =   Straddle

Steps to Trading a Straddle

1. Buy ATM strike puts, preferably with about three months to expiration.

2. Buy ATM strike calls with the same expiration.

Steps In

- Actively seek chart patterns that appear like pennant formations, signifying a consolidating price pattern.

- Try to concentrate on stocks with news events and earnings reports about to happen within two weeks.

- Choose a stock price range you feel comfortable with. For some traders, that's between $20.00 and $60.00.

Steps Out

- Manage your position according to the rules defined in your Trading Plan.

- Exit either a few days after the news event occurs where there is no movement, or after the news event where there has been profitable movement.

- If the stock thrusts up, sell the call (making a profit for the entire position) and wait for a retracement to profit from the put.

- If the stock thrusts down, sell the put (making a profit for the entire position) and wait for a retracement to profit from the call.

- Try to avoid holding into the last month; otherwise, you'll be exposed to serious time decay.

4.1.2 Context

Outlook

- With straddles, your outlook is **direction neutral.** You are looking for increasing volatility with the stock price moving explosively in either direction.

Rationale

- To execute a neutral trade for a capital gain while expecting a surge in volatility. Ideally you are looking for a scenario where Implied Volatility is currently very low, giving you low option prices, but the stock is about to make an explosive move—you just don't know which direction.

Net Position

- This is a **net debit** transaction because you have bought calls and puts.

- Your maximum risk on the trade itself is limited to the net debit of the bought calls and puts. Your maximum reward is potentially unlimited.

Effect of Time Decay

■ Time decay is harmful to the Straddle. Never keep a Straddle into the last month to expiration because this is when time decay accelerates the fastest.

Appropriate Time Period to Trade

■ We want to combine safety with prudence on cost. Therefore the optimum time period to trade straddles is with three months until expiration, but if the stock has not moved decisively, sell your position when there is one month to expiration. *Be wary of holding a Straddle into the last month.*

Selecting the Stock

■ Choose from stocks with adequate liquidity, preferably over 500,000 Average Daily Volume (ADV).

■ Actively seek chart patterns that appear like pennant formations, signifying a consolidating price pattern that may be about to explode.

■ Try to concentrate on stocks with news events and earnings reports about to happen within two weeks.

■ Choose a stock price range you feel comfortable with.

Selecting the Options

■ Choose options with adequate liquidity; open interest should be at least 100, preferably 500.

■ **Strike**—ATM for the put and call.

■ **Expiration**—Preferably around three months. Use the same expiration date for both legs.

4.1.3 Risk Profile

■ **Maximum Risk**   [Net debit paid]

■ **Maximum Reward** [Uncapped]

■ **Breakeven Down**   [Strike − net debit]

■ **Breakeven Up**   [Strike + net debit]

4.1.4 Greeks

Key:
Expiration   ....
Today – 3 months ————
Time(t) – 1 month – – –

Risk Profile
If the stock price remains around the strike price, we make our maximum loss. If it moves explosively in either direction, we make profits.

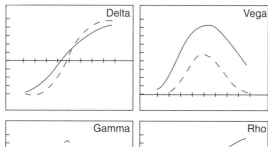

Theta
Time decay is most harmful when the position is unprofitable.

Delta
Delta (speed) is at its greatest when the position is making money in either direction. The negative Delta is purely an indication of direction; i.e., making profit as the stock falls.

Vega
Volatility is helpful to the position particularly at the strike price where the stock hasn't yet moved.

Gamma
Gamma (acceleration) peaks around the strike price, illustrating the position's turning point and the fastest rate of change.

Rho
Higher interest rates are generally helpful to the position when the stock rises and vice versa.

4.1.5 Advantages and Disadvantages

Advantages

- Profit from a volatile stock moving in either direction.

- Capped risk.

- Uncapped profit potential if the stock moves.

Disadvantages

- Expensive—you have to buy the ATM call and put.

- Significant movement of the stock and option prices is required to make a profit.

- Bid/Ask Spread can adversely affect the quality of the trade.

- Psychologically demanding strategy.

4.1.6 Exiting the Trade

Exiting the Position

- With this strategy, you can simply unravel the spread by selling your calls and puts.

- You can also exit only your profitable leg of the trade and hope that the stock retraces to favor the unprofitable side later on. For example, if the share has moved decisively upwards, thus making the call profitable, you will sell the calls and make a profit on the entire trade, but you will be left with almost valueless puts. Having now sold the calls, you will hope that the stock may retrace and enhance the value of the puts you are still holding, which you can then sell.

Mitigating a Loss

- Sell the position if you have only one month left to expiration. Do not hold on, hoping for the best, because you risk losing your entire stake.

4.1.7 Example

ABCD is trading at $25.37 on May 17, 2004.

Buy the August 2004 25 strike put for $1.70.

Buy the August 2004 25 strike call for $2.40.

Net Debit	Premiums bought **$1.70 + $2.40 = $4.10**
Maximum Risk	Net debit **$4.10**
Maximum Reward	Uncapped
Breakeven Down	Strike − net debit **$25.00 − $4.10 = $20.90**
Breakeven Up	Strike + net debit **$25.00 + $4.10 = $29.10**

So we can see that if we held on to expiration, our breakevens would be $20.90 and $29.10, respectively. In other words, the stock would have to fall to below $20.90 or rise above $29.10 in order for us to make a profit. In reality we don't hold on until expiration, and therefore, because both options will still contain some time value before that final month, our breakevens will be slightly more narrow, which of course helps us.

In the previous example, we haven't taken into account the rules, but let's assume that there was an earnings announcement on, say, May 21. Let's also assume that the three-month high had been $26.49 and the three-month low had been $16.39. The difference between the two is $10.10. Divide in half to get $5.05, which is greater than our Straddle cost of $4.10. Therefore we passed the rules, assuming of course that the chart pattern was acceptable!

4.2 Strangle

Proficiency	Direction	Volatility	Asset Legs	Max Risk	Max Reward	Strategy Type
Intermediate	Neutral	High	■ Long Put ■ Long Call	Capped	Uncapped	Capital Gain

4.2.1 Description

The Strangle is a simple adjustment to the Straddle to make it slightly cheaper. Instead of buying ATM options, we buy OTM calls and puts, which creates a lower cost basis and therefore potentially higher returns. The risk we run with a Strangle is that the breakevens can be pushed further apart, which is bad, but where the difference is not too great (and that's a judgment call), then the Strangle can be spectacular.

The Strangle is the second easiest volatility strategy to understand, and we only look at it if the Straddle criteria have been obeyed. We simply buy lower strike puts and higher strike calls with the same expiration date so that we can profit from the stock soaring up or plummeting down. As with the Straddle, each leg of the trade has limited downside (i.e., the call or put premium) but uncapped upside.

Again the same challenges apply regarding Bid/Ask Spreads and the psychology of the actual trade. Remember that time decay hurts long options positions because options are like wasting assets. The closer we get to expiration, the less time value there is in the option. Time decay accelerates exponentially during the last month before expiration, so we don't want to hold onto OTM or ATM options into the last month.

Use the Straddle rules but then make an adjustment for the Strangle:

1. Instead of trading the ATM calls and puts, choose the next strike lower for the put and the next strike higher for the call.

2. Now compare the breakeven scenarios for the Strangle to those for the Straddle. Typically the Strangle's breakevens will be slightly wider. Now you must make a judgment between the cost of the Strangle and the likelihood of the stock moving explosively up or down. Because the rules have already passed, you should have established a good likelihood of a move happening.

Again, it's important to follow the entry and exit rules, and psychologically speaking, it's another tough strategy to play after you're in. It's very easy to find reasons to exit, even though it's in breach of your trading plan. But you must remember that you got in for a certain reason (or reasons), and you must stay in until one of your other reasons compels you to exit.

| Buy OTM put | + | Buy OTM call | = | Strangle |

Steps to Trading a Strangle

1. Buy OTM (lower) strike puts, preferably with about three months to expiration.

2. Buy OTM (higher) strike calls with the same expiration.

Steps In

- Actively seek chart patterns that appear like pennant formations, signifying a consolidating price pattern.

- Try to concentrate on stocks with news events and earnings reports about to happen within two weeks.

- Choose a stock price range you feel comfortable with. For some traders, that's between $20.00 and $60.00.

Steps Out

- Manage your position according to the rules defined in your Trading Plan.

- Exit either a few days after the news event occurs where there is no movement or after the news event where there has been profitable movement.

- If the stock thrusts up, sell the call (making a profit for the entire position) and wait for a retracement to profit from the put.

- If the stock thrusts down, sell the put (making a profit for the entire position) and wait for a retracement to profit from the call.

- Try to avoid holding into the last month; otherwise, you'll be exposed to serious time decay.

4.2.2 Context

Outlook

- With strangles, your outlook is **direction neutral.** You are looking for increasing volatility with the stock price moving explosively in either direction.

Rationale

- To execute a neutral trade for a capital gain while expecting a surge in volatility. Ideally you are looking for a scenario where Implied Volatility is currently very low, giving you low option prices, but the stock is about to make an explosive move—you just don't know which direction.

■ Strangles are cheaper than Straddles because you are buying OTM options on both sides, as opposed to buying ATM options. This can also have the effect of widening your breakeven points.

Net Position

■ This is a **net debit** transaction because you have bought calls and puts.

■ Your maximum risk on the trade itself is limited to the net debit of the bought calls and puts. Your maximum reward is potentially unlimited.

Effect of Time Decay

■ Time decay is harmful to the Strangle. Never keep a Strangle into the last month to expiration because this is the time when time decay accelerates the fastest.

Appropriate Time Period to Trade

■ We want to combine safety with prudence on cost. Therefore, the optimum time period to trade Strangles is with three months until expiration, but if the stock has not moved decisively, sell your position when there is one month to expiration. *Be wary of holding a Strangle into the last month.*

Selecting the Stock

■ Choose from stocks with adequate liquidity, preferably over 500,000 Average Daily Volume (ADV).

■ Actively seek chart patterns that appear like pennant formations, signifying a consolidating price pattern that may be about to explode.

■ Try to concentrate on stocks with news events and earnings reports about to happen within two weeks.

■ Choose a stock price range you feel comfortable with.

Selecting the Options

■ Choose options with adequate liquidity; open interest should be at least 100, preferably 500.

■ **Put Strike**—Below the current stock price.

■ **Call Strike**—Above the current stock price.

■ **Expiration**—Preferably around three months. Use the same expiration date for both legs.

4.2.3 Risk Profile

- **Maximum Risk**   [Net debit paid]

- **Maximum Reward**   [Uncapped]

- **Breakeven Down**   [Lower strike − net debit]

- **Breakeven Up**   [Higher strike + net debit]

4.2.4 Greeks

Key:
Expiration   ....
Today − 3 months ————
Time(t) − 1 month — — —

Risk Profile
If the stock price remains between the strike prices, we make our maximum loss. If it moves explosively in either direction, we make profits.

Delta
Delta (speed) is at its greatest when the position is making money in either direction. The negative Delta is purely an indication of direction; i.e., making profit as the stock falls.

Gamma
Gamma (acceleration) peaks between the strike prices, illustrating the position's turning point and the fastest rate of change.

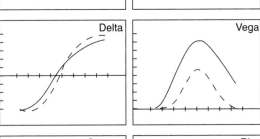
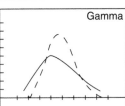
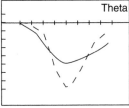
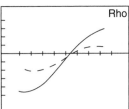

Theta
Time decay is most harmful when the position is unprofitable.

Vega
Volatility is helpful to the position, particularly between the strike prices.

Rho
Higher interest rates are generally helpful to the position when the stock rises and vice versa.

4.2.5 Advantages and Disadvantages

Advantages

- Profit from a volatile stock moving in either direction.

- Capped risk.

- Uncapped profit potential if the stock moves.

- Cheaper than a Straddle.

Disadvantages

■ Significant movement of the stock and option prices is required to make a profit.

■ Bid/Ask Spread can adversely affect the quality of the trade.

■ Psychologically demanding strategy.

4.2.6 Exiting the Trade

Exiting the Position

■ With this strategy, you can simply unravel the spread by selling your calls and puts.

■ You can also exit only your profitable leg of the trade and hope that the stock retraces to favor the unprofitable side later on. For example, if the share has moved decisively upwards, thus making the call profitable, you will sell the calls and make a profit on the entire trade, but you will be left with almost valueless puts. Having now sold the calls, you will hope that the stock may retrace and enhance the value of the puts you are still holding, which you can then sell.

Mitigating a Loss

■ Sell the position if you have only one month left to expiration. Do not hold on, hoping for the best, because you risk losing your entire stake.

4.2.7 Example

ABCD is trading at $25.37 on May 17, 2004.

Buy the August 2004 $22.50 strike put for $0.85.

Buy the August 2004 $27.50 strike call for $1.40.

Net Debit	Premiums bought **$0.85 − $1.40 = $2.25**
Maximum Risk	Net debit **$2.25**
Maximum Reward	Uncapped
Breakeven Down	Lower strike − net debit **$22.50 − $2.25 = $20.25**
Breakeven Up	Higher strike + net debit **$27.50 + $2.25 = $29.75**

Let's compare this trade to the Straddle in the previous section. The main differences in results are that the net debit is less and the breakevens are about $0.65 wider at expiration. The question is . . . would we prefer the Straddle or the Strangle?

This is a judgment call based on the potential movement of the stock, coupled with your experience and the news event you're anticipating. In this case, with no other information other than that the Straddle passed the rules, I'd be tempted!

4.3 Strip

Proficiency	Direction	Volatility	Asset Legs	Max Risk	Max Reward	Strategy Type
Expert	Bearish	High	■ Two Long Puts ■ One Long Call	Capped	Uncapped	Capital Gain

4.3.1 Description

The Strip is a simple adjustment to the Straddle to make it more biased toward the downside. In buying a second put, the strategy retains its preference for high volatility but now with a more bearish slant.

As with the Straddle, we choose the ATM strike for both legs, which means the strategy is expensive. We're therefore requiring a pretty big move, preferably with the stock plunging downwards. As such, our risk is greater than with the Straddle, and our reward is still uncapped. Because we bought double the number of puts, our position improves at double the speed, so the breakeven to the downside is slightly tighter. The breakeven to the upside is the strike plus the net debit, which is more than the Straddle because we've bought double the amount of puts.

Again the same challenges apply regarding Bid/Ask Spreads and the psychology of the actual trade. Remember that time decay hurts long options positions because options are like wasting assets. The closer we get to expiration, the less time value there is in the option. Time decay accelerates exponentially during the last month before expiration, so we don't want to hold onto OTM or ATM options into the last month.

Use the Straddle rules but buy twice as many puts as calls in order to make an adjustment for the Strip.

Again, it's important to follow the entry and exit rules (as for straddles), and psychologically speaking, this is another tough strategy to play after you're in. It's very easy to find reasons to exit, even though it's in breach of your trading plan. But you must remember that you got in for a certain reason (or reasons), and you must stay in until one of your other reasons compels you to exit.

Here's a reminder of the rules for trading straddles that you must also apply to strips:

1. Choose your preferred stock price range. Some traders choose stocks between $20.00 and $60.00, but that's a personal preference.

2. Only do a Strip on a stock that is close to making an announcement that may cause a surprise jump in the stock price either way, such as the week before an earnings report.

3. Buy ATM calls and puts with the expiration at least two months away, preferably three. You can get away with four months if nothing else is available.

4. The cost of the Straddle should be less than half of the stock's recent high less its recent low. By recent, we mean the last 40 trading days for a two-month Straddle, the last 60 trading days for a three-month Straddle, or the last 80 days for a four-month Straddle. The point here is that the cost of the Straddle should be low in comparison with the potential of the stock to move. If this works with the Straddle, then the Strip can be acceptable.

5. Exit within two weeks after the news event occurs. Never hold into the final month before expiration. During the final month, your options will suffer increasing time decay, which we don't want to be exposed to.

6. Try to find a stock that is forming a consolidation pattern, such as a flag or pennant, or in other words, where the stock price action has become tighter and where volatility has shrunk in advance of a big move in either direction. Typically we're looking for a pennant within the context of a downward trend.

| Buy two ATM puts | Buy ATM call | Strip |

Steps to Trading a Strip

1. Buy two ATM strike puts, preferably with about three months to expiration.

2. Buy one ATM strike call with the same expiration.

Keep the ratio as two puts for one call.

Steps In

■ Actively seek chart patterns that appear like pennant formations, signifying a consolidating price pattern.

■ Try to concentrate on stocks with news events and earnings reports about to happen within two weeks.

■ Choose a stock price range you feel comfortable with. For some traders, that's between $20.00 and $60.00.

Steps Out

■ Manage your position according to the rules defined in your Trading Plan.

■ Exit either a few days after the news event occurs where there is no movement, or after the news event where there has been profitable movement.

■ If the stock thrusts up, sell the call (making a profit for the entire position) and wait for a retracement to profit from the puts.

■ If the stock thrusts down, sell the puts (making a profit for the entire position) and wait for a retracement to profit from the call.

■ Try to avoid holding into the last month; otherwise, you'll be exposed to serious time decay.

4.3.2 Context

Outlook

■ With strips, your outlook is **neutral** to **bearish.** You are looking for increasing volatility with the stock price moving explosively in either direction, preferably to the downside.

Rationale

■ To execute a neutral to bearish trade for a capital gain while expecting a surge in volatility to the downside. Ideally you are looking for a scenario where Implied Volatility is currently very low, giving you low option prices, but the stock is about to make an explosive move—you don't know which direction, but you have a bias toward the downside.

Net Position

■ This is a **net debit** transaction because you have bought calls and puts.

■ Your maximum risk on the trade itself is limited to the net debit of the bought calls and puts. Your maximum reward is potentially unlimited.

Effect of Time Decay

■ Time decay is harmful to the Strip. Never keep a Strip into the last month to expiration because this is when time decay accelerates the fastest.

Appropriate Time Period to Trade

■ We want to combine safety with prudence on cost. Therefore, the optimum time period to trade strips is with three months until expiration, but if the stock has not moved decisively, sell your position when there is one month to expiration. *Be wary of holding a Strip into the last month.*

Selecting the Stock

■ Choose from stocks with adequate liquidity, preferably over 500,000 Average Daily Volume (ADV).

■ Actively seek chart patterns that appear like pennant formations, signifying a consolidating price pattern, preferably within a downward trend.

■ Try to concentrate on stocks with news events and earnings reports about to happen within two weeks.

■ Choose a stock price range you feel comfortable with.

Selecting the Options

■ Choose options with adequate liquidity; open interest should be at least 100, preferably 500.

■ **Strike**—ATM for the puts and call.

■ **Expiration**—Preferably around three months. Use the same expiration date for both legs.

4.3.3 Risk Profile

■ **Maximum Risk**   [Net debit paid]

■ **Maximum Reward**   [Uncapped]

■ **Breakeven Down**   [Strike − half the net debit]

■ **Breakeven Up**   [Strike + net debit]

4.3.4 Greeks

Key:
Expiration   ....
Today – 3 months ————
Time(t) – 1 month – – -

Risk Profile
If the stock price remains around the strike price, we make our maximum loss. If it moves explosively in either direction, we make profits, particularly if the stock moves down.

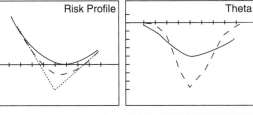

Theta
Time decay is most harmful when the position is unprofitable.

Delta
Delta (speed) is at its greatest when the position is making money in either direction. The negative Delta is purely an indication of direction; i.e., making profit as the stock falls.

Gamma
Gamma (acceleration) peaks around the strike price, illustrating the position's turning point and the fastest rate of change.

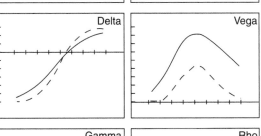

Vega
Volatility is helpful to the position, particularly at the strike price where the stock hasn't yet moved.

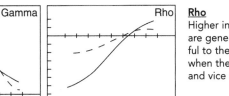

Rho
Higher interest rates are generally unhelpful to the position when the stock falls and vice versa.

4.3.5 Advantages and Disadvantages

Advantages

- Profit from a volatile stock moving in either direction.
- Capped risk.
- Uncapped profit potential if the stock moves.

Disadvantages

- Expensive—you have to buy the ATM call and puts.
- Significant movement of the stock and option prices is required to make a profit.
- Bid/Ask Spread can adversely affect the quality of the trade.
- Psychologically demanding strategy.

4.3.6 Exiting the Trade

Exiting the Position

- With this strategy, you can simply unravel the spread by selling your calls and puts.
- You can also exit only your profitable side of the trade and hope that the stock moves to favor the unprofitable side later on. For example, if the share has moved decisively downwards, thus making the puts profitable, you will sell the puts and make a profit on the entire trade, but you will be left with almost valueless calls. Having now sold the puts, you will hope that the stock may retrace upwards and enhance the value of the calls you are still holding, which you can then sell.

Mitigating a Loss

- Sell the position if you have only one month left to expiration. Do not hold on, hoping for the best, because you risk losing your entire stake.

4.3.7 Example

ABCD is trading at $25.37 on May 17, 2004.

Buy two August 2004 25 strike puts at $1.70.

Buy the August 2004 25 strike call for $2.40.

Net Debit	Premiums bought **$3.40 + $2.40 = $5.80**
Maximum Risk	Net debit **$5.80**
Maximum Reward	Uncapped
Breakeven Down	Strike − (net debit / 2) **$25.00 − $2.90 = $22.10**
Breakeven Up	Strike + net debit **$25.00 + $5.80 = $30.80**

We can see that if we held on to expiration, our breakevens would be $22.10 and $30.80, respectively. In other words, the stock would have to fall to below $22.10 or rise above $30.80 in order for us to make a profit. In reality, we don't hold on until expiration, and therefore because both options will still contain some time value before that final month, our breakevens will be slightly more narrow, which of course helps us.

In the previous example, we've assumed that the rules required to make a Straddle have been passed in order for us to contemplate the Strip!

4.4 Strap

Proficiency	Direction	Volatility	Asset Legs	Max Risk	Max Reward	Strategy Type
Expert	Bullish	High	■ One Long Put ■ Two Long Calls	Capped	Uncapped	Capital Gain

4.4.1 Description

The Strap is a simple adjustment to the Straddle to make it more biased to the upside. In buying a second call, the strategy retains its preference for high volatility but now with a more bullish slant.

As with the Straddle, we choose the ATM strike for both legs, which means the strategy is expensive. We're therefore requiring a pretty big move, preferably with the stock soaring upwards. As such, our risk is greater than with the Straddle, and our reward is still uncapped. Because we bought double the number of calls, our position improves at double the speed, so the breakeven to the upside is slightly tighter. The breakeven to the downside is the strike less the net debit, which is more than the Straddle because we've bought double the amount of calls.

Again the same challenges apply regarding Bid/Ask Spreads and the psychology of the actual trade. Remember that time decay hurts long options positions because options are like wasting assets. The closer we get to expiration, the less time value there is in the option. Time decay accelerates exponentially during the last month before expiration, so we don't want to hold onto OTM or ATM options into the last month.

Use the Straddle rules but buy twice as many calls as puts in order to make an adjustment for the Strap.

Again, it's important to follow the entry and exit rules (as for straddles), and psychologically speaking, it's another tough strategy to play after you're in. It's very easy to find reasons to exit, even though it's in breach of your trading plan. But you must remember that you got in for a certain reason (or reasons), and you must stay in until one of your other reasons compels you to exit.

Here's a reminder of the rules for trading straddles that you must also apply for straps:

1. Choose your preferred stock price range. Some traders choose stocks between $20.00 and $60.00, but that's a personal preference.

2. Only do a Strap on a stock that is close to making an announcement, such as the week before an earnings report.

3. Buy ATM calls and puts with the expiration at least two months away, preferably three. You can get away with four months if nothing else is available.

4. The cost of the Straddle should be less than half of the stock's recent high less its recent low. By recent, we mean the last 40 trading days for a two-month Straddle, the last 60 trading days for a three-month Straddle, or the last 80 days for a four-month Straddle. The point here is that the cost of the Straddle should be low in comparison with the potential of the stock to move. If this works with the Straddle, then the Strap can be acceptable.

5. Exit within two weeks after the news event occurs. Never hold into the final month before expiration. During the final month, your options will suffer increasing time decay, which we don't want to be exposed to.

6. Try to find a stock that is forming a consolidation pattern, such as a flag or pennant, or in other words where the stock price action has become tighter and where volatility has shrunk in advance of a big move in either direction. Typically we're looking for a pennant within the context of an upward trend.

Buy ATM put   Buy two ATM calls   Strap

Steps to Trading a Strap

1. Buy one ATM strike put with the same expiration.

2. Buy two ATM strike calls, preferably with about three months to expiration.

Keep the ratio as two calls for one put.

Steps In

- Actively seek chart patterns that appear like pennant formations, signifying a consolidating price pattern.

- Try to concentrate on stocks with news events and earnings reports about to happen within two weeks.

- Choose a stock price range you feel comfortable with. For some traders, that's between $20.00 and $60.00.

Steps Out

- Manage your position according to the rules defined in your Trading Plan.

- Exit either a few days after the news event occurs where there is no movement, or after the news event where there has been profitable movement.

- If the stock thrusts up, sell the calls (making a profit for the entire position) and wait for a retracement to profit from the put.

- If the stock thrusts down, sell the put (making a profit for the entire position) and wait for a retracement to profit from the calls.

- Try to avoid holding into the last month; otherwise, you'll be exposed to serious time decay.

4.4.2 Context

Outlook

- With straps, your outlook is **neutral** to **bullish.** You are looking for increasing volatility with the stock price moving explosively in either direction, preferably to the upside.

Rationale

- To execute a neutral to bullish trade for a capital gain while expecting a surge in volatility to the upside. Ideally you are looking for a scenario where Implied Volatility is currently very low, giving you low option prices, but the stock is about to make an explosive move—you don't know which direction, but you have a bias toward the upside.

Net Position

- This is a **net debit** transaction because you have bought calls and puts.

- Your maximum risk on the trade itself is limited to the net debit of the bought calls and puts. Your maximum reward is potentially unlimited.

Effect of Time Decay

■ Time decay is harmful to the Strap. Never keep a Strap into the last month to expiration because this is when time decay accelerates the fastest.

Appropriate Time Period to Trade

■ We want to combine safety with prudence on cost. Therefore, the optimum time period to trade straps is with three months until expiration, but if the stock has not moved decisively, sell your position when there is one month to expiration. *Never hold a Strap into the last month.*

Selecting the Stock

■ Choose from stocks with adequate liquidity, preferably over 500,000 Average Daily Volume (ADV).

■ Actively seek chart patterns that appear like pennant formations, signifying a consolidating price pattern, preferably within an upward trend.

■ Try to concentrate on stocks with news events and earnings reports about to happen within two weeks.

■ Choose a stock price range you feel comfortable with.

Selecting the Options

■ Choose options with adequate liquidity; open interest should be at least 100, preferably 500.

■ **Strike**—ATM for the put and calls.

■ **Expiration**—Preferably around three months. Use the same expiration date for both legs.

4.4.3 Risk Profile

■ **Maximum Risk**   [Net debit paid]

■ **Maximum Reward**   [Uncapped]

■ **Breakeven Down**   [Strike − net debit]

■ **Breakeven Up**   [Strike + half the net debit]

4.4.4 Greeks

Key:

Expiration   ....
Today – 3 months ————
Time(t) – 1 month – – –

Risk Profile
If the stock price remains around the strike price, we make our maximum loss. If it moves explosively in either direction, we make profits, particularly if the stock moves up.

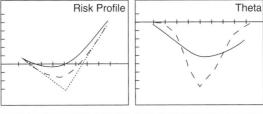

Theta
Time decay is most harmful when the position is unprofitable.

Delta
Delta (speed) is at its greatest when the position is making money in either direction. The negative Delta is purely an indication of direction; i.e., making profit as the stock falls.

Gamma
Gamma (acceleration) peaks around the strike price, illustrating the position's turning point and the fastest rate of change.

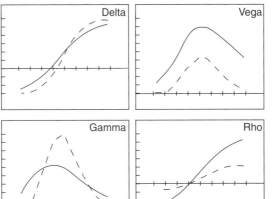

Vega
Volatility is helpful to the position, particularly at the strike price where the stock hasn't yet moved.

Rho
Higher interest rates are generally helpful to the position when the stock rises and vice versa.

4.4.5 Advantages and Disadvantages

Advantages

- Profit from a volatile stock moving in either direction.

- Capped risk.

- Uncapped profit potential if the stock moves.

Disadvantages

- Expensive—you have to buy the ATM calls and put.

- Significant movement of the stock and option prices is required to make a profit.

- Bid/Ask Spread can adversely affect the quality of the trade.

- Psychologically demanding strategy.

4.4.6 Exiting the Trade

Exiting the Position

- With this strategy, you can simply unravel the spread by selling your calls and puts.

- You can also exit only your profitable side of the trade and hope that the stock moves to favor the unprofitable side later on. For example, if the share has moved decisively upwards, thus making the calls profitable, you will sell the calls and make a profit on the entire trade, but you will be left with almost valueless puts. Having now sold the calls, you will hope that the stock may retrace upwards and enhance the value of the puts you are still holding, which you can then sell.

Mitigating a Loss

- Sell the position if you have only one month left to expiration. Do not hold on, hoping for the best, because you risk losing your entire stake.

4.4.7 Example

ABCD is trading at $25.37 on May 17, 2004.

Buy the August 2004 25 strike put at $1.70.

Buy two August 2004 25 strike calls for $2.40.

Net Debit	Premiums bought **$1.70 + $4.80 = $6.50**
Maximum Risk	Net debit **$6.50**
Maximum Reward	Uncapped
Breakeven Down	Strike − net debit **$25.00 − $6.50 = $18.50**
Breakeven Up	Strike + (net debit / 2) **$25.00 + $3.25 = $28.25**

We can see that if we held on to expiration, our breakevens would be $18.50 and $28.25, respectively. In other words, the stock would have to fall to below $18.50 or rise above $28.25 in order for us to make a profit. In reality, we don't hold on until expiration, and therefore because both options will still contain some time value before that final month, our breakevens will be slightly more narrow, which of course helps us.

In the previous example, we've assumed that the rules required to make a Straddle have been passed in order for us to contemplate the Strap!

4.5 Guts

Proficiency	Direction	Volatility	Asset Legs	Max Risk	Max Reward	Strategy Type
Expert	Neutral	High	■ Long Call ■ Long Put	Capped	Uncapped	Capital Gain

4.5.1 Description

The Guts is a simple adjustment to the Strangle, but this adjustment makes it more expensive. Instead of buying OTM options, we buy ITM calls and puts, which creates a higher cost basis. As with the Strangle, the risk we run with a Guts is that the breakevens can be pushed further apart than with a Straddle.

To even contemplate a Guts, the Straddle criteria must have been satisfied first. We buy higher strike puts and lower strike calls with the same expiration date so that we can profit from the stock soaring up or plummeting down. As with the Strangle, each leg of the trade has limited downside (i.e., the call or put premium) but uncapped upside.

Again the same challenges apply regarding Bid/Ask Spreads and the psychology of the actual trade. Remember that time decay hurts long options positions because options are like wasting assets. The closer we get to expiration, the less time value there is in the option.

Use the Straddle rules but then make an adjustment for the Guts:

1. Instead of trading the ATM calls and puts, choose the next strike higher for the put and the next strike lower for the call.

2. Now compare the breakeven scenarios for the Guts to the Straddle. Typically the Guts' breakevens will be slightly wider. The Guts isn't very attractive when compared to the Strangle, but you can always compare the two with the Straddle, using the Analyzer.

Again, it's important to follow the entry and exit rules, and psychologically speaking, it's another tough strategy to play after you're in. It's very easy to find reasons to exit, even though it's in breach of your Trading Plan. But you must remember that you got in for a certain reason (or reasons), and you must stay in until one of your other reasons compels you to exit.

Buy ITM call   +   Buy ITM put   =   Guts

Steps to Trading a Guts

1. Buy ITM (lower) strike calls, preferably with about three months to expiration.

2. Buy ITM (higher) strike puts with the same expiration.

Steps In

- Actively seek chart patterns that appear like pennant formations, signifying a consolidating price pattern.

- Try to concentrate on stocks with news events and earnings reports about to happen within two weeks.

- Choose a stock price range you feel comfortable with. For some traders, that's between $20.00 and $60.00.

Steps Out

- Manage your position according to the rules defined in your Trading Plan.

- Exit either a few days after the news event occurs where there is no movement or after the news event where there has been profitable movement.

- If the stock thrusts up, sell the call (making a profit for the entire position) and wait for a retracement to profit from the put.

- If the stock thrusts down, sell the put (making a profit for the entire position) and wait for a retracement to profit from the call.

- Try to avoid holding into the last month; otherwise, you'll be exposed to serious time decay.

4.5.2 Context

Outlook

- With Guts, your outlook is **direction neutral.** You are looking for increasing volatility with the stock price moving explosively in either direction.

Rationale

- To execute a neutral trade for a capital gain whilst expecting a surge in volatility. Ideally you are looking for a scenario where Implied Volatility is currently very low, giving you low option prices, but the stock is about to make an explosive move—you just don't know which direction.

- Guts are more expensive than Strangles because you are buying ITM options on both sides, as opposed to buying OTM options. Generally, a Guts is prohibitively expensive, and it would be better to carry out a long Strangle instead.

Net Position

- This is a **net debit** transaction because you have bought calls and puts.

- Your maximum risk on the trade itself is limited to the net debit of the bought calls and puts less the difference between the strikes. Your maximum reward is potentially unlimited.

Effect of Time Decay

- Time decay is harmful to the Guts. Never keep a Guts into the last month to expiration because this is when time decay accelerates the fastest.

Appropriate Time Period to Trade

- We want to combine safety with prudence on cost. Therefore the optimum time period to trade Guts is with three months until expiration, but if the stock has not moved decisively, sell your position when there is one month to expiration. *Never hold a Strangle into the last month.*

Selecting the Stock

- Choose from stocks with adequate liquidity, preferably over 500,000 Average Daily Volume (ADV).

- Actively seek chart patterns that appear like pennant formations, signifying a consolidating price pattern that may be about to explode.

- Try to concentrate on stocks with news events and earnings reports about to happen within two weeks.

- Choose a stock price range you feel comfortable with.

Selecting the Options

- Choose options with adequate liquidity; open interest should be at least 100, preferably 500.

- **Call Strike**—ITM—below the current stock price.

- **Put Strike**—ITM—above the current stock price.

- **Expiration**—Preferably around three months. Use the same expiration date for both legs.

4.5.3 Risk Profile

- **Maximum Risk**   [Net debit paid] − [Difference between strikes]

- **Maximum Reward** [Uncapped]

- **Breakeven Down**   Lower strike − [Net debit − difference between strikes]

- **Breakeven Up**   [Higher strike] + [Net debit − difference between strikes]

4.5.4 Greeks

Key:

Expiration	....
Today – 3 months	——————
Time(t) – 1 month	– – –

Risk Profile
If the stock price remains between the strike prices, we make our maximum loss. If it moves explosively in either direction, we make profits.

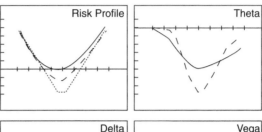

Theta
Time decay is most harmful when the position is unprofitable.

Delta
Delta (speed) is at its greatest when the position is making money in either direction. The negative Delta is purely an indication of direction; i.e., making profit as the stock falls.

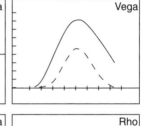

Vega
Volatility is helpful to the position particularly between the strike prices.

Gamma
Gamma (acceleration) peaks between the strike prices, illustrating the position's turning point and the fastest rate of change.

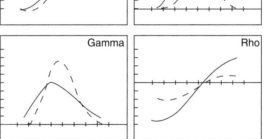

Rho
Higher interest rates are generally helpful to the position when the stock rises and vice versa.

4.5.5 Advantages and Disadvantages

Advantages

■ Profit from a volatile stock moving in either direction.

■ Capped risk.

■ Uncapped profit potential if the stock moves.

Disadvantages

■ Significant movement of the stock and option prices is required to make a profit.

■ Very expensive due to both options being ITM.

■ Bid/Ask Spread can adversely affect the quality of the trade.

■ Psychologically demanding strategy.

4.5.6 Exiting the Trade

Exiting the Position

■ With this strategy, you can simply unravel the spread by selling your calls and puts.

■ You can also exit only your profitable leg of the trade and hope that the stock retraces to favor the unprofitable side later on. For example, if the share has moved decisively upwards, thus making the call profitable, you will sell the calls and make a profit on the entire trade, but you will be left with almost valueless puts. Having now sold the calls, you will hope that the stock may retrace and enhance the value of the puts you are still holding, which you can then sell.

Mitigating a Loss

■ Sell the position if you have only one month left to expiration. Do not hold on, hoping for the best, because you risk losing your entire stake.

4.5.7 Example

ABCD is trading at $25.37 on May 17, 2004.

Buy the August 2004 $22.50 strike call for $4.20.

Buy the August 2004 $27.50 strike put for $3.80.

Net Debit	Premiums bought **$4.20 + $3.80 = $8.00**
Maximum Risk	Net debit − difference in strikes **$8.00 − $5.00 = $3.00**
Maximum Reward	Uncapped
Breakeven Down	Lower strike − maximum risk **$22.50 − $3.00 = $19.50**
Breakeven Up	Higher strike + maximum risk **$27.50 + $3.00 = $30.50**

It's very rare to even contemplate doing a Guts instead of a Strangle because the cost basis is too high.

4.6 Short Call Butterfly

Proficiency	Direction	Volatility	Asset Legs	Max Risk	Max Reward	Strategy Type
Intermediate	Neutral	High	■ Short Call ■ Two Long Calls ■ Short Call	Capped	Capped	Capital Gain

4.6.1 Description

The Short Call Butterfly is another volatility strategy and is the opposite of a Long Call Butterfly, which is a rangebound strategy. The reason that short butterflies aren't particularly popular is because even though they produce a net credit, they offer very small returns compared to straddles and strangles with only slightly less risk.

The Short Call Butterfly involves a low strike short call, two ATM long calls, and an OTM short call. The resulting position is profitable in the event of a big move by the stock. The problem is that the reward is seriously capped and is typically dwarfed by the potential risk if the stock fails to move.

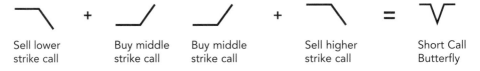

| Sell lower strike call | + | Buy middle strike call | Buy middle strike call | + | Sell higher strike call | = | Short Call Butterfly |

Steps to Trading a Short Call Butterfly

1. Sell one lower strike (ITM) call.

2. Buy two middle strike (ATM) calls.

3. Sell one higher strike (OTM) call.

   - All options share the same expiration date for this strategy.

   - For this strategy, you must use all calls.

   - Remember that there should be equal distance between each strike price. The maximum risk occurs if the stock is at the middle strike at expiration.

   Steps In

   - Actively seek chart patterns that appear like pennant formations, signifying a consolidating price pattern.

Steps Out

- Manage your position according to the rules defined in your Trading Plan.

- You can unravel the position just before expiration—remember to include all the commissions in your calculations.

4.6.2 Context

Outlook

- With short butterflies, your outlook is **direction neutral.** You are looking for large volatility in the stock price, but you are not concerned with the direction.

Rationale

- With short butterflies, you are looking to execute a limited yielding trade at a net credit whereby your maximum profits occur if the stock finishes on either side of the upper and lower strike prices at expiration.

- You are anticipating high volatility with the stock price, which will lead you to profit.

Net Position

- This is a **net credit** trade.

- Your maximum risk is the difference between the adjacent strike prices less the net credit. (Remember that the upper and lower strike prices are equidistant to the middle strike price.) Your maximum reward is the net credit you receive.

Effect of Time Decay

- Time decay is generally harmful to your trade here because you are looking for a lot of movement in the stock price. After the position has become profitable, time decay becomes helpful.

Appropriate Time Period to Trade

- At least three months out.

Selecting the Stock

- Choose from stocks with adequate liquidity, preferably over 500,000 Average Daily Volume (ADV).

- Actively seek chart patterns that appear like pennant formations, signifying a consolidating price pattern that may be about to explode.

Selecting the Options

- Choose options with adequate liquidity; open interest should be at least 100, preferably 500.

- **Lower Strike**—Below the current stock price.

- **Middle Strike**—As close to ATM (or where you think the stock will *not* be at expiration) as possible.

- **Higher Strike**—The same distance above the middle strike as the lower is below it; use online tools to find the optimum yields and breakeven points at and before expiration.

- **Expiration**—Preferably three months or more, but there is a trade-off between time, cost/net credit, and profit potential. Use the same expiration date for all legs.

4.6.3 Risk Profile

- **Maximum Risk**   [Difference in adjacent strikes − net credit]

- **Maximum Reward**   [Net credit received]

- **Breakeven Down**   [Lower strike + net credit]

- **Breakeven Up**   [Higher strike − net credit]

4.6.4 Greeks

Key:
Expiration   ....
Today – 3 months ———
Time(t) – 1 month — — -

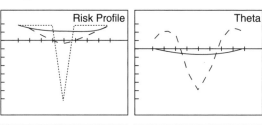

Risk Profile
As the stock price remains rangebound, the position is loss-making, with maximum loss occurring at the middle strike price.

Theta
Time decay is helpful to the position when it is profitable and unhelpful when it is unprofitable.

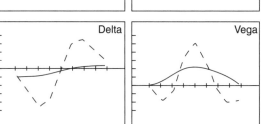

Delta
Delta (speed) is at its greatest around the outer strikes and is zero around the middle strike.

Gamma
Gamma (acceleration) peaks positively around the middle strike, highlighting the position's major turning point and middle Delta neutral point, and peaks inversely around the outside strikes.

Vega
Volatility is generally helpful to the position unless it the stock moves outside the outer strikes.

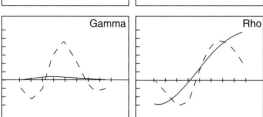

Rho
Higher interest rates are generally helpful to the position when the stock price is higher and vice versa.

4.6.5 Advantages and Disadvantages

Advantages

- Profit from a rangebound stock with no capital outlay.
- Capped risk.
- Comparatively high profit probability if the stock moves explosively.

Disadvantages

- The higher profit potential comes with a wider range between the strikes.
- The higher profit potential only comes nearer expiration.
- The potential loss is far greater than the amount by which you can profit.
- Bid/Ask Spread can adversely affect the quality of the trade.

4.6.6 Exiting the Trade

Exiting the Position

- With this strategy, you can simply unravel the spread by buying back the options you sold and selling the options you bought in the first place.
- Advanced traders may leg up and down or only partially unravel the spread as the underlying asset fluctuates up and down. In this way, the trader will be taking smaller incremental profits before the expiration of the trade.

Mitigating a Loss

- Unravel the trade as described previously.
- Advanced traders may choose to only partially unravel the spread leg-by-leg and create alternative risk profiles.

4.6.7 Example

ABCD is trading at $50.00 on May 17, 2004.

Sell the August 2004 45 strike call for $7.98.

Buy two August 2004 50 strike calls at $5.28.

Sell the August 2004 55 strike call for $3.35.

Net Credit	Premiums sold − premiums bought **$7.98 + $3.35 − $10.56 = $0.77**
Maximum Risk	Difference in adjacent strikes − net credit **$5.00 − $0.77 = $4.23**
Maximum Reward	Net credit **$0.77**
Breakeven Down	Lower strike + net credit **$45.00 + $0.77 = $45.77**
Breakeven Up	Higher strike − net credit **$55.00 − $0.77 = $54.23**
Max ROI	18.20% if the stock is either below $45.00 or above $55.00 at expiration.

4.7 Short Put Butterfly

Proficiency	Direction	Volatility	Asset Legs	Max Risk	Max Reward	Strategy Type
Intermediate	Neutral	High	■ Short Put ■ Two Long Puts ■ Short Put	Capped	Capped	Capital Gain

4.7.1 Description

The Short Put Butterfly is identical to the Short Call Butterfly, except that it uses puts instead of calls. It is the opposite of a Long Put Butterfly, which is a rangebound strategy. The reason that short butterflies aren't particularly popular is because even though they produce a net credit, they offer very small returns compared with straddles and strangles with only slightly less risk.

The Short Put Butterfly involves a low strike short put, two ATM long puts, and an ITM short put. The resulting position is profitable in the event of a big move by the stock. The problem is that the reward is seriously capped and is typically dwarfed by the potential risk if the stock fails to move.

Sell lower strike put + Buy middle strike put   Buy middle strike put + Sell higher strike put = Short Put Butterfly

Steps to Trading a Short Put Butterfly

1. Sell one lower strike (OTM) put.

2. Buy two middle strike (ATM) puts.

3. Sell one higher strike (ITM) put.

    ■ All options share the same expiration date for this strategy.

    ■ For this strategy, you must use all puts.

    ■ Remember that there should be equal distance between each strike price. The maximum risk occurs if the stock is at the middle strike at expiration.

    Steps In

    ■ Actively seek chart patterns that appear like pennant formations, signifying a consolidating price pattern.

    Steps Out

    ■ Manage your position according to the rules defined in your Trading Plan.

    ■ You can unravel the position just before expiration—remember to include all the commissions in your calculations.

4.7.2 Context

Outlook

■ With short butterflies, your outlook is **direction neutral.** You are looking for large volatility in the stock price, but you are not concerned with the direction.

Rationale

■ With short butterflies, you are looking to execute a limited yielding trade at a net credit whereby your maximum profits occur if the stock finishes on either side of the upper and lower strike prices at expiration.

■ You are anticipating high volatility with the stock price, which will lead you to profit.

Net Position

■ This is a **net credit** trade.

■ Your maximum risk is the difference between the adjacent strike prices less the net credit. (Remember that the upper and lower strike prices are equidistant to the middle strike price.) Your maximum reward is the net credit you receive.

Effect of Time Decay

■ Time decay is generally harmful to your trade here because you are looking for a lot of movement in the stock price. After the position has become profitable, time decay then becomes helpful.

Appropriate Time Period to Trade

■ At least three months out.

Selecting the Stock

■ Choose from stocks with adequate liquidity, preferably over 500,000 Average Daily Volume (ADV).

■ Actively seek chart patterns that appear like pennant formations, signifying a consolidating price pattern that may be about to explode.

Selecting the Options

■ Choose options with adequate liquidity; open interest should be at least 100, preferably 500.

■ **Lower Strike**—Below the current stock price.

■ **Middle Strike**—As close to ATM (or where you think the stock will *not* be at expiration) as possible.

■ **Higher Strike**—The same distance above the middle strike as the lower is below it; use online tools to find the optimum yields and breakeven points at and before expiration.

■ **Expiration**—Preferably three months or more, but there is a trade-off between time, cost/net credit, and profit potential. Use the same expiration date for all legs.

4.7.3 Risk Profile

■ **Maximum Risk**   [Difference in adjacent strikes − net credit]

■ **Maximum Reward**   [Net credit received]

■ **Breakeven Down**   [Lower strike + net credit]

■ **Breakeven Up**   [Higher strike − net credit]

4.7.4 Greeks

Key:
Expiration   ....
Today – 3 months ——————
Time(t) – 1 month – – –

Risk Profile
As the stock price remains rangebound, the position is loss-making, with maximum loss occurring at the middle strike price.

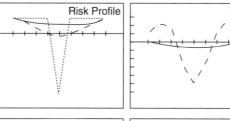

Theta
Time decay is helpful to the position when it is profitable and unhelpful when it is unprofitable.

Delta
Delta (speed) is at its greatest around the outer strikes and is zero around the middle strike.

Gamma
Gamma (acceleration) peaks positively around the middle strike, highlighting the position's major turning point and middle Delta neutral point, and peaks inversely around the outside strikes.

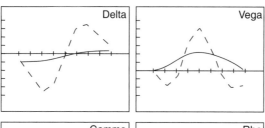

Vega
Volatility is generally helpful to the position unless it the stock moves outside the outer strikes.

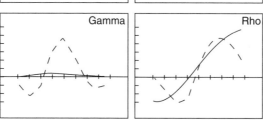

Rho
Higher interest rates are generally helpful to the position when the stock price is higher and vice versa.

4.7.5 Advantages and Disadvantages

Advantages

- Profit from a rangebound stock with no capital outlay.

- Capped risk.

- Comparatively high profit probability if the stock moves explosively.

Disadvantages

- The higher profit potential comes with a wider range between the strikes.

- The higher profit potential only comes nearer expiration.

- The potential loss is far greater than the amount by which you can profit.

- Bid/Ask Spread can adversely affect the quality of the trade.

4.7.6 Exiting the Trade

Exiting the Position

- With this strategy, you can simply unravel the spread by buying back the options you sold and selling the options you bought in the first place.

- Advanced traders may leg up and down or only partially unravel the spread as the underlying asset fluctuates up and down. In this way, the trader will be taking smaller incremental profits before the expiration of the trade.

Mitigating a Loss

- Unravel the trade as described previously.

- Advanced traders may choose to only partially unravel the spread leg-by-leg and create alternative risk profiles.

4.7.7 Example

ABCD is trading at $50.00 on May 17, 2004.

Sell the August 2004 45 strike put for $2.57.

Buy two August 2004 50 strike puts at $4.83.

Sell the August 2004 55 strike put for $7.85.

Net Credit	Premiums sold − premiums bought **$2.57 + $7.85 − $9.66 = $0.76**
Maximum Risk	Difference in adjacent strikes − net credit **$5.00 − $0.76 = $4.24**
Maximum Reward	Net credit **$0.76**
Breakeven Down	Lower strike + net credit **$45.00 + $0.76 = $45.76**
Breakeven Up	Higher strike − net credit **$55.00 − $0.76 = $54.24**
Max ROI	17.92% if the stock is either below $45.00 or above $55.00 at expiration.

4.8 Short Call Condor

Proficiency	Direction	Volatility	Asset Legs	Max Risk	Max Reward	Strategy Type
Ⓘ	ⓦ	ⓦ	◠ + ◡ ◡ + ◠	△	Ⓒ	⛁
Advanced	Neutral	High	▪ Short Call ▪ Long Call ▪ Long Call ▪ Short Call	Capped	Capped	Capital Gain

4.8.1 Description

Short condors are identical to short butterflies, with the exception that the two middle bought options have different strikes. The Short Call Condor is another volatility strategy and is the opposite of a Long Call Condor, which is a rangebound strategy. Short condors aren't particularly popular because even though they produce a net credit, they offer very small returns compared to straddles and strangles, with only slightly less risk.

The Short Call Condor involves a low strike short call, a lower middle ITM long call, a higher middle OTM long call, and a higher OTM short call. The resulting position yields a position that is profitable in the event of a big move by the stock. Again, the problem is that the reward is seriously capped and is typically dwarfed by the potential risk if the stock fails to move.

Sell lower strike call	Buy middle strike call	Buy middle strike call	Sell higher strike call	Short Call Condor

Steps to Trading a Short Call Condor

1. Sell one lower strike (ITM) call.
2. Buy one lower middle strike (ITM) call.
3. Buy one higher middle strike (OTM) call.
4. Sell one higher strike (OTM) call.

   ▪ All options share the same expiration date for this strategy.

   ▪ For this strategy, you must use all calls.

   ▪ Remember that there should be equal distance between each strike price. The maximum risk occurs if the stock is at the middle strike at expiration.

   Steps In

   ▪ Actively seek chart patterns that appear like pennant formations, signifying a consolidating price pattern.

Steps Out

■ Manage your position according to the rules defined in your Trading Plan.

■ You can unravel the position just before expiration—remember to include all the commissions in your calculations.

4.8.2 Context

Outlook

■ With short condors, your outlook is **direction neutral.** You are looking for large volatility in the stock price, but you are not concerned with the direction.

Rationale

■ With short condors, you are looking to execute a limited yielding trade at a net credit, whereby your maximum profits occur if the stock finishes on either side of the upper and lower strike prices at expiration.

■ You are anticipating high volatility with the stock price, which will lead you to profit.

Net Position

■ This is a **net credit** trade.

■ Your maximum risk is the difference between the adjacent strike prices less the net credit. (Remember that all strike prices are equidistant to each other.) Your maximum reward is the net credit you receive.

Effect of Time Decay

■ Time decay is generally harmful to your trade here because you are looking for a lot of movement in the stock price. After the position has become profitable, time decay becomes helpful.

Appropriate Time Period to Trade

■ At least three months out.

Selecting the Stock

■ Choose from stocks with adequate liquidity, preferably over 500,000 Average Daily Volume (ADV).

■ Actively seek chart patterns that appear like pennant formations, signifying a consolidating price pattern that may be about to explode.

Selecting the Options

■ Choose options with adequate liquidity; open interest should be at least 100, preferably 500.

■ **Lower Strike**—At least two strikes below the current stock price.

■ **Lower Middle Strike**—At least one strike below the current stock price.

■ **Higher Middle Strike**—At least one strike above the current stock price.

■ **Higher Strike**—At least two strikes above the current stock price.

■ **Expiration**—Preferably three months or more, but there is a trade-off between time, cost/net credit, and profit potential. Use the same expiration date for all legs.

4.8.3 Risk Profile

■ **Maximum Risk**   [Difference in adjacent strikes − net credit]

■ **Maximum Reward**   [Net credit received]

■ **Breakeven Down**   [Lowest strike + net credit]

■ **Breakeven Up**   [Highest strike − net credit]

4.8.4 Greeks

Key:
Expiration   ....
Today – 3 months   ——————
Time(t) – 1 month   — — -

Risk Profile
As the stock price remains rangebound, the position is loss-making, with maximum loss occurring between the middle strikes.

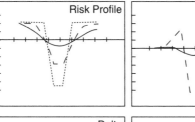

Theta
Time decay is helpful to the position when it is profitable and unhelpful when it is unprofitable.

Delta
Delta (speed) is at its greatest around the outer strikes and is zero between the middle strikes.

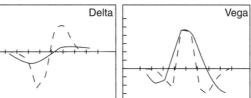

Vega
Volatility is generally helpful to the position unless it the stock moves outside the outer strikes.

Gamma
Gamma (acceleration) peaks positively around the middle strikes, and peaks inversely around the outside strikes.

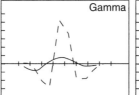
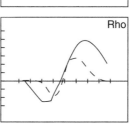

Rho
Higher interest rates are generally helpful to the position when the stock price is higher and vice versa.

4.8.5 Advantages and Disadvantages

Advantages

- Profit from a rangebound stock with no capital outlay.
- Capped risk.

Disadvantages

- The higher profit potential comes with a wider range between the middle strikes.
- The higher profit potential only comes nearer expiration.
- The potential loss is far greater than the amount by which you can profit.
- Bid/Ask Spread can adversely affect the quality of the trade.

4.8.6 Exiting the Trade

Exiting the Position

- With this strategy, you can simply unravel the spread by buying back the options you sold and selling the options you bought in the first place.
- Advanced traders may leg up and down or only partially unravel the spread as the underlying asset fluctuates up and down. In this way, the trader will be taking smaller incremental profits before the expiration of the trade.

Mitigating a Loss

- Unravel the trade as described previously.
- Advanced traders may choose to only partially unravel the spread leg-by-leg and create alternative risk profiles.

4.8.7 Example

ABCD is trading at $52.87 on May 17, 2004.

Sell the August 2004 45 strike call for $10.16.

Buy the August 2004 50 strike call at $7.05.

Buy the August 2004 55 strike call at $4.70.

Sell the August 2004 60 strike call for $3.02.

Net Credit	Premiums sold − premiums bought $10.16 + $3.02 − $7.05 − $4.70 = $1.43
Maximum Risk	Difference in adjacent strikes − net credit $5.00 − $1.43 = $3.57
Maximum Reward	Net credit $1.43
Breakeven Down	Lower strike + net credit $45.00 + $1.43 = $46.43
Breakeven Up	Higher strike − net credit $60.00 − $1.43 = $58.57
Max ROI	40.06% if the stock is either below $45.00 or above $60.00 at expiration.

4.9 Short Put Condor

Proficiency	Direction	Volatility	Asset Legs	Max Risk	Max Reward	Strategy Type
Advanced	Neutral	High	■ Short Put ■ Long Put ■ Long Put ■ Short Put	Capped	Capped	Capital Gain

4.9.1 Description

The Short Put Condor is identical to the Short Call Condor except that it uses puts instead of calls. It is the opposite of a Long Put Condor, which is a rangebound strategy. Short condors aren't particularly popular because even though they produce a net credit, they offer very small returns compared to straddles and strangles with only slightly less risk.

The Short Put Condor involves a low strike short put, a lower middle OTM long put, a higher middle ITM long put, and a higher ITM short put. The resulting position is profitable in the event of a big move by the stock. Again, the problem is that the reward is seriously capped and is typically dwarfed by the potential risk if the stock fails to move.

| Sell lower strike put | + | Buy middle strike put | + | Buy middle strike put | + | Sell higher strike put | = | Short Put Condor |

Steps to Trading a Short Put Condor

1. Sell one lower strike (OTM) put.

2. Buy one lower middle strike (OTM) put.

3. Buy one higher middle strike (ITM) put.

4. Sell one higher strike (ITM) put.

   ■ All options share the same expiration date for this strategy.

   ■ For this strategy, you must use all puts.

   ■ Remember that there should be equal distance between each strike price. The maximum risk occurs if the stock is at the middle strike at expiration.

   Steps In

   ■ Actively seek chart patterns that appear like pennant formations, signifying a consolidating price pattern.

   Steps Out

   ■ Manage your position according to the rules defined in your Trading Plan.

   ■ You can unravel the position just before expiration—remember to include all the commissions in your calculations.

4.9.2 Context

Outlook

■ With short condors, your outlook is **direction neutral.** You are looking for large volatility in the stock price, but you are not concerned with the direction.

Rationale

■ With short condors, you are looking to execute a limited yielding trade at a net credit, whereby your maximum profits occur if the stock finishes on either side of the upper and lower strike prices at expiration.

■ You are anticipating high volatility with the stock price, which will lead you to profit.

Net Position

■ This is a **net credit** trade.

■ Your maximum risk is the difference between the adjacent strike prices less the net credit. (Remember that all strike prices are equidistant to each other.) Your maximum reward is the net credit you receive.

Effect of Time Decay

■ Time decay is generally harmful to your trade here because you are looking for a lot of movement in the stock price. After the position has become profitable, time decay becomes helpful.

Appropriate Time Period to Trade

■ At least three months out.

Selecting the Stock

■ Choose from stocks with adequate liquidity, preferably over 500,000 Average Daily Volume (ADV).

■ Actively seek chart patterns that appear like pennant formations, signifying a consolidating price pattern that may be about to explode.

Selecting the Options

■ Choose options with adequate liquidity; open interest should be at least 100, preferably 500.

■ **Lower Strike**—At least two strikes below the current stock price.

■ **Lower Middle Strike**—At least one strike below the current stock price.

■ **Higher Middle Strike**—At least one strike above the current stock price.

■ **Higher Strike**—At least two strikes above the current stock price.

■ **Expiration**—Preferably three months or more, but there is a trade-off between time, cost/net credit, and profit potential. Use the same expiration date for all legs.

4.9.3 Risk Profile

■ **Maximum Risk**   [Difference in adjacent strikes − net credit]

■ **Maximum Reward**   [Net credit received]

■ **Breakeven Down**   [Lowest strike + net credit]

■ **Breakeven Up**   [Highest strike − net credit]

4.9.4 Greeks

Key:
Expiration   ············
Today – 3 months ————
Time(t) – 1 month – – –

Risk Profile
As the stock price remains rangebound, the position is loss-making, with maximum loss occurring between the middle strikes.

Delta
Delta (speed) is at its greatest around the outer strikes and is zero between the middle strikes.

Gamma
Gamma (acceleration) peaks positively around the middle strikes, and peaks inversely around the outside strikes.

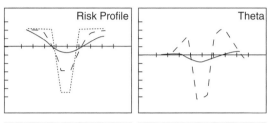
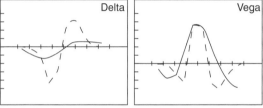
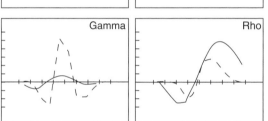

Theta
Time decay is helpful to the position when it is profitable and unhelpful when it is unprofitable.

Vega
Volatility is generally helpful to the position unless it the stock moves outside the outer strikes.

Rho
Higher interest rates are generally helpful to the position when the stock price is higher and vice versa.

4.9.5 Advantages and Disadvantages

Advantages

- Profit from a rangebound stock with no capital outlay.
- Capped risk.

Disadvantages

- The higher profit potential comes with a wider range between the middle strikes.
- The higher profit potential only comes nearer expiration.

■ The potential loss is far greater than the amount by which you can profit.

■ Bid/Ask Spread can adversely affect the quality of the trade.

4.9.6 Exiting the Trade

Exiting the Position

■ With this strategy, you can simply unravel the spread by buying back the options you sold and selling the options you bought in the first place.

■ Advanced traders may leg up and down or only partially unravel the spread as the underlying asset fluctuates up and down. In this way, the trader will be taking smaller incremental profits before the expiration of the trade.

Mitigating a Loss

■ Unravel the trade as described previously.

■ Advanced traders may choose to only partially unravel the spread leg-by-leg and create alternative risk profiles.

4.9.7 Example

ABCD is trading at $52.87 on May 17, 2004.

Sell the August 2004 45 strike put for $1.88.

Buy the August 2004 50 strike put at $3.73.

Buy the August 2004 55 strike put at $6.33.

Sell the August 2004 60 strike put for $9.60.

Net Credit	Premiums sold − premiums bought **$1.88 + $9.60 − $3.73 − $6.33 = $1.42**
Maximum Risk	Difference in adjacent strikes − net credit **$5.00 − $1.42 = $3.58**
Maximum Reward	Net credit **$1.42**
Breakeven Down	Lower strike + net credit **$45.00 + $1.42 = $46.42**
Breakeven Up	Higher strike − net credit **$60.00 − $1.42 = $58.58**
Max ROI	39.66% if the stock is either below $45.00 or above $60.00 at expiration.

4.10 Short Iron Butterfly

Proficiency	Direction	Volatility	Asset Legs	Max Risk	Max Reward	Strategy Type
Advanced	Neutral	High	■ Short Put ■ Long Put ■ Long Call ■ Short Call	Capped	Capped	Capital Gain

4.10.1 Description

The Short Iron Butterfly is another volatility strategy and is the opposite of a Long Iron Butterfly, which is a rangebound strategy.

Short iron butterflies aren't particularly popular because they produce a net debit and offer very small returns compared to straddles and strangles with only slightly less risk.

The Short Iron Butterfly involves putting together a Bear Put Spread and a Bull Call Spread. The higher strike put shares the same strike as the lower strike call to create the Short Butterfly shape. The resulting position is profitable in the event of a big move by the stock. The problem is that the reward is seriously capped and is typically dwarfed by the potential risk if the stock fails to move.

| Sell lower strike put | Buy middle strike put | Buy middle strike call | Sell higher strike call | Short Iron Butterfly |

Steps to Trading a Short Iron Butterfly

1. Sell one lower strike (OTM) put.
2. Buy one middle strike (ATM) put.
3. Buy one middle strike (ATM) call.
4. Sell one higher strike OTM call.

   ■ All options share the same expiration date for this strategy.

   ■ For this strategy, you must use both calls and puts. A Short Iron Butterfly is the combination of a Bear Put Spread and a Bull Call Spread.

   ■ The short put and the short call share the same middle (ATM) strike price.

   ■ Remember that there should be equal distance between the three strikes.

Steps In

   ■ Actively seek chart patterns that appear like pennant formations, signifying a consolidating price pattern.

Steps Out

- Manage your position according to the rules defined in your Trading Plan.

- Remember that the Short Iron Butterfly is a combination of other strategies, so it can be unraveled in two-leg chunks.

4.10.2 Context

Outlook

- With short iron butterflies, your outlook is **direction neutral.** You are looking for increased volatility in the stock price, but you are not concerned with the direction.

Rationale

- With short iron butterflies, you are looking to execute an inexpensive, capped yield trade where your maximum profits occur if the stock finishes on either side of the upper and lower strike prices at expiration.

- You are anticipating greater volatility in the stock price.

Net Position

- This is a **net debit** trade.

- Your maximum risk is your net debit you pay. Your maximum reward is the difference between any adjacent strike prices less the net debit.

Effect of Time Decay

- Time decay is generally harmful to your trade here because you are looking for a lot of movement in the stock price. After the position has become profitable, time decay becomes helpful.

Appropriate Time Period to Trade

- At least three months out. Exit the position before the final month preceding expiration.

Selecting the Stock

- Choose from stocks with adequate liquidity, preferably over 500,000 Average Daily Volume (ADV).

- Actively seek chart patterns that appear like pennant formations, signifying a consolidating price pattern that may be about to explode.

Selecting the Options

- Choose options with adequate liquidity; open interest should be at least 100, preferably 500.

- **Lower Strike**—Below the current stock price.

- **Middle Strike**—As close to ATM as possible (or where you think the stock will *not* be at expiration).

- **Higher Strike**—The same distance above the middle strike as the lower is below it; use online tools to find the optimum yields and breakeven points at and before expiration.

- **Expiration**—Preferably three months or more, but there is a trade-off between time, cost, and profit potential. Use the same expiration for all legs.

4.10.3 Risk Profile

- **Maximum Risk**   [Net debit]

- **Maximum Reward**   [Difference between adjacent strikes − net debit]

- **Breakeven Down**   [Middle strike − net debit]

- **Breakeven Up**   [Middle strike + net debit]

4.10.4 Greeks

Key:
Expiration   ············
Today – 3 months ————
Time(t) – 1 month – – –

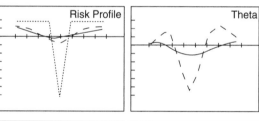

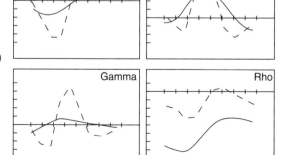

Risk Profile
As the stock price remains rangebound, the position is unprofitable, with maximum loss occurring at the middle strike price.

Delta
Delta (speed) is at its greatest the outer strikes and is zero around the middle strike.

Gamma
Gamma (acceleration) peaks positively around the middle strike, highlighting the position's major turning point and middle Delta neutral point, and peaks inversely outside the outer strikes.

Theta
Time decay is helpful to the position when it is profitable and unhelpful when it is unprofitable.

Vega
Volatility is generally helpful to the position unless the stock moves outside the outer strikes.

Rho
Higher interest rates are generally unhelpful to the position, particularly when the stock price is lower.

4.10.5 Advantages and Disadvantages

Advantages

- Profit from a volatile stock with little capital outlay.
- Capped risk.
- Comparatively high profit probability if the stock moves.

Disadvantages

- The higher profit potential comes with a wider range between the strikes.
- The higher profit potential only comes nearer expiration.
- The potential loss is far greater than the amount by which you can profit.
- Bid/Ask Spread can adversely affect the quality of the trade.
- Complicated strategy for the intermediate trader.

4.10.6 Exiting the Trade

Exiting the Position

- With this strategy, you can simply unravel the spread by buying back the options you sold and selling the options you bought in the first place.
- Advanced traders may leg up and down or only partially unravel the spread as the underlying asset fluctuates up and down. In this way, the trader will be taking smaller incremental profits before the expiration of the trade.

Mitigating a Loss

- Unravel the trade as described previously.
- Advanced traders may choose to only partially unravel the spread leg-by-leg and create alternative risk profiles.

4.10.7 Example

ABCD is trading at $52.87 on May 17, 2004.

Sell the August 2004 45 strike put for $1.88.

Buy the August 2004 50 strike put for $3.73.

Buy the August 2004 50 strike call for $7.03.

Sell the August 2004 55 strike call for $4.67.

Net Debit	Premiums bought − premiums sold **$3.73 + $7.03 − $1.88 − $4.67 = $4.21**
Maximum Risk	Net debit **$4.21**
Maximum Reward	Difference in adjacent strikes − net debit **$5.00 − $4.21 = $0.79**
Breakeven Down	Middle strike − net debit **$50.00 − $4.21 = $45.79**
Breakeven Up	Middle strike + net debit **$50.00 + $4.21 = $54.21**
Max ROI	18.76% if the stock is either below $45.00 or above $55.00 at expiration.

4.11 Short Iron Condor

Proficiency	Direction	Volatility	Asset Legs	Max Risk	Max Reward	Strategy Type
Advanced	Neutral	High	■ Short Put ■ Long Put ■ Long Call ■ Short Call	Capped	Capped	Capital Gain

4.11.1 Description

The Short Iron Condor another volatility strategy and is the opposite of a Long Iron Condor, which is a rangebound strategy. The Short Iron Condor differs from the Short Iron Butterfly in that the middle strikes are separated.

Short iron condors aren't particularly popular because they produce a net debit and offer very small returns compared to straddles and strangles with only slightly less risk.

The Short Iron Condor involves putting together a Bear Put Spread and a higher strike Bull Call Spread. The higher strike put has a lower strike than the lower strike call to create the Short Condor shape. The resulting position is profitable in the event of a big move by the stock. The problem is that the reward is seriously capped and is typically dwarfed by the potential risk if the stock fails to move.

Sell lower strike put	Buy middle strike put	Buy middle strike call	Sell higher strike call	Short Iron Condor

Steps to Trading a Short Iron Condor

1. Sell one lower strike (OTM) put.

2. Buy one middle strike (OTM) put.

3. Buy one middle strike (OTM) call.

4. Sell one higher strike OTM call.

    ■ All options share the same expiration date for this strategy.

    ■ For this strategy, you must use both calls and puts. A Short Iron Condor is the combination of a Bear Put Spread and a Bull Call Spread.

    ■ The long put strike is lower than the long call strike.

    ■ Remember that there should be equal distance between each strike price.

Steps In

■ Actively seek chart patterns that appear like pennant formations, signifying a consolidating price pattern that may be about to explode.

Steps Out

■ Manage your position according to the rules defined in your Trading Plan.

■ Remember that the Short Iron Condor is a combination of other strategies, so it can be unraveled in two-leg chunks.

■ You can unravel the position just before expiration—remember to include all the commissions in your calculations.

4.11.2 Context

Outlook

■ With short iron condors, your profile is **direction neutral.** You are looking for increased volatility in the stock price, but you are not concerned with the direction.

Rationale

■ With short iron condors, you are looking to execute an inexpensive, capped yield trade where your maximum profits occur if the stock finishes on either side of the upper and lower strike prices at expiration.

■ You are anticipating greater volatility in the stock price.

Net Position

- This is a **net debit** trade.

- Your maximum risk is your net debit you pay. Your maximum reward is the difference between adjacent strike prices less the net debit.

Effect of Time Decay

- Time decay is generally harmful to your trade here because you are looking for a lot of movement in the stock price. After the position has become profitable, time decay becomes helpful.

Appropriate Time Period to Trade

- At least three months out. Exit the position before the final month preceding expiration.

Selecting the Stock

- Choose from stocks with adequate liquidity, preferably over 500,000 Average Daily Volume (ADV).

- Actively seek chart patterns that appear like pennant formations, signifying a consolidating price pattern that may be about to explode.

Selecting the Options

- Choose options with adequate liquidity; open interest should be at least 100, preferably 500.

- **Lower (Put) Strikes**—Below the current stock price.

- **Higher (Call) Strikes**—Above the current stock price.

- **Expiration**—Preferably three months or more, but there is a trade-off between time, cost, and profit potential. Use the same expiration for all legs.

4.11.3 Risk Profile

- **Maximum Risk**   [Net debit paid]

- **Maximum Reward**   [Difference in adjacent strikes − net debit]

- **Breakeven Down**   [Middle long put strike − net debit]

- **Breakeven Up**   [Middle long call strike + net debit]

4.11.4 Greeks

Key:
Expiration   ....
Today – 3 months ———
Time(t) – 1 month – – -

Risk Profile
As the stock price remains rangebound, the position is unprofitable, with maximum loss occurring between the middle strikes.

Delta
Delta (speed) is at its greatest the outer strikes and is zero between the middle strikes.

Gamma
Gamma (acceleration) peaks positively between the middle strikes, highlighting the position's major turning point and middle Delta neutral point, and peaks inversely around the outside strikes.

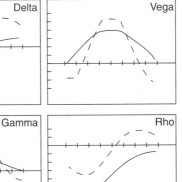

Theta
Time decay is helpful to the position when it is profitable and unhelpful when it is unprofitable.

Vega
Volatility is generally helpful to the position unless the stock moves outside the outer strikes.

Rho
Higher interest rates are generally unhelpful to the position when the stock price is lower and vice versa.

4.11.5 Advantages and Disadvantages

Advantages

- Profit from a volatile stock with little capital outlay.

- Capped risk.

- Comparatively high profit probability if the stock moves.

Disadvantages

- The higher profit potential comes with a wider range between the strikes.

- The higher profit potential only comes nearer expiration.

- The potential loss is far greater than the amount by which you can profit.

- Bid/Ask Spread can adversely affect the quality of the trade.

- Complicated strategy for the intermediate trader.

4.11.6 Exiting the Trade

Exiting the Position

- With this strategy, you can simply unravel the spread by buying back the options you sold and selling the options you bought in the first place.

- Advanced traders may leg up and down or only partially unravel the spread as the underlying asset fluctuates up and down. In this way, the trader will be taking smaller incremental profits before the expiration of the trade.

Mitigating a Loss

- Unravel the trade as described previously.

- Advanced traders may choose to only partially unravel the spread leg-by-leg and create alternative risk profiles.

4.11.7 Example

ABCD is trading at $52.87 on May 17, 2004.

Sell the August 2004 45 strike put for $1.88.

Buy the August 2004 50 strike put for $3.73.

Buy the August 2004 55 strike call for $4.70.

Sell the August 2004 60 strike call for $3.02.

Net Debit	Premiums bought − premiums sold **$3.73 + $4.70 − $1.88 − $3.02 = $3.53**
Maximum Risk	Net debit **$3.53**
Maximum Reward	Difference in adjacent strikes − net debit **$5.00 − $3.53 = $1.47**
Breakeven Down	Lower middle strike − net debit **$50.00 − $3.53 = $46.47**
Breakeven Up	Higher middle strike + net debit **$55.00 + $3.53 = $58.53**
Max ROI	41.64% if the stock is either below $45.00 or above $60.00 at expiration.

5

Sideways Strategies

Introduction

Sideways strategies are defined as those where you make a profit provided that the stock remains rangebound. We're looking for a stock that is not going to explode with high volatility; rather, it's going to trade in a tight channel, preferably between clear levels of support and resistance.

So, bearing that in mind, would you look to trade a sideways strategy shortly before a news event like an earnings report? Heck, no! Get the news out of the way first, and then we have a greater chance of the stock meandering sideways, hopefully.

Sideways strategies can be challenging to trade, psychologically speaking. The reason is that as the stock touches support, we don't actually know if support will hold or not; likewise for resistance. So there can be some anxious moments at those times where support or resistance is within touching distance.

For this reason, it's best for the inexperienced trader *not* to consider uncapped risk strategies such as the Short Straddles, Short Strangles, and Short Guts. These are the precise opposite of their long versions we reviewed in Chapter 4, "Volatility Strategies." In this section, we'll cover those risky strategies first and then show how we can reduce the risk by adding *buy* legs to create more balanced strategies that have more attractive risk/reward ratios.

Sideways Strategies Staircase

This diagram shows how the various sideways strategies link together, highlighting their similarities and differences. You may want to complete the chapter first before coming back to this diagram so you can better appreciate the links.

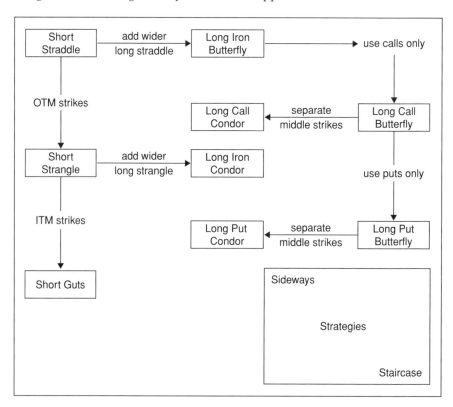

Combining Strategies

The Long Iron Butterfly can be created either by combining a Short Straddle with a wider Long Strangle or by combining a Bull Put Spread with a Bear Call Spread. In this way, we can begin to see how new strategies are created simply by adding or subtracting legs from one strategy to another.

5.1 Short Straddle

Proficiency	Direction	Volatility	Asset Legs	Max Risk	Max Reward	Strategy Type
![icon]	![icon]	![icon]	![icon] + ![icon]	![icon]	![icon]	![icon]
Advanced	Neutral	Low	■ Short Put ■ Short Call	Uncapped	Capped	Income

5.1.1 Description

The Short Straddle is precisely the opposite of a (Long) Straddle. We short ATM puts and calls with a short time to expiration (one month or less) in order to pick up income. Because we're short options, time decay works for us, so we only select short-term expiration dates. Also we're exposed to potentially unlimited risk, which is another reason for making this a short-term strategy. As such, it's *not* one I'd recommend to inexperienced traders. The problem is that you could be successful at it for months, picking up modest income over and over again, and then whooomph, one big loss will wipe out years worth of gains. It's not worth it.

Each leg of the trade has uncapped downside. If the stock starts going ballistic in either direction, then your position is precarious to say the least. If the stock remains rangebound, then we'll make a limited profit. But it's not enough for me to get excited. If the stock gaps in either direction, we're history!

As such, this module will be largely academic (I hope) to your practical trading experience; however, it's worth studying so you can compare it to the other rangebound strategies in this chapter. One thing to note is that you would *never* trade this strategy right before a news event like an earnings report. You certainly wouldn't want any nasty surprises to be lurking around the corner.

Sell ATM put   Sell ATM call   Short Straddle

Steps to Trading a Short Straddle

1. Sell ATM strike puts, preferably with one month or less to expiration.

2. Sell ATM strike calls with the same expiration.

    Steps In

    ■ Try to ensure that the trend is rangebound and identify clear areas of support and resistance.

    ■ Try to ensure that no news is coming out soon for the stock.

    Steps Out

    ■ Manage your position according to the rules defined in your Trading Plan.

    ■ Close the losing side by buying back the relevant option if the stock breaks support or resistance.

    ■ Buy back both options if the position is profitable but you think news may emerge about the underlying stock.

5.1.2 Context

Outlook

■ With Short Straddles, your outlook is **direction neutral**—you are looking for no movement in the stock.

Rationale

■ To execute a direction-neutral **income** strategy for a net credit while expecting a future decline in volatility. Ideally you are looking for a scenario where the immediate Implied Volatility has been high, giving you above average options premiums, but where you anticipate the stock to consolidate (become less volatile) and remain rangebound for the duration of your trade.

Net Position

■ This is a **net credit** trade because you have sold calls and puts.

■ Your maximum risk on the trade itself is unlimited, whereas your maximum reward is limited to the net credit you receive for selling the calls and puts.

Effect of Time Decay

■ Time decay is helpful to short straddles. Because you are short in options, and because you are exposed to unlimited downside, you want to be exposed to this position for as little time as possible.

Appropriate Time Period to Trade

■ One month or less.

Selecting the Stock

■ Choose from stocks with adequate liquidity, preferably over 500,000 Average Daily Volume (ADV).

■ Try to ensure that the trend is rangebound and identify clear areas of support and resistance.

■ Try to ensure that no news is coming out soon for the stock.

Selecting the Options

■ Choose options with adequate liquidity; open interest should be at least 100, preferably 500.

■ **Strike**—ATM for the put and call.

■ **Expiration**—Preferably one month or less. Use the same expiration for both legs.

5.1.3 Risk Profile

■ **Maximum Risk**   [Uncapped]

■ **Maximum Reward**   [Net credit received]

■ **Breakeven Down**   [Strike − net credit]

■ **Breakeven Up**   [Strike + net credit]

5.1.4 Greeks

Key:
Expiration   ············
Today – 1 month ———
Time(t) – 5 days – – -

Risk Profile
If the stock price remains around the strike price, we make our maximum profit. If it moves explosively in either direction, we make uncapped losses.

Delta
Delta (speed) is at its greatest when the position is losing money in either direction.

Gamma
Gamma (acceleration) peaks inversely around the strike price, illustrating the position's turning point and the fastest rate of change.

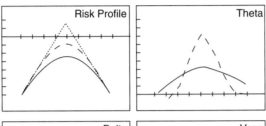
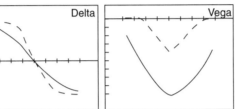
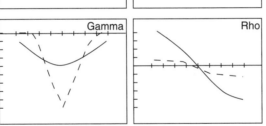

Theta
Time decay is most helpful when the position is profitable.

Vega
Volatility is unhelpful when the position is profitable and vice versa.

Rho
Higher interest rates are generally unhelpful to the position when the stock rises and vice versa.

5.1.5 Advantages and Disadvantages

Advantages

- Profit from a rangebound stock.
- Comparatively high-yielding income strategy.

Disadvantages

- Uncapped risk if the stock moves in either direction.
- Capped reward.
- Almost certain exercise at expiration.
- Bid/Ask Spread can adversely affect the quality of the trade.
- High-risk strategy; *not* for novices or intermediates.

5.1.6 Exiting the Trade

Exiting the Position

- With this strategy, you can simply unravel the spread by buying back your calls and puts.

Mitigating a Loss

- Buy back your sold options.

- Advanced traders may consider buying further OTM calls and puts on either side in order to create a Long Iron Butterfly, which is more conservative.

5.1.7 Example

ABCD is trading at $25.37 on May 17, 2004.

Sell the June 2004 25 strike put for $1.20.

Sell the June 2004 25 strike call for $1.50.

Net Credit	Premiums sold **$1.20 + $1.50 = $2.70**
Maximum Risk	Uncapped
Maximum Reward	Net credit **$2.70**
Breakeven Down	Strike − net credit **$25.00 − $2.70 = $22.30**
Breakeven Up	Strike + net credit **$25.00 + $2.70 = $27.70**

The major problem with this strategy is the uncapped risk position. Any surprise concerning the stock could leave you with a serious problem, and frankly, it simply isn't worth the risk unless you have a lot of experience.

5.2 Short Strangle

Proficiency	Direction	Volatility	Asset Legs	Max Risk	Max Reward	Strategy Type
Advanced	Neutral	Low	■ Short Put ■ Short Call	Uncapped	Capped	Income

5.2.1 Description

The Short Strangle is a simple adjustment to the Short Straddle to improve the probability of a profitable trade by widening the strikes and therefore the breakeven points. Instead of selling ATM options, we sell OTM calls and puts, which means a lower net credit but typically wider breakeven points.

The Short Strangle is precisely the opposite of a (Long) Strangle. We short OTM puts and calls with a short time to expiration (one month or less) in order to pick up income. Because we're short options, time decay works for us, so we only select short-term expiration dates. Also we're exposed to potentially unlimited risk, which is another reason for making this a short-term strategy. Again, it's *not* one I'd recommend to inexperienced traders. It's worth reemphasizing that the problem is that you could be successful at it for months, picking up modest income over and over again, and then wham, one big loss will wipe out years worth of gains.

Each leg of the trade has uncapped downside. If the stock starts going ballistic in either direction, then your position is precarious to say the least. If the stock remains rangebound, then we'll make a limited profit. But it's not enough for me to get excited. If the stock gaps in either direction, we're history!

You would *never* trade this strategy right before a news event like an earnings report. You certainly wouldn't want any nasty surprises to be lurking around the corner.

| Sell OTM put | + | Sell OTM call | = | Short Strangle |

Steps to Trading a Short Strangle

1. Sell OTM (lower) strike puts, preferably with one month or less to expiration.

2. Sell OTM (higher) strike calls with the same expiration.

   Steps In

   ■ Try to ensure that the trend is rangebound and identify clear areas of support and resistance.

   ■ Try to ensure that no news is coming out soon for the stock.

   Steps Out

   ■ Manage your position according to the rules defined in your Trading Plan.

   ■ Close the losing side by buying back the relevant option if the stock breaks support or resistance.

   ■ Buy back both options if the position is profitable but you think news may emerge about the underlying stock.

5.2.2 Context

Outlook

■ With Short Strangles, your outlook is **direction neutral**—you are looking for no movement in the stock.

Rationale

■ To execute a direction-neutral **income** strategy for a net credit while expecting a future decline in volatility. Ideally you are looking for a scenario where the immediate Implied Volatility has been high, giving you above average options premiums, but where you anticipate the stock to consolidate (become less volatile) and remain rangebound for the duration of your trade.

Net Position

■ This is a **net credit** trade because you have sold calls and puts.

■ Your maximum risk on the trade itself is unlimited, whereas your maximum reward is limited to the net credit you receive for selling the calls and puts.

Effect of Time Decay

■ Time decay is helpful to Short Strangles. Because you are short in options, and because you are exposed to unlimited downside, you want to be exposed to this position for as little time as possible.

Appropriate Time Period to Trade

■ One month or less.

Selecting the Stock

■ Choose from stocks with adequate liquidity, preferably over 500,000 Average Daily Volume (ADV).

■ Try to ensure that the trend is rangebound and identify clear areas of support and resistance.

■ Try to ensure that no news is coming out soon for the stock.

Selecting the Options

■ Choose options with adequate liquidity; open interest should be at least 100, preferably 500.

■ **Put Strike**—OTM—below the current stock price.

■ **Call Strike**—OTM—above the current stock price.

■ **Expiration**—Preferably one month or less. Use the same expiration for both legs.

5.2.3 Risk Profile

■ **Maximum Risk**   [Uncapped]

■ **Maximum Reward**   [Net credit received]

■ **Breakeven Down**   [Lower strike − net credit]

■ **Breakeven Up**   [Higher strike + net credit]

5.2.4 Greeks

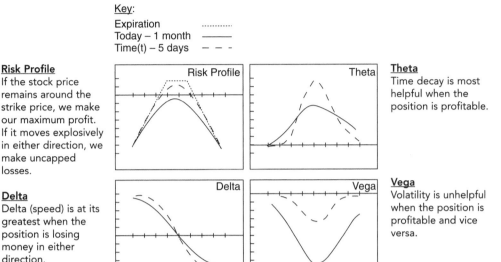

Key:
Expiration   ....
Today – 1 month   ——————
Time(t) – 5 days – – –

Risk Profile
If the stock price remains around the strike price, we make our maximum profit. If it moves explosively in either direction, we make uncapped losses.

Delta
Delta (speed) is at its greatest when the position is losing money in either direction.

Gamma
Gamma (acceleration) peaks inversely between the strike prices, and falls to zero when the position is deep OTM on either side.

Theta
Time decay is most helpful when the position is profitable.

Vega
Volatility is unhelpful when the position is profitable and vice versa.

Rho
Higher interest rates are generally unhelpful to the position when the stock rises and vice versa.

5.2.5 Advantages and Disadvantages

Advantages

■ Profit from a rangebound stock.

■ Comparatively high-yielding income strategy.

Disadvantages

■ Uncapped risk if the stock moves in either direction.

■ Capped reward.

■ Bid/Ask Spread can adversely affect the quality of the trade.

■ High-risk strategy; *not* for novices or intermediates.

5.2.6 Exiting the Trade

Exiting the Position

■ With this strategy, you can simply unravel the spread by buying back your calls and puts.

Mitigating a Loss

■ Buy back your sold options.

■ Advanced traders may consider buying further OTM calls and puts on either side in order to create a Long Iron Condor, which is more conservative.

5.2.7 Example

ABCD is trading at $25.37 on May 17, 2004.

Sell the June 2004 $22.50 strike put for $0.35.

Sell the June 2004 $27.50 strike call for $0.65.

Net Credit	Premiums sold **$0.35 + $0.65 = $1.00**
Maximum Risk	Uncapped
Maximum Reward	Net credit **$1.00**
Breakeven Down	Lower strike − net credit **$22.50 − $1.00 = $21.50**
Breakeven Up	Higher strike + net credit **$27.50 + $1.00 = $28.50**

Compare this to the previous Short Straddle. We've sacrificed some net credit for more safety in terms of our wider breakeven points on both sides.

As with the Short Straddle, the major problem with this strategy is the uncapped risk position. Any surprise concerning the stock could leave you with a serious problem, and frankly, it simply isn't worth the risk.

5.3 Short Guts

Proficiency	Direction	Volatility	Asset Legs	Max Risk	Max Reward	Strategy Type
Expert	Neutral	Low	■ Short Call ■ Short Put	Uncapped	Capped	Income

5.3.1 Description

The Short Guts is a simple adjustment to the Short Strangle that increases the net credit. Instead of selling OTM options, we sell ITM calls and puts, which creates a higher net credit. As with Short Straddles and Short Strangles, the risk we run with a Short Guts is uncapped on either side.

The Short Guts is precisely the opposite of a (Long) Guts. We short ITM puts and calls with a short time to expiration (one month or less) in order to pick up income. Because we're short options, time decay works for us, so we only select short-term expiration dates. Also we're exposed to potentially unlimited risk, which is another reason for making this a short-term strategy. It's *not* one I'd recommend. The additional risk you face with a Short Guts is that each of the strikes is ITM, and therefore you could be exercised early, so stay away from this strategy!

Each leg of the trade has uncapped downside. If the stock starts going ballistic in either direction, then your position is precarious to say the least. If the stock remains rangebound, then we'll make a limited profit.

You would *never* trade this strategy right before a news event like an earnings report. You certainly wouldn't want any nasty surprises to be lurking around the corner.

Sell ITM call   +   Sell ITM put   =   Short Guts

Steps to Trading a Short Guts

1. Sell ITM (lower) strike calls, preferably with one month or less to expiration.

2. Sell ITM (higher) strike puts with the same expiration.

   Steps In

   ■ Try to ensure that the trend is rangebound and identify clear areas of support and resistance.

   ■ Try to ensure that no news is coming out soon for the stock.

   Steps Out

   ■ Manage your position according to the rules defined in your Trading Plan.

   ■ Close the losing side by buying back the relevant option if the stock breaks support or resistance.

   ■ Buy back both options if the position is profitable but you think news may emerge about the underlying stock.

5.3.2 Context

Outlook

■ With Short Guts, your outlook is **direction neutral**—you are looking for no movement in the stock.

Rationale

■ To execute a direction-neutral **income** strategy for a net credit while expecting a future decline in volatility. Ideally you are looking for a scenario where the immediate Implied Volatility has been high, giving you above average options premiums, but where you anticipate the stock to consolidate (become less volatile) and remain rangebound for the duration of your trade.

■ Because the options are ITM, a Short Guts can raise a significant net credit into your account. This makes a Short Guts a plausible hedging strategy against something like a long Straddle or long Strangle, for example.

Net Position

■ This is a **net credit** trade because you have sold calls and puts.

■ Your maximum risk on the trade itself is unlimited, whereas your maximum reward is limited to the net credit you receive for selling the calls and puts less the difference in strike prices.

Effect of Time Decay

■ Time decay is helpful to a Short Guts. Because you are short in options, and because you are exposed to unlimited downside, you want to be exposed to this position for as little time as possible.

Appropriate Time Period to Trade

■ One month or less.

Selecting the Stock

■ Choose from stocks with adequate liquidity, preferably over 500,000 Average Daily Volume (ADV).

■ Try to ensure that the trend is rangebound and identify clear areas of support and resistance.

■ Try to ensure that no news is coming out soon for the stock.

Selecting the Options

■ Choose options with adequate liquidity; open interest should be at least 100, preferably 500.

■ **Call Strike**—ITM—below the current stock price.

■ **Put Strike**—ITM—above the current stock price.

■ **Expiration**—Preferably one month or less. Use the same expiration for both legs.

5.3.3 Risk Profile

- **Maximum Risk**   [Uncapped]

- **Maximum Reward** [Net credit received − difference in strikes]

- **Breakeven Down**   [Lower strike − net credit + difference in strikes]

- **Breakeven Up**   [Higher strike + net credit − difference in strikes]

5.3.4 Greeks

Key:
Expiration   ....
Today − 1 month ————
Time(t) − 5 days   − − −

Risk Profile
If the stock price remains around the strike price, we make our maximum profit. If it moves explosively in either direction, we make uncapped losses.

Delta
Delta (speed) is at its greatest when the position is losing money in either direction.

Gamma
Gamma (acceleration) peaks inversely between the strike prices and falls to zero when the position is loss making on either side.

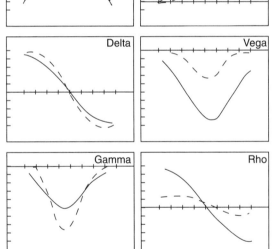

Theta
Time decay is most helpful when the position is profitable.

Vega
Volatility is unhelpful when the position is profitable and vice versa.

Rho
Higher interest rates are generally unhelpful to the position when the stock rises and vice versa.

5.3.5 Advantages and Disadvantages

Advantages

- Profit from a rangebound stock.

- Comparatively high-yielding income strategy.

- High premiums because both options are ITM.

Disadvantages

- Uncapped risk if the stock moves in either direction.
- Capped reward.
- Certain exercise at expiration whatever the movement of the stock.
- Bid/Ask Spread can adversely affect the quality of the trade.
- High-risk strategy; *not* for novices or intermediates.

5.3.6 Exiting the Trade

Exiting the Position

- With this strategy, you can simply unravel the spread by buying back your calls and puts.

Mitigating a Loss

- Buy back your sold options.

5.3.7 Example

ABCD is trading at $25.37 on May 17, 2004.

Sell the June 2004 $22.50 strike call for $3.30.

Sell the June 2004 $27.50 strike put for $2.80.

Net Credit	Premiums sold **$3.30 + $2.80 = $6.10**
Maximum Risk	Uncapped
Maximum Reward	Net credit − difference in strikes **$6.10 − $5.00 = $1.10**
Breakeven Down	Lower strike − net credit + difference in strikes **$22.50 − $6.10 + $5.00 = $21.40**
Breakeven Up	Higher strike + net credit − difference in strikes **$27.50 + $6.10 − $5.00 = $28.60**

5.4 Long Call Butterfly

Proficiency	Direction	Volatility	Asset Legs	Max Risk	Max Reward	Strategy Type
Intermediate	Neutral	Low	■ Long Call ■ Two Short Calls ■ Long Call	Capped	Capped	Capital Gain

5.4.1 Description

The Long Call Butterfly is another rangebound strategy and is the opposite of a Short Call Butterfly, which is a volatility strategy. Long butterflies are quite popular because they offer a good risk/reward ratio, together with low cost. The long options at the outside strikes ensure that the risk is capped on both sides, and this is a much more conservative strategy than the Short Straddle.

The Long Call Butterfly involves a low strike long call, two ATM short calls, and an OTM long call. The resulting is profitable in the event of rangebound action by the stock. Although the risk/reward ratio is attractive, the problem is that the maximum reward is restricted to the scenario where the stock is at the middle strike at expiration.

| Buy lower strike call | Sell middle strike call | Sell middle strike call | Buy higher strike call | Long Call Butterfly |

Steps to Trading a Long Call Butterfly

1. Buy one lower strike (ITM) call.

2. Sell two middle strike (ATM) calls.

3. Buy one higher strike (OTM) call.

- All options share the same expiration date for this strategy.

- For this strategy, you must use all calls.

- Remember that there should be equal distance between each strike price. The maximum reward occurs if the stock is at the middle strike at expiration.

Steps In

- Try to ensure that the trend is rangebound and identify clear areas of support and resistance.

- Try to ensure that no news is coming out soon for the stock.

Steps Out

- Manage your position according to the rules defined in your Trading Plan.

- If the stock veers outside your stop loss areas above or below the stock price, then unravel the entire position.

- You can unravel the position just before expiration—remember to include all the commissions in your calculations.

5.4.2 Context

Outlook

- With long butterflies, your profile is **direction neutral**—you expect very little movement in the stock price.

Rationale

■ With long butterflies, you are looking to execute a potentially high-yielding trade at very low cost, where your maximum profits occur if the stock is at the middle strike price at expiration.

■ You are anticipating very low volatility in the stock price.

Net Position

■ This is a **net debit** trade, although the net cost is typically low.

■ Your maximum risk is the net debit of the bought and sold options. Your maximum reward is the difference between adjacent strike prices less the net debit. (Remember that the upper and lower strike prices are equidistant to the middle strike price).

Effect of Time Decay

■ Time decay is helpful to this position when it is profitable and harmful when the position is unprofitable. When you enter the trade, typically the stock price will be in the profitable area of the risk profile, so from that perspective, time decay harms the position.

Appropriate Time Period to Trade

■ One month or less.

Selecting the Stock

■ Choose from stocks with adequate liquidity, preferably over 500,000 Average Daily Volume (ADV).

■ Try to ensure that the trend is rangebound and identify clear areas of support and resistance.

■ Select a stock price range you feel comfortable with. Some traders look to avoid stocks under $20.00, claiming the need for adequate wingspan between the breakeven points for the best chance of success. Ultimately it's more important that the stock remains rangebound.

Selecting the Options

■ Choose options with adequate liquidity; open interest should be at least 100, preferably 500.

■ **Lower Strike**—Below the current stock price.

■ **Middle Strike**—As close to ATM (or where you think the stock will be at expiration) as possible.

■ **Higher Strike**—The same distance above the middle strike as the lower is below it; use online tools to find the optimum yields and breakeven points at and before expiration.

■ **Expiration**—Preferably one month or less, but there is a trade-off between time and profit potential. Use the same expiration for all legs.

5.4.3 Risk Profile

■ **Maximum Risk**   [Net debit paid]

■ **Maximum Reward**   [Difference between adjacent strikes − net debit]

■ **Breakeven Down**   [Lower strike + net debit]

■ **Breakeven Up**   [Higher strike − net debit]

5.4.4 Greeks

Key:
Expiration   ....
Today – 3 months ————
Time(t) – 1 month – – –

Risk Profile
As the stock price remains rangebound, the position is profitable, with maximum reward occurring at the middle strike price.

Delta
Delta (speed) is at its greatest around the outer strikes and is zero around the middle strike.

Gamma
Gamma (acceleration) peaks inversely around the middle strike, highlighting the position's major turning point and middle Delta neutral point, and peaks positively around the outside strikes.

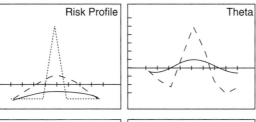
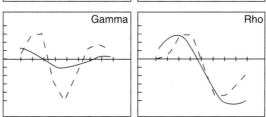

Theta
Time decay is helpful to the position when it is profitable and unhelpful when it is unprofitable.

Vega
Volatility is generally unhelpful to the position unless it the stock moves outside the outer strikes.

Rho
Higher interest rates are generally helpful to the position when the stock price is lower and vice versa.

5.4.5 Advantages and Disadvantages

Advantages

- Profit from a rangebound stock for very little cost.

- Capped and low risk.

- Comparatively high risk/reward ratio if the stock remains rangebound.

Disadvantages

- The higher profit potential comes with a narrow range between the wing strikes.

- The higher profit potential only comes nearer expiration.

- Bid/Ask Spread can adversely affect the quality of the trade.

5.4.6 Exiting the Trade

Exiting the Position

- With this strategy, you can simply unravel the spread by buying back the options you sold and selling the options you bought in the first place.

- Advanced traders may leg up and down or only partially unravel the spread as the underlying asset fluctuates up and down. In this way, the trader will be taking smaller incremental profits before the expiration of the trade.

Mitigating a Loss

- Unravel the trade as described previously.

- Advanced traders may choose to only partially unravel the spread leg-by-leg and create alternative risk profiles.

5.4.7 Example

ABCD is trading at $50.00 on May 17, 2004.

Buy the June 2004 45 strike call for $6.12.

Sell two June 2004 50 strike calls at $3.07.

Buy the June 2004 55 strike call for $1.30.

Net Debit	Premiums bought − premiums sold **$6.12 + $1.30 − $6.14 = $1.28**
Maximum Risk	Net debit **$1.28**
Maximum Reward	Difference in adjacent strikes − net debit **$5.00 − $1.28 = $3.72**
Breakeven Down	Lower strike + net debit **$45.00 + $1.28 = $46.28**
Breakeven Up	Higher strike − net debit **$55.00 − $1.28 = $53.72**
Max ROI	290.63% if the stock is priced at $50.00 at expiration.

5.5 Long Put Butterfly

Proficiency	Direction	Volatility	Asset Legs	Max Risk	Max Reward	Strategy Type
Intermediate	Neutral	Low	■ Long Put ■ Two Short Puts ■ Long Put	Capped	Capped	Capital Gain

5.5.1 Description

The Long Put Butterfly is another rangebound strategy and is the opposite of a Short Put Butterfly, which is a volatility strategy. Long butterflies are quite popular because they offer a good risk/reward ratio, together with low cost. The long options at the outside strikes ensure that the risk is capped on both sides, and this is a much more conservative strategy than the Short Straddle.

The Long Put Butterfly involves a low strike long put, two ATM short puts, and an ITM long put. The resulting positionis profitable in the event of rangebound action by the stock. Although the risk/reward ratio is attractive, the problem is that the maximum reward is restricted to the scenario where the stock is at the middle strike at expiration.

| Buy lower
strike put | + | Sell middle
strike put | Sell middle
strike put | + | Buy higher
strike put | = | Long Put
Butterfly |

Steps to Trading a Long Put Butterfly

1. Buy one lower strike (OTM) put.

2. Sell two middle strike (ATM) puts.

3. Buy one higher strike (ITM) put.

   - All options share the same expiration date for this strategy.

   - For this strategy, you must use all puts.

   - Remember that there should be equal distance between each strike price. The maximum reward occurs if the stock is at the middle strike at expiration.

   Steps In

   - Try to ensure that the trend is rangebound and identify clear areas of support and resistance.

   - Try to ensure that no news is coming out soon for the stock.

   Steps Out

   - Manage your position according to the rules defined in your Trading Plan.

   - If the stock veers outside your stop loss areas above or below the stock price, then unravel the entire position.

   - You can unravel the position just before expiration—remember to include all the commissions in your calculations.

5.5.2 Context

Outlook

- With long butterflies, your profile is **direction neutral**—you expect very little movement in the stock price.

Rationale

- With long butterflies, you are looking to execute a potentially high-yielding trade at very low cost, where your maximum profits occur if the stock finishes at the middle strike price at expiration.

- You are anticipating very low volatility in the stock price.

Net Position

- This is a **net debit** trade, although the net cost is typically low.

- Your maximum risk is the net debit of the bought and sold options. Your maximum reward is the difference between adjacent strike prices less the net debit.

(Remember that the upper and lower strike prices are equidistant to the middle strike price.)

Effect of Time Decay

■ Time decay is helpful to this position when it is profitable and harmful when the position is unprofitable. When you enter the trade, typically the stock price will be in the profitable area of the risk profile, so from that perspective, time decay harms the position.

Appropriate Time Period to Trade

■ One month or less.

Selecting the Stock

■ Choose from stocks with adequate liquidity, preferably over 500,000 Average Daily Volume (ADV).

■ Try to ensure that the trend is rangebound and identify clear areas of support and resistance.

■ Select a stock price range you feel comfortable with. Some traders look to avoid stocks under $20.00, claiming the need for adequate wingspan between the breakeven points for the best chance of success. Ultimately it's more important that the stock remains rangebound.

Selecting the Options

■ Choose options with adequate liquidity; open interest should be at least 100, preferably 500.

■ **Lower Strike**—Below the current stock price.

■ **Middle Strike**—As close to ATM (or where you think the stock will be at expiration) as possible.

■ **Higher Strike**—The same distance above the middle strike as the lower is below it; use online tools to find the optimum yields and breakeven points at and before expiration.

■ **Expiration**—Preferably one month or less, but there is a trade-off between time and profit potential. Use the same expiration for all legs.

5.5.3 Risk Profile

■ **Maximum Risk**   [Net debit paid]

■ **Maximum Reward**   [Difference between adjacent strikes − net debit]

■ **Breakeven Down**   [Lower strike + net debit]

■ **Breakeven Up**   [Higher strike − net debit]

5.5.4 Greeks

Key:
Expiration   ....
Today – 3 months ————
Time(t) – 1 month – – –

Risk Profile
As the stock price remains rangebound, the position is profitable, with maximum reward occurring at the middle strike price.

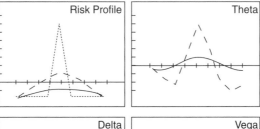

Theta
Time decay is helpful to the position when it is profitable and unhelpful when it is unprofitable.

Delta
Delta (speed) is at its greatest around the outer strikes and is zero around the middle strike.

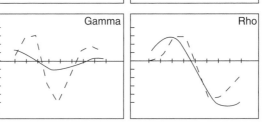

Vega
Volatility is generally unhelpful to the position unless it the stock moves outside the outer strikes.

Gamma
Gamma (acceleration) peaks inversely around the middle strike, highlighting the position's major turning point and middle Delta neutral point, and peaks positively around the outside strikes.

Rho
Higher interest rates are generally helpful to the position when the stock price is lower and vice versa.

5.5.5 Advantages and Disadvantages

Advantages

- Profit from a rangebound stock for very little cost.

- Capped and low risk.

- Comparatively high risk/reward ratio if the stock remains rangebound.

Disadvantages

- The higher profit potential comes with a narrow range between the wing strikes.

- The higher profit potential only comes nearer expiration.

- Bid/Ask Spread can adversely affect the quality of the trade.

5.5.6 Exiting the Trade

Exiting the Position

- With this strategy, you can simply unravel the spread by buying back the options you sold and selling the options you bought in the first place.

- Advanced traders may leg up and down or only partially unravel the spread as the underlying asset fluctuates up and down. In this way, the trader will be taking smaller incremental profits before the expiration of the trade.

Mitigating a Loss

- Unravel the trade as described previously.

- Advanced traders may choose to only partially unravel the spread leg-by-leg and create alternative risk profiles.

5.5.7 Example

ABCD is trading at $50.00 on May 17, 2004.

Buy the June 2004 45 strike put for $0.98.

Sell two June 2004 50 strike puts at $2.91.

Buy the June 2004 55 strike put for $6.12.

Net Debit	Premiums bought − premiums sold **$0.98 + $6.12 − $5.82 = $1.28**
Maximum Risk	Net debit **$1.28**
Maximum Reward	Difference in adjacent strikes − net debit **$5.00 − $1.28 = $3.72**
Breakeven Down	Lower strike + net debit **$45.00 + $1.28 = $46.28**
Breakeven Up	Higher strike − net debit **$55.00 − $1.28 = $53.72**
Max ROI	290.63% if the stock is priced at $50.00 at expiration.

5.6 Long Call Condor

Proficiency	Direction	Volatility	Asset Legs		Max Risk	Max Reward	Strategy Type
Advanced	Neutral	Low	■ Long Call ■ Short Call ■ Short Call ■ Long Call		Capped	Capped	Capital Gain

5.6.1 Description

Long condors are identical to long butterflies, with the exception that the two middle options have different strikes. The Long Call Condor is another range-bound strategy and is the opposite of a Short Call Condor, which is a volatility strategy. Long condors are quite popular because they offer a good risk/reward ratio, together with low cost. The long options at the outside strikes ensure that the risk is capped on both sides, and this is a much more conservative strategy than the Short Strangle.

The Long Call Condor involves a low strike long call, a lower middle ITM short call, a higher middle OTM short call, and a higher OTM long call. The resulting position is profitable in the event of the stock remaining rangebound. Here the risk/reward ratio is attractive, and the profitable area of the risk profile is wider than that of the Long Butterfly.

| Buy lower strike call | + | Sell middle strike call | + | Sell middle strike call | + | Buy higher strike call | = | Long Call Condor |

Steps to Trading a Long Call Condor

1. Buy one lower strike (ITM) call.

2. Sell one lower middle strike (ITM) call.

3. Sell one higher middle strike (OTM) call.

4. Buy one higher strike (OTM) call.

   ■ All options share the same expiration date for this strategy.

   ■ For this strategy, you must use all calls.

- Remember that there should be equal distance between each strike price. The maximum reward occurs if the stock is at the middle strike at expiration.

Steps In

- Try to ensure that the trend is rangebound and identify clear areas of support and resistance.

- Try to ensure that no news is coming out soon for the stock.

Steps Out

- Manage your position according to the rules defined in your Trading Plan.

- If the stock veers outside your stop loss areas above or below the stock price, then unravel the entire position.

- You can unravel the position just before expiration—remember to include all the commissions in your calculations.

5.6.2 Context

Outlook

- With long condors, your profile is **direction neutral**—you expect very little movement in the stock price.

Rationale

- With long condors, you are looking to execute a potentially high-yielding trade at very low cost, where your maximum profits occur if the stock finishes between the middle strike prices at expiration.

- You are anticipating very low volatility in the stock price.

Net Position

- This is a **net debit** trade, although the net cost is typically low.

- Your maximum risk is the net debit of the bought and sold options. Your maximum reward is the difference between adjacent strike prices less the net debit. (Remember that all strike prices are equidistant to each other.)

Effect of Time Decay

- Time decay is helpful to this position when it is profitable and harmful when the position is unprofitable. When you enter the trade, typically the stock price will be in the profitable area of the risk profile, so from that perspective, time decay harms the position.

Appropriate Time Period to Trade

- One month or less.

Selecting the Stock

- Choose from stocks with adequate liquidity, preferably over 500,000 Average Daily Volume (ADV).

- Try to ensure that the trend is rangebound and identify clear areas of support and resistance.

- Select a stock price range you feel comfortable with. Some traders look to avoid stocks under $20.00, claiming the need for adequate wingspan between the breakeven points for the best chance of success. Ultimately, it's more important that the stock remains rangebound.

Selecting the Options

- Choose options with adequate liquidity; open interest should be at least 100, preferably 500.

- **Lower Strike**—At least two strikes below the current stock price.

- **Lower Middle Strike**—At least one strike below the current stock price.

- **Higher Middle Strike**—At least one strike above the current stock price.

- **Higher Strike**—At least two strikes above the current stock price.

- **Expiration**—Preferably one month or less, but there is a trade-off between time and profit potential. Use the same expiration for all legs.

5.6.3 Risk Profile

- **Maximum Risk**   [Net debit paid]
- **Maximum Reward**   [Difference between adjacent strikes − net debit]
- **Breakeven Down**   [Lower strike + net debit]
- **Breakeven Up**   [Higher strike − net debit]

5.6.4 Greeks

Key:
Expiration   ....
Today – 3 months ————
Time(t) – 1 month – – –

Risk Profile
As the stock price remains rangebound, the position is profitable, with maximum reward occurring between middle strike prices.

Delta
Delta (speed) is at its greatest around the outer strikes and is zero between the middle strikes.

Gamma
Gamma (acceleration) peaks inversely between the middle strikes and peaks positively around the outside strikes.

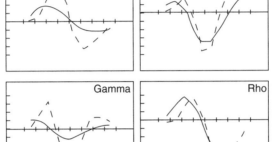

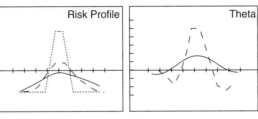

Theta
Time decay is helpful to the position when it is profitable and unhelpful when it is unprofitable.

Vega
Volatility is generally unhelpful to the position unless it the stock moves outside the outer strikes.

Rho
Higher interest rates are generally helpful to the position when the stock price is lower and vice versa.

5.6.5 Advantages and Disadvantages

Advantages

■ Profit from a rangebound stock for very little cost.

■ Capped and low risk.

■ Comparatively high risk/reward ratio if the stock remains rangebound.

Disadvantages

■ The higher profit potential comes with a narrow range between the wing strikes.

■ The higher profit potential only comes nearer expiration.

■ Bid/Ask Spread can adversely affect the quality of the trade.

5.6.6 Exiting the Trade

Exiting the Position

- With this strategy, you can simply unravel the spread by buying back the options you sold and selling the options you bought in the first place.

- Advanced traders may leg up and down or only partially unravel the spread as the underlying asset fluctuates up and down. In this way, the trader will be taking smaller incremental profits before the expiration of the trade.

Mitigating a Loss

- Unravel the trade as described previously.

- Advanced traders may choose to only partially unravel the spread leg-by-leg and create alternative risk profiles.

5.6.7 Example

ABCD is trading at $52.87 on May 17, 2004.

Buy the June 2004 45 strike call for $8.52.

Sell the June 2004 50 strike call at $4.82.

Sell the June 2004 55 strike call at $2.34.

Buy the June 2004 60 strike call for $0.98.

Net Debit	Premiums bought − premiums sold **$8.52 + $0.98 − $4.82 − $2.34 = $2.34**
Maximum Risk	Net debit **$2.34**
Maximum Reward	Difference in adjacent strikes − net debit **$5.00 − $2.34 = $2.66**
Breakeven Down	Lower strike + net debit **$45.00 + $2.34 = $47.34**
Breakeven Up	Higher strike − net debit **$60.00 − $2.34 = $57.66**
Max ROI	113.68% if the stock is between $50.00 and $55.00 at expiration.

5.7 Long Put Condor

Proficiency	Direction	Volatility	Asset Legs	Max Risk	Max Reward	Strategy Type
Advanced	Neutral	Low	■ Long Put ■ Short Put ■ Short Put ■ Long Put	Capped	Capped	Capital Gain

5.7.1 Description

The Long Put Condor is another rangebound strategy and is the opposite of a Short Put Condor, which is a volatility strategy. Long condors are quite popular because they offer a good risk/reward ratio, together with low cost. The long options at the outside strikes ensure that the risk is capped on both sides, and this is a much more conservative strategy than the Short Strangle.

The Long Put Condor involves a low strike long put, a lower middle OTM Short Put, a higher middle ITM Short Put, and a higher ITM Long Put. The resulting position yields a position that is profitable in the event of the stock remaining rangebound. Here the risk/reward ratio is attractive, and the profitable area of the risk profile is wider than that of the Long Butterfly.

Buy lower strike put + Sell middle strike put + Sell middle strike put + Buy higher strike put = Long Put Condor

Steps to Trading a Long Put Condor

1. Buy one lower strike (OTM) put.

2. Sell one lower middle strike (OTM) put.

3. Sell one higher middle strike (ITM) put.

4. Buy one higher strike (ITM) put.

   ■ All options share the same expiration date for this strategy.

   ■ For this strategy, you must use all puts.

■ Remember that there should be equal distance between each strike price. The maximum reward occurs if the stock is at the middle strike at expiration.

Steps In

■ Try to ensure that the trend is rangebound and identify clear areas of support and resistance.

■ Try to ensure that no news is coming out soon for the stock.

Steps Out

■ Manage your position according to the rules defined in your Trading Plan.

■ If the stock veers outside your stop loss areas above or below the stock price, then unravel the entire position.

■ You can unravel the position just before expiration—remember to include all the commissions in your calculations.

5.7.2 Context

Outlook

■ With long condors, your profile is **direction neutral**—you expect very little movement in the stock price.

Rationale

■ With long condors, you are looking to execute a potentially high-yielding trade at very low cost, where your maximum profits occur if the stock finishes between the middle strike prices at expiration.

■ You are anticipating very low volatility in the stock price.

Net Position

■ This is a **net debit** trade, although the net cost is typically low.

■ Your maximum risk is the net debit of the bought and sold options. Your maximum reward is the difference between adjacent strike prices less the net debit. (Remember that all strike prices are equidistant to each other.)

Effect of Time Decay

■ Time decay is helpful to this position when it is profitable and harmful when the position is unprofitable. When you enter the trade, typically the stock price will be in the profitable area of the risk profile, so from that perspective, time decay harms the position.

Appropriate Time Period to Trade

■ One month or less.

Selecting the Stock

■ Choose from stocks with adequate liquidity, preferably over 500,000 Average Daily Volume (ADV).

■ Try to ensure that the trend is rangebound and identify clear areas of support and resistance.

■ Select a stock price range you feel comfortable with. Some traders look to avoid stocks under $20.00, claiming the need for adequate wingspan between the breakeven points for the best chance of success. Ultimately it's more important that the stock remains rangebound.

Selecting the Options

■ Choose options with adequate liquidity; open interest should be at least 100, preferably 500.

■ **Lower Strike**—At least two strikes below the current stock price.

■ **Lower Middle Strike**—At least one strike below the current stock price.

■ **Higher Middle Strike**—At least one strike above the current stock price.

■ **Higher Strike**—At least two strikes above the current stock price.

■ **Expiration**—Preferably one month or less, but there is a trade-off between time and profit potential. Use the same expiration for all legs.

5.7.3 Risk Profile

■ **Maximum Risk**   [Net debit paid]

■ **Maximum Reward**   [Difference between adjacent strikes − net debit]

■ **Breakeven Down**   [Lower strike + net debit]

■ **Breakeven Up**   [Higher strike − net debit]

5.7.4 Grereeks

Key:

Expiration   ....
Today – 3 months ————
Time(t) – 1 month – – –

Risk Profile
As the stock price remains rangebound, the position is profitable, with maximum reward occurring between middle strike prices.

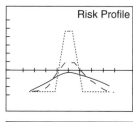

Theta
Time decay is helpful to the position when it is profitable and unhelpful when it is unprofitable.

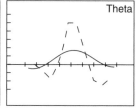

Delta
Delta (speed) is at its greatest around the outer strikes and is zero between the middle strikes.

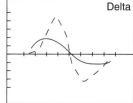

Vega
Volatility is generally unhelpful to the position unless it the stock moves outside the outer strikes.

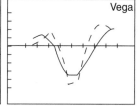

Gamma
Gamma (acceleration) peaks inversely between the middle strikes and peaks positively around the outside strikes.

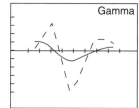

Rho
Higher interest rates are generally helpful to the position when the stock price is lower and vice versa.

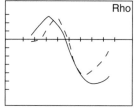

5.7.5 Advantages and Disadvantages

Advantages

- Profit from a rangebound stock for very little cost.

- Capped and low risk.

- Comparatively high risk/reward ratio if the stock remains rangebound.

Disadvantages

- The higher profit potential comes with a narrow range between the wing strikes.

- The higher profit potential only comes nearer expiration.

- Bid/Ask Spread can adversely affect the quality of the trade.

5.7.6 Exiting the Trade

Exiting the Position

- With this strategy, you can simply unravel the spread by buying back the options you sold and selling the options you bought in the first place.

- Advanced traders may leg up and down or only partially unravel the spread as the underlying asset fluctuates up and down. In this way, the trader will be taking smaller incremental profits before the expiration of the trade.

Mitigating a Loss

- Unravel the trade as described previously.

- Advanced traders may choose to only partially unravel the spread leg-by-leg and create alternative risk profiles.

5.7.7 Example

ABCD is trading at $52.87 on May 17, 2004.

Buy the June 2004 45 strike put for $0.51.

Sell the June 2004 50 strike put at $1.80.

Sell the June 2004 55 strike put at $4.30.

Buy the June 2004 60 strike put for $7.92.

Net Debit	Premiums bought − premiums sold **$0.51 + $7.92 − $1.80 − $4.30 = $2.33**
Maximum Risk	Net debit **$2.33**
Maximum Reward	Difference in adjacent strikes − net debit **$5.00 − $2.33 = $2.67**
Breakeven Down	Lower strike + net debit **$45.00 + $2.33 = $47.33**
Breakeven Up	Higher strike − net debit **$60.00 − $2.33 = $57.67**
Max ROI	114.59% if the stock is between $50.00 and $55.00 at expiration.

5.8 Modified Call Butterfly

Proficiency	Direction	Volatility	Asset Legs		Max Risk	Max Reward	Strategy Type
Expert	Bullish	Low	◼ Long Call ◼ Two Short Calls ◼ Long Call		Capped	Capped	Capital Gain

5.8.1 Description

The Modified Call Butterfly is identical to the Long Call Butterfly with the exception that the distance between the middle and higher strike calls is closer than that of the lower and middle strikes.

The net effect of this is that the position changes to a rangebound strategy with a bullish bias. As such, we make our biggest profits if the stock remains around the middle strike, but we can still make a profit if the stock breaks to the upside.

This is a fiddly strategy and should only be used if you have an analyzer handy; otherwise, it would be easy to miscalculate your risk profile. But in terms of its usefulness, the Modified Butterfly is extremely useful for butterfly enthusiasts who need some flexibility.

The Modified Call Butterfly involves a low strike long call, two ATM short calls, and an OTM long call. The resulting position is profitable in the event of rangebound or rising action by the stock. Although the risk/reward ratio is attractive, the problem remains that the maximum reward is restricted to the scenario where the stock is at the middle strike at expiration.

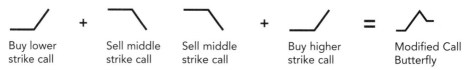

Buy lower strike call + Sell middle strike call Sell middle strike call + Buy higher strike call = Modified Call Butterfly

Steps to Trading a Modified Call Butterfly

1. Buy one lower strike (ITM) call.

2. Sell two middle strike (ATM) calls.

3. Buy one higher strike (OTM) call.

   ◼ All options share the same expiration date for this strategy.

   ◼ For this strategy, you must use all calls.

   ◼ Remember that the distance between the higher and middle strikes is closer than the distance between the lower and middle strikes. The maximum reward occurs if the stock is at the middle strike at expiration.

Steps In

- Try to ensure that the trend is rangebound and identify a clear area of support.

Steps Out

- Manage your position according to the rules defined in your Trading Plan.

- If the stock falls below your stop loss below the current stock price, then unravel the entire position.

- You can unravel the position just before expiration—remember to include all the commissions in your calculations.

5.8.2 Context

Outlook

- With modified butterflies, your profile is **direction neutral to moderately bullish**—you expect a moderate rise.

Rationale

- With modified butterflies, you are looking to execute a potentially high-yielding trade at very low cost, where your maximum profits occur if the stock finishes at the middle strike price at expiration.

- You are anticipating moderately low volatility in the stock price.

Net Position

- This is a **net debit** trade.

- Your maximum risk is the net debit of the bought and sold options. Your maximum reward is the difference between the lower and middle strikes less the net debit.

Effect of Time Decay

- Time decay is helpful to this position when it is profitable and harmful when the position is unprofitable. When you enter the trade, typically the stock price will be in the profitable area of the risk profile, so from that perspective, time decay harms the position.

Appropriate Time Period to Trade

- One month or less.

Selecting the Stock

- Choose from stocks with adequate liquidity, preferably over 500,000 Average Daily Volume (ADV).

- Try to ensure that the trend is rangebound and identify a clear area of support.

Selecting the Options

- Choose options with adequate liquidity; open interest should be at least 100, preferably 500.

- **Lower Strike**—Below the current stock price.

- **Middle Strike**—As close to ATM as possible.

- **Higher Strike**—Closer to the middle strike than the lower is below it; use online tools to find the optimum yields and breakeven points at and before expiration.

- **Expiration**—Preferably one month or less, but there is a trade-off between time and profit potential. Use the same expiration for all legs.

5.8.3 Risk Profile

- **Maximum Risk**   [Net debit paid]

- **Maximum Reward**   [Difference between lower and middle strikes − net debit]

- **Breakeven**   [Lower strike + net debit]

5.8.4 Greeks

Key:
Expiration   ....
Today – 3 months ———
Time(t) – 1 month – – –

Risk Profile
As the stock price remains rangebound, the position is profitable, with maximum reward occurring at the middle strike price.

Delta
Delta (speed) peaks positively around the lower strike and inversely around the upper strike.

Gamma
Gamma (acceleration) peaks positively as the risk profile begins to climb into a profitable position and peaks inversely around the upper strike.

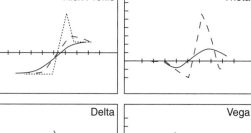
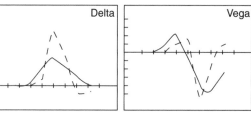
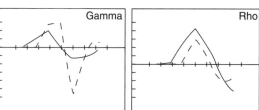

Theta
Time decay is helpful to the position when it is profitable and unhelpful when it is unprofitable.

Vega
Volatility is generally unhelpful to the position unless it the stock moves outside the outer strikes.

Rho
Higher interest rates are generally helpful to the position when the stock price is lower and vice versa.

5.8.5 Advantages and Disadvantages

Advantages

■ Profit from a sideways or rising stock for very little cost.

■ Capped and low risk.

■ Comparatively high risk/reward ratio if the stock remains rangebound.

Disadvantages

■ The higher profit potential comes with a narrow range between the wing strikes.

■ The higher profit potential only comes nearer expiration.

■ Bid/Ask Spread can adversely affect the quality of the trade.

5.8.6 Exiting the Trade

Exiting the Position

■ With this strategy, you can simply unravel the spread by buying back the options you sold and selling the options you bought in the first place.

■ Advanced traders may leg up and down or only partially unravel the spread as the underlying asset fluctuates up and down. In this way, the trader will be taking smaller incremental profits before the expiration of the trade.

Mitigating a Loss

■ Unravel the trade as described previously.

■ Advanced traders may choose to only partially unravel the spread leg-by-leg and create alternative risk profiles.

5.8.7 Example

ABCD is trading at $50.00 on May 17, 2004.

Buy the June 2004 45 strike call for $6.12.

Sell two June 2004 55 strike calls at $1.30.

Buy the June 2004 60 strike call for $0.50.

Net Debit	Premiums bought − premiums sold **$6.12 + $0.50 − $2.60 = $4.02**
Maximum Risk	Net debit **$4.02**
Maximum Reward	Middle strike − lower strike strikes − net debit **$55.00 − $45.00 − $4.02 = $5.98**
Interim Risk / Reward	(Higher strike − middle strike) − (middle strike − lower strike) − net debit **$10.00 − $5.00 − $4.02 = $0.98 (reward)**
Breakeven Down	Lower strike + net debit **$45.00 + $4.02 = $49.02**
Breakeven Up	N/A here.
Max ROI	148.76% if the stock is priced at $55.00 at expiration.
Interim ROI	24.38% if the stock is priced above $60.00 at expiration.

It's possible to have two breakevens with the Modified Butterfly, although it's infinitely preferable to structure the trade so that there is no upper breakeven at all. After all, this is a neutral to bullish strategy, and it wouldn't make sense for us to lose money if the stock breaks the way we anticipated, even if we are still cautious about the amount it could move.

5.9 Modified Put Butterfly

Proficiency	Direction	Volatility	Asset Legs	Max Risk	Max Reward	Strategy Type
Expert	Bullish	Low	■ Long Put ■ Two Short Puts ■ Long Put	Capped	Capped	Capital Gain

5.9.1 Description

The Modified Put Butterfly is identical to the Long Put Butterfly with the exception that the distance between the middle and higher strike calls is closer than that of the lower and middle strikes. The Modified Put Butterfly is virtually identical to the Modified Call Butterfly.

The net effect of this is that the position changes to a rangebound strategy with a bullish bias. As such, we make our biggest profits if the stock remains around the middle strike, but we can still make a profit if the stock breaks to the upside.

This is a fiddly strategy and should only be used if you have an analyzer handy; otherwise, it would be easy to miscalculate your risk profile. But in terms of its usefulness, the Modified Butterfly is extremely useful for butterfly enthusiasts who need some flexibility.

The Modified Put Butterfly involves a low strike long put, two ATM short puts, and an OTM long put. The resulting position is profitable in the event of rangebound or rising action by the stock. Although the risk/reward ratio is attractive, the problem remains that the maximum reward is restricted to the scenario where the stock is at the middle strike at expiration.

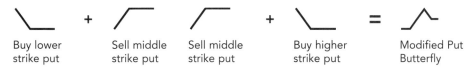

Buy lower
strike put

Sell middle
strike put

Sell middle
strike put

Buy higher
strike put

Modified Put
Butterfly

Steps to Trading a Modified Put Butterfly

1. Buy one lower strike (OTM) put.

2. Sell two middle strike (ATM) puts.

3. Buy one higher strike (ITM) put.

   ■ All options share the same expiration date for this strategy.

   ■ For this strategy, you must use all puts.

   ■ Remember that the distance between the higher and middle strikes is closer than the distance between the lower and middle strikes. The maximum reward occurs if the stock is at the middle strike at expiration.

Steps In

■ Choose from stocks with adequate liquidity, preferably over 500,000 Average Daily Volume (ADV).

■ Try to ensure that the trend is rangebound and identify a clear area of support.

Steps Out

■ Manage your position according to the rules defined in your Trading Plan.

■ If the stock falls below your stop loss below the current stock price, then unravel the entire position.

■ You can unravel the position just before expiration—remember to include all the commissions in your calculations.

5.9.2 Context

Outlook

■ With modified butterflies, your profile is **direction neutral to moderately bullish**—you expect a moderate rise.

Rationale

- With modified butterflies, you are looking to execute a potentially high-yielding trade at very low cost, where your maximum profits occur if the stock finishes at the middle strike price at expiration.

- You are anticipating moderately low volatility in the stock price.

Net Position

- You should aim to create a **net credit** trade, though this is not always the case.

- Your maximum risk is the [difference between the lowest and middle strikes] less the [difference between the middle and highest strikes], [plus net debit] or [minus net credit]. Your maximum reward is the [difference between the middle and highest strikes] plus the net credit or minus the net debit.

Effect of Time Decay

- Time decay is helpful to this position when it is profitable and harmful when the position is unprofitable. When you enter the trade, typically the stock price will be in the profitable area of the risk profile, so from that perspective, time decay harms the position.

Appropriate Time Period to Trade

- One month or less.

Selecting the Stock

- Choose from stocks with adequate liquidity, preferably over 500,000 Average Daily Volume (ADV).

- Try to ensure that the trend is rangebound and identify a clear area of support.

Selecting the Options

- Choose options with adequate liquidity; open interest should be at least 100, preferably 500.

- **Lower Strike**—Below the current stock price.

- **Middle Strike**—As close to ATM as possible.

- **Higher Strike**—Closer to the middle strike than the lower is below it; use online tools to find the optimum yields and breakeven points at and before expiration.

- **Expiration**—Preferably one month or less, but there is a trade-off between time and profit potential. Use the same expiration for all legs.

5.9.3 Risk Profile

- **Maximum Risk**   [Middle strike − lower strike] − [higher strike − middle strike] − net credit

- **Maximum Reward**   [Higher strike − middle strike] + net credit

- **Breakeven**   [Lower strike + max risk]

5.9.4 Greeks

Key:
Expiration   ....
Today – 3 months   ————
Time(t) – 1 month   – – -

Risk Profile
As the stock price remains rangebound, the position is profitable, with maximum reward occurring at the middle strike price.

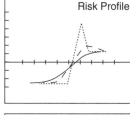

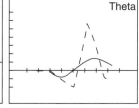

Theta
Time decay is helpful to the position when it is profitable and unhelpful when it is unprofitable.

Delta
Delta (speed) peaks positively around the lower strike and inversely around the upper strike.

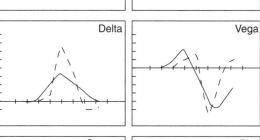

Vega
Volatility is generally unhelpful to the position unless it the stock moves outside the outer strikes.

Gamma
Gamma (acceleration) peaks positively as the risk profile begins to climb into a profitable position and peaks inversely around the upper strike.

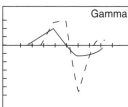

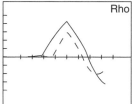

Rho
Higher interest rates are generally helpful to the position when the stock price is lower and vice versa.

5.9.5 Advantages and Disadvantages

Advantages

- Profit from a sideways or rising stock for very little cost.

- Capped and low risk.

- Comparatively high risk/reward ratio if the stock remains rangebound.

Disadvantages

■ The higher profit potential comes with a narrow range between the wing strikes.

■ The higher profit potential only comes nearer expiration.

■ Bid/Ask Spread can adversely affect the quality of the trade.

5.9.6 Exiting the Trade

Exiting the Position

■ With this strategy, you can simply unravel the spread by buying back the options you sold and selling the options you bought in the first place.

■ Advanced traders may leg up and down or only partially unravel the spread as the underlying asset fluctuates up and down. In this way, the trader will be taking smaller incremental profits before the expiration of the trade.

Mitigating a Loss

■ Unravel the trade as described previously.

■ Advanced traders may choose to only partially unravel the spread leg-by-leg and create alternative risk profiles.

5.9.7 Example

ABCD is trading at $55.00 on May 17, 2004.

Buy the June 2004 45 strike put for $0.98.

Sell two June 2004 55 strike puts at $6.12.

Buy the June 2004 60 strike put for $10.28.

Net Credit	Premiums sold − premiums bought **$12.24 − $0.98 − $10.28 = $0.98**
Maximum Risk	[Middle strike − lower strike] − [higher strike − middle strike] − net credit **$10.00 − $5.00 − $0.98 = $4.02**
Maximum Reward	Higher strike − middle strike − net credit **$60.00 − $55.00 − $0.98 = $4.02**
Interim Risk / Reward	Net credit **$0.98**
Breakeven Down	Lower strike + maximum risk **$45.00 + $4.02 = $49.02**
Breakeven Up	N/A here.
Max ROI	148.76% if the stock is priced at $55.00 at expiration.
Interim ROI	24.38% if the stock is priced above $60.00 at expiration.

It's possible to have two breakevens with the Modified Butterfly, although it's infinitely preferable to structure the trade so that there is no upper breakeven at all. After all, this is a neutral to bullish strategy, and it wouldn't make sense for us to lose money if the stock breaks the way we anticipated, even if we are still cautious about the amount it could move.

Note that you should always aim to achieve a net credit with the Modified Put Butterfly.

5.10 Long Iron Butterfly

The Long Iron Butterfly is a rangebound income strategy that we covered in Chapter 2, "Income Strategies." We won't repeat an entire section on it here because it's more suitably placed among the other income strategies. However, this is also a natural place for it to be so that you can compare it to the other rangebound and butterfly strategies.

Go to Section 2.5 if you want to review this strategy before moving on to the next.

5.11 Long Iron Condor

The Long Iron Condor is also a rangebound income strategy that we covered in Chapter 2. We won't repeat an entire section on it here because it's more suitably placed among the other income strategies. However, this is also a natural place for it to be so that you can compare it to the other rangebound and condor strategies.

Go to Section 2.6 if you want to review this strategy before moving on to the next chapter.

6

Leveraged Strategies

Introduction

By *leveraged* strategies, we mean the ratio backspreads and ratio spreads. These are strategies where your profits (or losses) are increasingly leveraged because of the different number of options you're buying or selling as part of the strategy.

In this chapter we're only reviewing four strategies. The ratio backspreads involve buying more options than selling, so there is uncapped upside at an accelerated rate. The ratio spreads involve selling more options than buying, so there is uncapped downside at an accelerated rate. No prizes for guessing which type is preferable!

If we're to concentrate on the ratio backspreads, we'll quickly discover that they give us limited risk and unlimited reward potential and that they require increasing volatility, together with a large move in the stock price. Ratio backspreads are advanced strategies and are fun to play when you've mastered other, more straightforward strategies. If you win, you can win big, but whatever happens to the stock, you want it to be dramatic either way!

6.1 Call Ratio Backspread

Proficiency	Direction	Volatility	Asset Legs	Max Risk	Max Reward	Strategy Type
Advanced	Bullish	High	■ Short Call* ■ Two Long Calls	Capped	Uncapped	Capital Gain

* Or can be two short calls with three long calls.

6.1.1 Description

The Call Ratio Backspread is an exciting strategy that enables us to make accelerated profits provided that the stock moves sharply upwards. Increasing volatility is very helpful because we're net long in calls. The worst thing that can happen is that the stock doesn't move at all, and even a sharp move down can be profitable, or at the very least, preferable to no movement at all.

The Call Ratio Backspread involves buying and selling different numbers of the same expiration calls. Typically we buy and sell calls in a ratio of 2:1 or 3:2, so we are always a net buyer. This gives us the uncapped profit potential. It also reduces the net cost of doing the deal such that we can even create a net credit! Furthermore, our risk is capped, though we need to investigate the strategy further in order to understand it more.

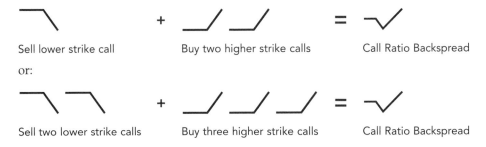

| Sell lower strike call | Buy two higher strike calls | Call Ratio Backspread |

or:

| Sell two lower strike calls | Buy three higher strike calls | Call Ratio Backspread |

Steps to Trading a Call Ratio Backspread

1. Sell one or two lower strike calls.

2. Buy two or three higher strike calls with the same expiration date. The ratio of bought to sold calls must be 2:1 or 3:2.

   ■ You will be trying to execute this trade at no cost or for a slight net credit.

   Steps In

   ■ Try to ensure that the trend is upward and identify a clear area of support.

   Steps Out

   ■ Manage your position according to the rules defined in your Trading Plan.

   ■ If the stock falls below your stop loss, then unravel the entire position.

   ■ In any event, look to unravel the trade at least one month before expiration, either to capture your profit or to contain your losses.

6.1.2 Context

Outlook

   ■ With call ratio backspreads, your outlook is **aggressively bullish**—you are looking for increasing volatility with the stock price moving explosively upwards.

Rationale

- To execute a bullish trade for little to no cost while reducing your maximum risk. You are looking for the stock to rise significantly.

Net Position

- You want to do this as a **net credit** or zero cost transaction in order to minimize your maximum risk and cost.

- Your maximum risk on the trade itself is limited to the difference in strikes less your net credit, all multiplied by the number of contracts you are selling. Your reward on the trade is unlimited.

Effect of Time Decay

- Time decay is generally harmful to your position—you want as much time to be right as possible because you are looking for such a large move.

Appropriate Time Period to Trade

- You will be safer to choose a longer time to expiration, preferably at least six months.

Selecting the Stock

- Choose from stocks with adequate liquidity, preferably over 500,000 Average Daily Volume (ADV).

- Try to ensure that the trend is upward and identify a clear area of support.

Selecting the Options

- Choose options with adequate liquidity; open interest should be at least 100, preferably 500.

- **Lower Strike**—Around ATM; use online tools to find the optimum point.

- **Higher Strike**—One or two strikes higher than the sold strike; use online tools to find the optimum yields and breakeven points at and before expiration.

- **Expiration**—Preferably over six months. Use the same expiration date for both legs.

6.1.3 Risk Profile

Please note that these calculations differ for when the strategy is traded with a 2:1 ratio or a 3:2 ratio.

- **Maximum Risk**   [Difference in strike prices] − [net credit received] or + [net debit paid]

- **Maximum Reward**   [Uncapped]

- **Breakeven Down**   [Lower strike + net credit]

- **Breakeven Up**   [Higher strike price + (difference in strike prices * number of short calls)/(number of long calls − number of short calls) − [net credit received] or + [net debit paid]]

6.1.4 Greeks

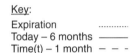

Key:
Expiration   ....
Today – 6 months   ————
Time(t) – 1 month   – – –

Risk Profile
If the stock price remains around the higher strike price, we make our maximum loss. If it moves explosively upwards, we make uncapped profits.

Delta
Delta (speed) is at its greatest the more the stock rises. The more the stock falls, the slower the position becomes, and hence Delta slows to zero.

Gamma
Gamma (acceleration) peaks around the higher strike price, illustrating the position's major turning point and the fastest rate of change.

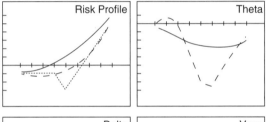

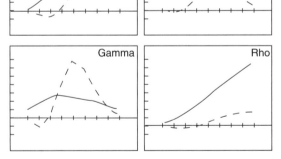

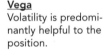

Theta
Time decay is predominantly harmful to the position unless the stock falls dramatically.

Vega
Volatility is predominantly helpful to the position.

Rho
Higher interest rates are generally helpful to the position, particularly when the stock rises.

6.1.5 Advantages and Disadvantages

Advantages

- Reduced cost of making the trade.

- Capped risk (especially if the underlying stock moves with high volatility).

- Uncapped and high leverage reward if the stock price rises.

Disadvantages

- ▨ More risk if the stock does not move.

- ▨ Comparatively complicated trade for the intermediate trader.

6.1.6 Exiting the Trade

Exiting the Position

- ▨ With this strategy, you can simply unravel the spread by buying back the calls you sold and selling the calls you bought in the first place.

- ▨ Advanced traders may leg up and down or only partially unravel the spread as the underlying asset fluctuates up and down. In this way, the trader will be taking smaller incremental profits before the expiration of the trade. By selling one of the bought calls, you will be creating a Bear Call Spread, a less aggressive trade but one that also involves a change of directional sentiment.

Mitigating a Loss

- ▨ Unravel the trade as described previously.

- ▨ Advanced traders may choose to only partially unravel the spread leg-by-leg and create alternative risk profiles (for example, a Bear Call risk profile).

6.1.7 Example

ABCD is trading at $27.65 on May 25, 2004.

Sell one January 2005 25 strike call at $4.90.

Buy two January 2005 30 strike calls at $2.50.

Net Debit	Premium bought − premium sold **$5.00 − $4.90 = $0.10**
Maximum Risk	Difference in strikes + net debit **$5.00 + $0.10 = $5.10**
Maximum Reward	Uncapped
Breakeven Down	Lower strike + net credit **N/A because net debit here**
Breakeven Up	Higher strike + (difference in strikes) / (long calls − short calls) + net debit (or − net credit) **$30.00 + ($5.00 / 1) + $0.10 = $35.10**

Or:

Sell two January 2005 25 strike calls at $4.90.

Buy three January 2005 30 strike calls at $2.50.

Net Credit	Premiums sold − premiums bought **$9.80 − $7.50 = $2.30**
Maximum Risk	Number of short calls * difference in strikes − net credit **(2 * $5.00) − $2.30 = $7.70**
Maximum Reward	Uncapped
Breakeven Down	Lower strike + (net credit / 2) **$25.00 + $1.15 = $26.15**
Breakeven Up	Higher strike + (difference in strikes * 2) / (long calls − short calls) + net debit (or − net credit) **$30.00 + ($10.00 / 1) − $2.30 = $37.70**

Here we can see the difference between the 2:1 and 3:2 ratios.

The 3:2 ratio here gives us a net credit, but our breakeven is pushed out further, and we accept more risk. The 2:1 only costs $0.10 and gives us less risk with a lower breakeven point. Without a shadow of doubt, we'd go for the 2:1 in this example. In reality we'd try a number of strikes ITM, ATM, and OTM in order to determine our optimum trade. Typically, the best way to do this is to compare the upper breakeven points and maximum risk for each alternative.

6.2 Put Ratio Backspread

Proficiency	Direction	Volatility	Asset Legs	Max Risk	Max Reward	Strategy Type
Advanced	Bearish	High	■ Two Long Puts ■ Short Put*	Capped	Uncapped	Capital Gain

* Or can be two Short Puts with three Long Puts.

6.2.1 Description

The Put Ratio Backspread is almost the precise opposite of the Call Ratio Backspread. It enables us to make accelerated profits, provided that the stock moves sharply downwards. Increasing volatility is very helpful because we're net long in puts. The worst thing that can happen is that the stock doesn't move at all, and even a sharp move up can be profitable, or at the very least, preferable to no movement at all.

The Put Ratio Backspread involves buying and selling different numbers of the same expiration puts. Typically we buy and sell puts in a ratio of 2:1 or 3:2, so we are always a net buyer. This gives us the uncapped profit potential. It also reduces the net cost of doing the deal such that we can even create a net credit! Furthermore, our risk is capped, though we need to investigate the strategy further in order to understand it better.

Buy two lower strike puts   +   Sell higher strike put   =   Put Ratio Backspread

or:

Buy three lower strike puts   +   Sell two higher strike puts   =   Put Ratio Backspread

Steps to Trading a Put Ratio Backspread

1. Buy two or three lower strike puts.

2. Sell one or two higher strike puts with the same expiration date. The ratio of bought to sold puts must be 2:1 or 3:2.

   ■ You will be trying to execute this trade at no cost or for a slight net credit.

   Steps In

   ■ Try to ensure that the trend is downward and identify a clear area of resistance.

   Steps Out

   ■ Manage your position according to the rules defined in your Trading Plan.

   ■ If the stock rises above your stop loss, then unravel the entire position.

   ■ In any event, look to unravel the trade at least one month before expiration, either to capture your profit or to contain your losses.

6.2.2 Context

Outlook

■ With put ratio backspreads, your outlook is **aggressively bearish**—you are looking for increasing volatility with the stock price moving explosively downwards.

Rationale

■ To execute a bearish trade for little to no cost while reducing your maximum risk. You are looking for the stock to fall significantly.

Net Position

■ You want to do this as a **net credit** or zero cost transaction in order to minimize your maximum risk and cost.

■ Your maximum risk on the trade itself is limited to the difference in strikes less your net credit, all multiplied by the number of contracts you are selling. Your reward on the trade is uncapped until the stock falls to zero.

Effect of Time Decay

■ Time decay is generally harmful to your position—you want as much time to be right as possible because you are looking for such a large move.

Appropriate Time Period to Trade

■ You will be safer to choose a longer time to expiration, preferably at least six months.

Selecting the Stock

■ Choose from stocks with adequate liquidity, preferably over 500,000 Average Daily Volume (ADV).

■ Try to ensure that the trend is downward and identify a clear area of resistance.

Selecting the Options

■ Choose options with adequate liquidity; open interest should be at least 100, preferably 500.

■ **Lower Strike**—One or two strikes lower than the sold strike; use online tools to find the optimum yields and breakeven points at and before expiration.

■ **Higher Strike**—Around ATM; use online tools to find the optimum point.

■ **Expiration**—Preferably over six months. Use the same expiration date for both legs.

6.2.3 Risk Profile

Please note that these calculations differ for when the strategy is traded with a 2:1 ratio or a 3:2 ratio.

■ **Maximum Risk**	[Difference in strike prices] − [net credit received] or + [net debit paid]
■ **Maximum Reward**	[Uncapped] until the stock falls to zero
■ **Breakeven Down**	[Lower strike price − (difference in strike prices * number of short puts) / (number of long puts − number of short puts) + [net credit received] or − [net debit paid]]
■ **Breakeven Up**	[Higher strike less net credit]

6.2.4 Greeks

Key:
Expiration   ....
Today – 6 months   ——
Time(t) – 1 month   – – -

Risk Profile
If the stock price remains around the lower strike price, we make our maximum loss. If it moves explosively downwards, we make uncapped profits.

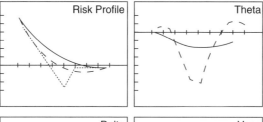

Theta
Time decay is predominantly harmful to the position unless the stock rises dramatically.

Delta
Delta (speed) is at its greatest (inversely) the more the stock falls. The more the stock rises, the slower the position becomes, and hence Delta slows to zero.

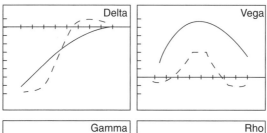

Vega
Volatility is predominantly helpful to the position.

Gamma
Gamma (acceleration) peaks around the lower strike price, illustrating the position's major turning point and the fastest rate of change.

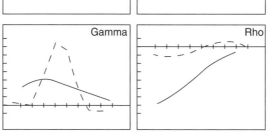

Rho
Higher interest rates are generally unhelpful to the position, particularly when the stock falls.

6.2.5 Advantages and Disadvantages

Advantages

- Reduced cost of making the trade.
- Capped risk (especially if the underlying stock moves with high volatility).
- Uncapped and high leverage reward if the stock price declines.

Disadvantages

- More risk if the stock does not move.
- Comparatively complicated trade for the intermediate trader.

6.2.6 Exiting the Trade

Exiting the Position

- With this strategy, you can simply unravel the spread by buying back the puts you sold and selling the puts you bought in the first place.

■ Advanced traders may leg up and down or only partially unravel the spread as the underlying asset fluctuates up and down. In this way, the trader will be taking smaller incremental profits before the expiration of the trade. By selling one of the bought puts, you will be creating a Bull Put Spread, a less aggressive trade but one that also involves a change of directional sentiment.

Mitigating a Loss

■ Unravel the trade as described previously.

■ Advanced traders may choose to only partially unravel the spread leg-by-leg and create alternative risk profiles (for example, a Bull Put risk profile).

6.2.7 Example

ABCD is trading at $27.98 on May 25, 2004.

Buy two January 2005 25 strike puts at $2.15.

Sell one January 2005 30 strike put at $4.20.

Net Debit	Premium bought − premium sold **$4.30 − $4.20 = $0.10**
Maximum Risk	Difference in strikes + net debit **$5.00 + $0.10 = $5.10**
Maximum Reward	Lower strike − maximum risk **$25.00 − $5.10 = $19.90**
Breakeven Down	Lower strike − maximum risk **$25.00 − $5.10 = $19.90**
Breakeven Up	**N/A because we have a net debit here.**

Or:

Buy three January 2005 25 strike puts at $2.15.

Sell two January 2005 30 strike put at $4.20.

Net Credit	Premiums sold − premiums bought **$8.40 − $6.45 = $1.95**
Maximum Risk	Number of short puts * difference in strikes − net credit **(2 * $5.00) − $1.95 = $8.05**
Maximum Reward	Lower strike − maximum risk **$25.00 − $8.05 = $16.95**
Breakeven Down	Lower strike − maximum risk **$25.00 − $8.05 = $16.95**
Breakeven Up	Higher strike − (net credit / 2) **$30.00 − $0.975 = $29.03 (rounded)**

Here we can see the difference between the 2:1 and 3:2 ratios.

The 3:2 ratio here gives us a net credit, but our breakeven is pushed down further, and we accept more risk. The 2:1 only costs $0.10 and gives us less risk with a more favorable breakeven point. Without a shadow of doubt, we'd go for the 2:1 ratio in this example. In reality, we'd try a number of strikes ITM, ATM, and OTM in order to determine our optimum trade. Typically, the best way to do this is to compare the lower breakeven points and maximum risk for each alternative.

6.3 Ratio Call Spread

Proficiency	Direction	Volatility	Asset Legs		Max Risk	Max Reward	Strategy Type
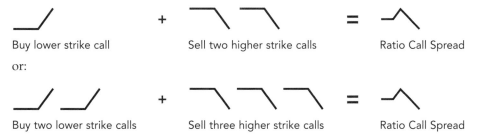			+				
			+				
Expert	Bearish	Low	▪ Long Call* ▪ Two Short Calls		Uncapped	Capped	Income

* Or can be two long calls with three short calls.

6.3.1 Description

The Ratio Call Spread is the opposite of a Call Ratio Backspread in that we're net short options. This means we're exposed to uncapped risk and can only make a limited reward. As such, this is an undesirable strategy, and you'd be better off trading one of the long butterflies.

Increasing volatility is harmful to this strategy because of our exposure to uncapped risk. The best thing that can happen is that the stock doesn't move at all.

The Ratio Call Spread involves buying and selling different numbers of the same expiration calls. Typically we sell and buy calls in a ratio of 2:1 or 3:2, so we are always a net seller. This gives us the uncapped risk potential. It also reduces the net cost of doing the deal such that we create a net credit.

Buy lower strike call	+	Sell two higher strike calls	=	Ratio Call Spread

or:

Buy two lower strike calls	+	Sell three higher strike calls	=	Ratio Call Spread

Steps to Trading a Ratio Call Spread

1. Buy one or two lower strike calls.

2. Sell two or three higher strike calls with the same expiration date. The ratio of bought to sold calls must be 1:2 or 2:3.

    ▪ You will be trying to execute this trade for a net credit.

    Steps In

    ▪ Try to ensure that the trend is downward and identify a clear area of resistance.

Steps Out

- Manage your position according to the rules defined in your Trading Plan.

- If the stock rises above your stop loss, then unravel the entire position.

- In any event, look to unravel the trade at least one month before expiration, either to capture your profit or to contain your losses.

6.3.2 Context

Outlook

- With Ratio Call Spreads, your outlook is **neutral to bearish**—you are looking for decreasing volatility with the stock price remaining rangebound.

Rationale

- To execute a neutral to bearish **income** trade for a net credit. You are looking for the stock to remain below the upper breakeven point.

Net Position

- You want to do this as a **net credit** to maximum your profit potential.

- Your maximum risk on the trade itself is unlimited. Your maximum reward on the trade is limited to the difference between the strike prices plus the net credit (all multiplied by the number of long contracts).

Effect of Time Decay

- Time decay is helpful to your position—because you are a net seller here (you are selling more contracts than you are buying), you want to be exposed to as little time as possible, preferably one month or less. Also remember that you are exposed to unlimited risk here, so you do not want that exposure to last for long.

Appropriate Time Period to Trade

- You will be safer to choose a shorter time to expiration, preferably just a month.

Selecting the Stock

- Choose from stocks with adequate liquidity, preferably over 500,000 Average Daily Volume (ADV).

- Try to ensure that the trend is downward and identify a clear area of resistance.

Selecting the Options

- Choose options with adequate liquidity; open interest should be at least 100, preferably 500.

- **Lower Strike**—ITM (below or at the current stock price); use online tools to find the optimum point.

- **Higher Strike**—ATM—one or two strikes higher than the bought strike; use online tools to find the optimum yields and breakeven points at and before expiration.

- **Expiration**—Preferably less than one month. Use the same expiration date for both legs.

6.3.3 Risk Profile

Please note that these calculations differ for when the strategy is traded with a 2:1 ratio or a 3:2 ratio.

- **Maximum Risk**   [Uncapped]

- **Maximum Reward**   [Difference in strike prices] + [net debit] or − [net debit]

- **Breakeven Down**   [Lower strike − (net debit/number of long contracts)]

- **Breakeven Up**   [Lower strike price] + [difference between strikes * number of short contracts] / [number of short contracts − number of long contracts] + [net credit received] or − [net debit paid]

6.3.4 Greeks

Key:
Expiration   ············
Today – 2 months   ————
Time(t) – 1 week   − − −

Risk Profile
If the stock price remains around the higher strike price, we make our maximum profit. If it moves explosively upwards, we make uncapped losses.

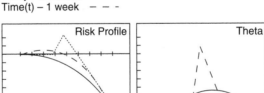

Delta
Delta (speed) is at its greatest (inversely) the more the stock rises. The more the stock falls, the slower the position becomes, and hence Delta slows to zero.

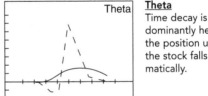

Gamma
Gamma (acceleration) peaks inversely around the higher strike price, illustrating the position's major turning point and the fastest rate of change.

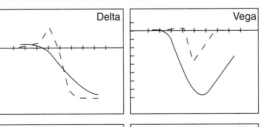

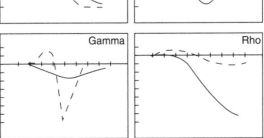

Theta
Time decay is predominantly helpful to the position unless the stock falls dramatically.

Vega
Volatility is predominantly harmful to the position.

Rho
Higher interest rates are generally unhelpful to the position, particularly when the stock rises.

6.3.5 Advantages and Disadvantages

Advantages

- Net credit raised.

- Profitable if the stock remains rangebound.

Disadvantages

- Uncapped risk if the stock price rises.

- More risk if the stock moves.

- Comparatively complicated trade for the intermediate trader.

6.3.6 Exiting the Trade

Exiting the Position

- With this strategy, you can simply unravel the spread by buying back the calls you sold and selling the calls you bought in the first place.

- Advanced traders may leg up and down or only partially unravel the spread as the underlying asset fluctuates up and down. In this way, the trader will be taking smaller incremental profits before the expiration of the trade. By buying back one of the sold calls, you will be creating a Bull Call Spread, a much safer trade but one that also involves a change of directional sentiment.

Mitigating a Loss

- Unravel the trade as described previously.

- Advanced traders may choose to only partially unravel the spread leg-by-leg and create alternative risk profiles (for example, a Bull Call risk profile).

6.3.7 Example

ABCD is trading at $27.65 on May 25, 2004.

Buy one June 2004 25 strike call at $3.11.

Sell two June 2004 $27.50 strike calls at $1.52.

Net Debit	Premium bought − premium sold **$3.11 − $3.04 = $0.07**
Maximum Risk	Uncapped
Maximum Reward	[Difference in strikes] − net debit **$2.50 − $0.07 = $2.43**
Breakeven Down	Lower strike + net debit **$25.00 + $0.07 = $25.07**
Breakeven Up	Higher strike + maximum reward **$27.50 + $2.43 = $29.93**

Or:

Buy two June 2004 25 strike call at $3.11.

Sell three June 2004 $27.50 strike calls at $1.52.

Net Debit	Premium bought − premium sold **$6.22 − $4.56 = $1.66**
Maximum Risk	Uncapped
Maximum Reward	[Number of long calls * difference in strikes] − net debit **(2 * $2.50) − $1.66 = $3.34**
Breakeven Down	Lower strike + (net debit / 2) **$25.00 + $0.825 = $25.83 (rounded)**
Breakeven Up	Higher strike + maximum reward **$27.50 + $3.34 = $30.84**

Here we can see the difference between the 2:1 and 3:2 ratios, but ultimately neither example is an attractive trade.

6.4 Ratio Put Spread

Proficiency	Direction	Volatility	Asset Legs	Max Risk	Max Reward	Strategy Type
Expert	Bullish	Low	■ Two Short Puts ■ Long Put*	Uncapped	Capped	Income

* Or can be three Short Puts with two Long Puts.

6.4.1 Description

The Ratio Put Spread is the opposite of a Put Ratio Backspread in that we're net short options. This means we're exposed to uncapped risk and can only make a limited reward. As such, this is an undesirable strategy, and you'd be better off trading one of the long butterflies.

Increasing volatility is harmful to this strategy because of our exposure to uncapped risk. The best thing that can happen is that the stock doesn't move at all.

The Ratio Put Spread involves buying and selling different numbers of the same expiration puts. Typically we sell and buy puts in a ratio of 2:1 or 3:2, so we are always a net seller. This gives us the uncapped risk potential. It also reduces the net cost of doing the deal such that we create a net credit.

| Sell two lower strike puts | Buy higher strike put | Ratio Put Spread |

or:

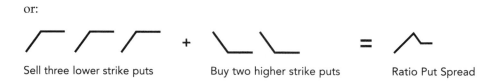

Sell three lower strike puts   Buy two higher strike puts   Ratio Put Spread

Steps to Trading a Ratio Put Spread

1. Sell two or three lower strike puts.

2. Buy one or two higher strike puts with the same expiration date. The ratio of bought to sold puts must be 1:2 or 2:3.

   ■ You will be trying to execute this trade for a net credit.

   Steps In

   ■ Try to ensure that the trend is upward and identify a clear area of support.

   Steps Out

   ■ Manage your position according to the rules defined in your Trading Plan.

   ■ If the stock falls below your stop loss, then unravel the entire position or at least buy back the short puts.

   ■ In any event, look to unravel the trade at least one month before expiration, either to capture your profit or to contain your losses.

6.4.2 Context

Outlook

■ With Ratio Put Spreads, your outlook is **neutral to bullish**—you are looking for decreasing volatility with the stock price remaining rangebound.

Rationale

■ To execute a neutral to bullish **income** trade for a net credit. You are looking for the stock to remain at or above the upper breakeven point.

Net Position

■ You want to do this as a **net credit** to maximize your profit potential.

■ Your maximum risk on the trade itself is unlimited. Your maximum reward on the trade is limited to the difference between the strike prices plus the net credit (all multiplied by the number of long contracts).

Effect of Time Decay

■ Time decay is helpful to your position—because you are a net seller here (you are selling more contracts than you are buying), you want to be exposed to as little time as possible, preferably one month or less. Also remember that you are exposed to unlimited risk here, so you do not want that exposure to last for long.

Appropriate Time Period to Trade

■ You will be safer to choose a shorter time to expiration, preferably just a month.

Selecting the Stock

■ Choose from stocks with adequate liquidity, preferably over 500,000 Average Daily Volume (ADV).

■ Try to ensure that the trend is upward and identify a clear area of support.

Selecting the Options

■ Choose options with adequate liquidity; open interest should be at least 100, preferably 500.

■ **Lower Strike**—Around ATM—use online tools to find the optimum point.

■ **Higher Strike**—One or two strikes higher than the sold strike—use online tools to find the optimum yields and breakeven points at and before expiration.

■ **Expiration**—Preferably less than one month. Use the same expiration date for both legs.

6.4.3 Risk Profile

Please note that these calculations differ for when the strategy is traded with a 2:1 ratio or a 3:2 ratio.

■ **Maximum Risk** [Higher strike − difference in strikes * sold contracts] + net debit

■ **Maximum Reward** [Bought puts * difference in strikes] − net debit (or + net credit)

■ **Breakeven Down** [Higher strike] less [difference in strikes * number of short contracts] / [number of short contracts less long contracts] less [net credit received] or plus [net debit paid]

■ **Breakeven Up** [Higher strike] − [net debit * number of long contracts]

6.4.4 Greeks

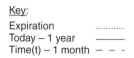

Key:
Expiration   ....
Today – 1 year   ———
Time(t) – 1 month – – –

Risk Profile
If the stock price remains around the lower strike price, we make our maximum profit. If it moves explosively downwards, we make uncapped losses.

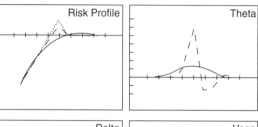

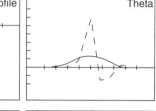

Theta
Time decay is predominantly helpful to the position unless the stock rises dramatically.

Delta
Delta (speed) is at its greatest the lower the stock reaches. The more the stock rises, the slower the position becomes, and hence Delta slows to zero.

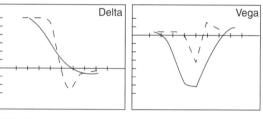

Vega
Volatility is predominantly harmful to the position.

Gamma
Gamma (acceleration) peaks inversely around the lower strike price, illustrating the position's major turning point and the fastest rate of change.

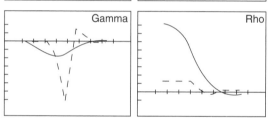

Rho
Higher interest rates are generally helpful to the position, particularly when the stock falls.

6.4.5 Advantages and Disadvantages

Advantages

- Net credit raised.

- Profitable if the stock remains rangebound.

Disadvantages

- Uncapped risk if the stock rises.

- More risk if the stock moves.

- Comparatively complicated trade for the intermediate trader.

6.4.6 Exiting the Trade

Exiting the Position

- With this strategy, you can simply unravel the spread by buying back the puts you sold and selling the puts you bought in the first place.

- Advanced traders may leg up and down or only partially unravel the spread as the underlying asset fluctuates up and down. In this way, the trader will be taking smaller incremental profits before the expiration of the trade. By buying back one of the sold puts, you will be creating a Bear Put Spread, a much safer trade but one that also involves a change of directional sentiment.

Mitigating a Loss

- Unravel the trade as described previously.

- Advanced traders may choose to only partially unravel the spread leg-by-leg and create alternative risk profiles (for example, a Bear Put risk profile).

6.4.7 Example

ABCD is trading at $27.65 on May 25, 2004.

Sell two June 2004 25 strike puts at $0.42.

Buy one June 2004 $27.50 strike put at $1.33.

Net Debit	Premium bought − premium sold **$1.33 − $0.84 = $0.49**
Maximum Risk	[Higher strike − difference in strikes * sold contracts] + net debit **$27.50 − $5.00 + $0.49 = $22.99**
Maximum Reward	[Bought puts * difference in strikes] − net debit **1 * $2.50 − $0.49 = $2.01**
Breakeven Down	[Higher strike − difference in strikes * sold contracts] + net debit **$27.50 − $5.00 + $0.49 = $22.99**
Breakeven Up	Higher strike − [net debit * bought contracts] **$27.50 − $0.49 = $27.01**

Or:

Sell three June 2004 25 strike puts at $0.42.

Buy two June 2004 $27.50 strike puts at $1.33.

Net Debit	Premium bought − premium sold **$2.66 − $1.26 = $1.40**
Maximum Risk	[Higher strike − difference in strikes * sold contracts] + net debit **$27.50 − $7.50 + $1.40 = $21.40**
Maximum Reward	[Bought puts * difference in strikes] − net debit **[2 * $2.50] − $1.40 = $3.60**
Breakeven Down	[Higher strike − difference in strikes * sold contracts] + net debit **$27.50 − $7.50 + $1.40 = $21.40**
Breakeven Up	Higher strike − (net debit / 2) **$27.50 − $0.70 = $26.80**

Here we can see the difference between the 2:1 and 3:2 ratios, but ultimately neither example is an attractive trade.

Synthetic Strategies

Introduction

Synthetic strategies are generally those that attempt to mimic other stock, futures, or options strategies and use other securities to create the new strategy. As such, we can re-create the underlying asset *synthetically* using only options. We can re-create long and short positions for straddles by using a combination of buying and selling stocks and options together. We can re-create the same risk profile shape as a Long Call or Long Put by combining other assets together. Often, these synthetic strategies come into being when you're looking to repair an existing strategy.

In this chapter, we'll cover the long and short synthetic straddles, which mimic those that we discussed in Chapter 4, "Volatility Strategies." Whereas a long straddle involves buying an ATM call and put together, a Long Synthetic Straddle can be constructed using the stock with calls or the stock with puts. The advantage of understanding how these synthetic strategies are created is not only the flexibility it affords us as traders but also the adaptability to morph an existing position into something else simply by adding or taking away a leg of the trade. For example, if you're already long in a stock, but you think it may be about to reverse, you could buy puts to create either a Synthetic Call or double the number of puts, which would create a Long Put Synthetic Straddle.

Consequently, even Long Call and Put positions have their synthetic equivalents. The beauty of options is that we can create virtually any risk profile, although that beauty largely exists in an academic sense if you have the time and passion to pursue it! When it comes to actual trading, it's best to keep things simple while having a grasp of the more complex. It's always best to trade "within yourself," or in other words, to know that your intellect isn't being stretched by the trade you're currently involved in. The "stretching" should happen outside trading hours. When you're making trading decisions, you need to concentrate purely on the trading plan in question.

Aside from the synthetic calls, puts, and straddles, we'll also cover the Long and Short Synthetic Futures, which use options to synthetically re-create the underlying position. The combos are variations of the synthetic futures, which both have long and short versions.

However, the first strategy we're going to cover in this chapter is the Collar. The Collar is a great strategy that somehow doesn't fit into any other chapter of this book! The Collar is similar to a long dated Covered Call, but we add a long put to insure the downside. The effect is that we buy the stock, insure it with a Long Put, and finance the insurance with a higher strike short call. Where volatility is high and sentiment is bullish, it's possible to create risk-free collars, notwithstanding the fact that there is the net debit (largely of buying the stock) to consider. As such, the Collar is a low-risk but expensive strategy.

In some senses, this is the most challenging chapter to follow, and these are certainly among the more awkward strategies to produce algorithms for, particularly the synthetic straddles. When you're attempting these strategies, paper trading or otherwise, use online tools so that you can take the math for granted, and just concentrate on the risk profile you're creating and whether it fits your intended trading plan and expectations. Many of the strategies in this chapter will have far-reaching tax consequences of which you and your accountant will need to be aware.

7.1 Collar

Proficiency	Direction	Volatility	Asset Legs	Max Risk	Max Reward	Strategy Type
(icon)	(icon)	N/A	(icon) + (icon)	(icon)	(icon)	(icon)
			+ (icon)			
Intermediate	Bullish		■ Long Stock	Capped	Capped	Capital Gain
			■ Long Put			
			■ Short Call			

7.1.1 Description

The Collar is similar to a Covered Call but typically works over a much longer time period and involves another leg—buying a put to insure against the stock falling. The effect is of buying a stock, insuring against a down-move by buying puts, and then insuring the trade by selling calls.

Buy stock	→	Buy asset
Buy puts	→	Insure it from falling
Sell calls	→	Finance the insurance

The risk profile therefore contains a capped downside because of the Long Put and a capped upside because of the Short Call. The level of insurance depends on where you place the put strike and the cost of the put. The amount of upside depends on the position of the higher strike call and how much you receive for selling the call. As such, there is an art to creating a good collar! Typically, high volatility is helpful, particularly in a bull market where demand for calls is higher and where they are priced higher than the equivalent puts.

The nature of a Collar is cautious. Don't expect wild returns, because the sold calls will prevent that from happening. The Collar works best over a longer period of time, so you're rarely looking a more than a 20% return over a year, depending on how much risk you're prepared to take. However, the trade-off is that the risk, in terms of your outlay on the stock, will be tiny. And that's the beauty of a Collar.

The Collar is particularly useful when you can't afford to lose much on a trade, but you still want to participate in upside market action over, say, a 12- to 18-month period. You're happy to place the trade and simply leave it alone until expiration or very close to it. The disadvantage to a Collar is that you really do have to wait until (near) expiration to fully benefit from the strategy, but bearing in mind that the Collar gives you such low risk, it's a price you're willing to pay.

Buy stock   Buy ATM put   Sell OTM call   Collar

Steps to Trading a Collar

1. Buy the stock.

2. Buy ATM (or OTM) puts.

3. Sell OTM calls.

   ▪ The closer the put strike is to the price you bought the stock for, the better insurance you'll have if the stock falls. However, the better insurance you have in that regard, the more it will cost you!

Steps In

▪ Some traders prefer to select stocks between $10.00 and $50.00, considering that above $50.00 would be expensive to buy the stock. Ultimately it's what you feel comfortable with.

▪ Try to ensure that the trend is upward and identify a clear area of support.

Steps Out

▪ Manage your position according to the rules defined in your Trading Plan.

▪ At expiration, you hope that your call will be exercised and that you've made your maximum profit.

▪ If the stock remains below the call strike but above your stop loss, let the call expire worthless and keep the entire premium.

- The point of a Collar is that you set the put strike at or above your stop loss, creating a minimum risk trade. Therefore, you are at liberty to keep the position until expiration.

7.1.2 Context

Outlook

- With Collars, your outlook is **conservatively bullish.** This is supposed to be a very low-risk strategy.

Rationale

- To execute a long-term trade that is inherently low-risk. You will have to use online tools to determine how little risk you're going to take.

- Obviously, with any long-term trade that takes money out of your account, there is "opportunity cost." This is the interest that you could have made on the net debit amount had you invested it in bonds or received simple interest payments on it.

Net Position

- This is a **net debit** trade because money will come out of your account to pay for the stock. This is different from actual risk. If you select the right strike prices for the bought put and sold call, you may even be able to execute this trade with no risk at expiration, even though money has been debited from your account in order to make the trade. You will need to verify the risk profile with the option prices and available strikes—it's not always possible to create a risk-free trade, but your best chance will come with longer to expiration during bullish market conditions, where puts are priced cheaper than calls!

- If you are lucky with the availability of both friendly options premiums and strikes, you may be able to structure a low-risk, risk-free, or even a guaranteed return trade. This is because your long position in the stock will rise up to the point of the sold call strike price, giving you a profitable (albeit limited) upside. If the stock falls, then the ATM put (your insurance) will rise in value, and you will retain the premium received by having sold the OTM call. This combination will offset the fall in value of the long stock.

Effect of Time Decay

- Time decay will be helpful with the sold call; it will be unhelpful to the bought put and will have no effect on the stock you have bought.

- The net effect is that time decay is helpful here when the position is profitable and harmful when the position is loss-making.

Appropriate Time Period to Trade

- It's more likely that you will find the better Collar opportunities (in terms of risk containment) further out in time. Between one to two years is recommended to give yourself more opportunities for a Collar to be successful. Do not expect inordinately high yields here—this is a risk-averse strategy!

Selecting the Stock

- Choose from stocks with adequate liquidity, preferably over 500,000 Average Daily Volume (ADV).

- Select a stock price range you feel comfortable with. Some traders prefer lower priced stocks; others don't care. Ultimately it's more important that the stock rises . . . or at least doesn't fall.

- Try to ensure that the trend is upward and identify a clear area of support.

Selecting the Options

- Choose options with adequate liquidity; open interest should be at least 100, preferably 500.

- **Put Strike**—Look for either the ATM or just OTM (lower) strike below the current stock price; it depends how much insurance you want.

- **Call Strike**—Look for one or two (or more) strikes above the current stock price. Use online tools to evaluate your risk/reward scenarios.

- **Expiration**—Typically the best Collars can be found with at least one year to expiration. You can, if you want to experiment, buy only a six-month put if you think you only need insurance for a set period of time, but the authentic Collar uses the same expiration dates for both put and call. Use online tools to experiment with the strikes and expiration dates for your optimum trade.

7.1.3 Risk Profile

- **Maximum Risk**   [Stock price + put premium] − [Put strike − call premium].

  If this gives a negative figure, then you have a risk-free trade.

- **Maximum Reward** [Call strike − put strike − the risk of the trade]

- **Breakeven**   [Stock price − call premium + put premium]

Look to create a strategy with minimal risk.

7.1.4 Greeks

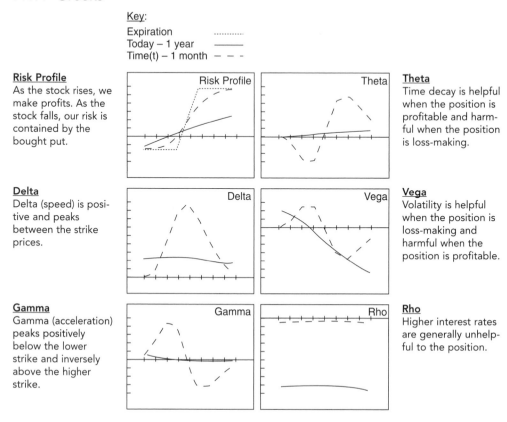

Key:
Expiration   ....
Today – 1 year   ———
Time(t) – 1 month – – –

Risk Profile
As the stock rises, we make profits. As the stock falls, our risk is contained by the bought put.

Theta
Time decay is helpful when the position is profitable and harmful when the position is loss-making.

Delta
Delta (speed) is positive and peaks between the strike prices.

Vega
Volatility is helpful when the position is loss-making and harmful when the position is profitable.

Gamma
Gamma (acceleration) peaks positively below the lower strike and inversely above the higher strike.

Rho
Higher interest rates are generally unhelpful to the position.

7.1.5 Advantages and Disadvantages

Advantages

■ Give yourself maximum protection against a fall in the underlying stock price.

■ With volatile stocks, you can create a very low risk or even risk-free trade.

■ You can create a high yield on risk.

Disadvantages

■ Works best for long-term strategies (over one year), so it is slow.

■ Maximum upside only occurs at expiration.

■ Creates only a low reward on capital expended.

7.1.6 Exiting the Trade

Exiting the Position

- ■ If executed correctly, you will not need to exit this trade early because there should be very little risk. If you used margin and require the margined cash urgently, you may need to unwind the trade; however, this strategy is unsuitable if you need the cash before expiration.

- ■ Advanced traders may leg up and down as the underlying asset fluctuates up and down. In this way the trader will be taking smaller incremental profits before the expiration of the trade.

Mitigating a Loss

- ■ This shouldn't be an issue with the Collar!

7.1.7 Example

ABCD is trading at $19.45 on May 29, 2004.

Buy 1,000 shares of stock at $19.45.

Buy 10 January 2006 20 strike puts at $6.50.

Sell 10 January 2006 25 strike calls at $5.00.

Net Debit	Stock bought + premium bought − premium sold $19.45 + $6.50 − $5.00 = $20.95 $20,950
Maximum Risk	Stock price + put premium − put strike − call premium $19.45 + $6.50 − $20.00 − $5.00 = $0.95 $950.00
Maximum Reward	Call strike − put strike − risk of trade $25.00 − $20.00 − $0.95 = $4.05 $4,050
Breakeven	Stock price − call premium + put premium $19.45 − $5.00 + $6.50 = $20.95
Max Yield on Risk	426.32%
Max Yield on Net Debit	19.33%

Notice how low the maximum risk is: just $950.00 compared to the net debit of $20,950. As such, the yield on risk is very high in comparison with the maximum yield on the net debit. However, because you're buying the stock, the Collar is an expensive strategy, but depending on your situation, it can be a great way to participate in a market upturn without risking much.

7.2 Synthetic Call

Proficiency	Direction	Volatility	Asset Legs	Max Risk	Max Reward	Strategy Type
Novice	Bullish	N/A	■ Long Stock ■ Long Put	Capped	Uncapped	Capital Gain

7.2.1 Description

I know we touched on this before, but . . . have you ever taken a red-hot stock tip? Did you buy the stock? Did it go up or down? If it went down, I'll bet you wished you'd bought some insurance! Well, that's what a Synthetic Call is. Basically, we buy the stock, but we insure against a downturn by buying an ATM or slightly OTM (lower strike) put. The net effect is that of creating the same *shape* as a standard long call but with the same leverage as buying the stock.

In simple terms, this means that we're capping our downside in case the stock unexpectedly drops through our stop loss. The long put will increase in value if the stock collapses, thereby countering the loss in value of the long stock position. This makes the Synthetic Call a very useful strategy for backing a hunch (not a very scientific way to trade, but that's why you'd look to insure it) or for speculating before, say, an earnings report or an FDA decision (for a drug stock).

The risk profile therefore contains a capped downside because of the long put and an uncapped upside because of the long stock position. The result *looks like* a long call but isn't one! The level of insurance depends on where you place the put strike and the cost of the put.

Buy stock	Buy put	Synthetic Call

Steps to Trading a Synthetic Call

1. Buy the stock.
2. Buy ATM (or OTM) puts.

   ■ The closer the put strike is to the price you bought the stock for, the better insurance you'll have if the stock falls. However, the better insurance you have in that regard, the more it will cost you!

   ■ Notice that you have created the risk profile of a call option (but you have paid a lot more for it). What you are doing is capping your downside risk by buying the put option, having bought the stock.

Steps In

■ Some traders prefer to select stocks between $10.00 and $50.00, considering that above $50.00 would be expensive to buy the stock. Ultimately it's what you feel comfortable with.

■ Try to ensure that the trend is upward and identify a clear area of support.

Steps Out

- Manage your position according to the rules defined in your Trading Plan.

- If the stock falls, then you may need to unravel the entire trade because the stock is behaving contrary to your expectations.

- Remember to buy more time than you strictly require so that you avoid the final month of time decay.

- If the stock falls below your stop loss, then either sell the stock and keep the put or unravel the entire position.

7.2.2 Context

Outlook

- With synthetic calls, your outlook is **conservatively bullish.** This is a low-risk strategy.

Rationale

- To buy a stock for the medium or long term with the aim of underwriting your downside in the meantime.

- If the stock rises, you will make profit.

- If the stock falls, you will lose money, but your losses will be capped at the level of the put strike price.

Net Position

- This is a **net debit** trade because you're buying both the stock and the put.

- Your maximum risk is limited if the stock falls.

Effect of Time Decay

- Time decay is harmful to the value of the put you bought.

Appropriate Time Period to Trade

- Buy the puts with as long a time to expiration as you need the insurance for, plus at least one extra month so that you can avoid the worst effects of time decay.

Selecting the Stock

- Choose from stocks with adequate liquidity, preferably over 500,000 Average Daily Volume (ADV).

- Select a stock price range you feel comfortable with. Some traders prefer lower priced stocks; others don't care. Ultimately it's more important that the stock rises . . . or at least doesn't fall.

- Try to ensure that the trend is upward and identify a clear area of support.

Selecting the Options

- ■ Choose options with adequate liquidity; open interest should be at least 100, preferably 500.

- ■ **Strike**—Look for either the ATM or just OTM (lower) strike below the current stock. If you're confident of the stock rising, then choose a lower strike; if you want maximum insurance, choose the ATM strike, which will be more expensive.

- ■ **Expiration**—Depends on how long you want the insurance for. If it's just to get past an earnings report, then just buy enough time to cover that event plus one more month to avoid the worst effects of time decay.

7.2.3 Risk Profile

- ■ **Maximum Risk**   [Stock price + put premium − put strike price]

- ■ **Maximum Reward**   [Uncapped]

- ■ **Breakeven**   [Strike price + put premium + stock price − put strike price]

7.2.4 Greeks

Key:
Expiration   ....
Today – 6 months ————
Time(t) – 1 month – – –

Risk Profile
As the stock rises, we make profits. As the stock falls, our risk is contained by the bought put.

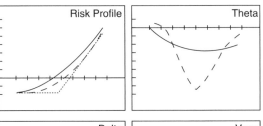

Theta
Time decay is harmful to the position because we are long in options.

Delta
Delta (speed) is positive and peaks as we get deep ITM.

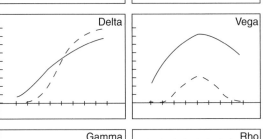

Vega
Volatility is helpful to the position because we are long in options.

Gamma
Gamma (acceleration) peaks positively around the strike price.

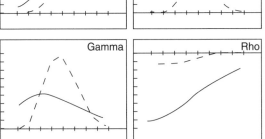

Rho
Higher interest rates are generally unhelpful to the position.

7.2.5 Advantages and Disadvantages

Advantages

■ Buying the put insures your long stock against a catastrophic decline, thus capping your downside risk more effectively than just a stop loss on the stock alone, particularly in the event of a gap down.

■ Upside is uncapped.

Disadvantages

■ The rate of leverage is much slower than simply buying a call.

■ This can be considered expensive because you have to buy the stock and the put.

7.2.6 Exiting the Trade

Exiting the Position

■ If the share falls below the strike price, you will make a limited loss.

■ If the share rises above the strike price plus the put premium you paid, you will make a profit.

■ For any exit, you can either sell the stock or sell the put, or both. If the share rises and you believe that it may fall afterwards, then you can just sell the stock and wait for the put to regain some of its value before selling that, too.

Mitigating a Loss

■ You have already mitigated your losses by buying the puts to insure your long stock position.

7.2.7 Example

ABCD is trading at $35.50 on June 1, 2004.

Buy 1,000 shares of stock at $35.50.

Buy 10 August 2004 35 strike puts at $2.55.

Net Debit	Stock bought + premium bought **$35.50 + $2.55 = $38.05** **$38,050**
Maximum Risk	Stock price + put premium − put strike **$35.50 + $2.55 − $35.00 = $3.05** **$3,050**
Maximum Reward	Uncapped
Breakeven	Put strike + put premium + stock price − put strike **$35.00 + $2.55 + $35.50 − $35.00 = $38.05**

Notice how low the maximum risk is: just $3,050 compared to the net debit of $38,050. That's the effect of the insurance you've bought for only 2.55 (or $2,550).

Now let's see what would happen if we tried a lower strike put.

Buy 1,000 shares of stock at $35.50.

Buy 10 August 2004 30 strike puts at $0.80.

Net Debit	Stock bought + premium bought $35.50 + $0.80 = $36.30 $36,300
Maximum Risk	Stock price + put premium − put strike $35.50 + $0.80 − $30.00 = $6.30 $6,300
Maximum Reward	Uncapped
Breakeven	Put strike + put premium + stock price − put strike $30.00 + $0.80 + $35.50 − $30.00 = $36.30

The lower put strike is cheaper, but it gives us less insurance on the downside. Our breakeven is also friendlier with the lower put strike trade, so you should buy as much insurance as you think you'll need. The more insurance you require, the more expensive it will be, but the less risk you'll be taking.

7.3 Synthetic Put

Proficiency	Direction	Volatility	Asset Legs	Max Risk	Max Reward	Strategy Type
Novice	Bearish	N/A	■ Short Stock ■ Long Call	Capped	Uncapped	Capital Gain

7.3.1 Description

Effectively an insurance policy for covering a short position, the Synthetic Put is the opposite of a Synthetic Call. Basically, we short the stock and buy an ATM or slightly OTM (higher strike) call. The net effect is that of creating the same *shape* as a standard Long Put but with the same leverage as shorting the stock, and we create a net credit instead of a net debit.

In simple terms, this means that we're capping our downside in case the stock unexpectedly rises through our stop loss. The Long Call will increase in value if the stock rises, thereby countering the loss in value of the short stock position.

Sell stock	Buy call	Synthetic Put

Steps to Trading a Synthetic Put

1. Short the stock.
2. Buy ATM (or OTM) calls.

- Notice that you have created the risk profile of a put option, but you have received a net credit for the trade by virtue of shorting the stock.

Steps In

- Try to ensure that the trend is downward and identify a clear area of resistance.

Steps Out

- Manage your position according to the rules defined in your Trading Plan.
- If the stock falls by more than the call premium, then you'll make a profit at expiration.
- If the stock rises above your stop loss, then exit by either reversing your position or simply buying back the stock and keeping the Long Call up to a new profit objective.

7.3.2 Context

Outlook

- With Synthetic Puts, your outlook is **bearish.**

Rationale

- To create the bearish risk profile of a put option but to take in a net credit by selling the stock short.
- If the stock falls, you can make a profit.
- If the stock rises, you will lose money, but your losses will be capped at the level of the call strike price to the call premium plus the difference between the stock price and call strike price.

Net Position

- If you're trading stocks, this is a **net credit** trade.
- Your maximum risk is limited if the stock rises.

Effect of Time Decay

- Time decay is harmful to the value of the call you bought.

Appropriate Time Period to Trade

- Buy the calls with as long a time to expiration as you need the short cover for, plus at least one extra month so that you can avoid the worst effects of time decay.

Selecting the Stock

- Choose from stocks with adequate liquidity, preferably over 500,000 Average Daily Volume (ADV).
- Try to ensure that the trend is downward and identify a clear area of resistance.

Selecting the Options

- Choose options with adequate liquidity; open interest should be at least 100, preferably 500.

- **Strike**—Look for either the ATM or just OTM (higher) strike above the current stock. If you're confident of the stock falling, then choose a higher strike call; if you want maximum short cover, choose the ATM strike call, which will be more expensive.

- **Expiration**—Depends on how long you want the short cover insurance for. If it's just to get past an earnings report, then just buy enough time to cover that event plus one more month to avoid the worst effects of time decay.

7.3.3 Risk Profile

- **Maximum Risk**   [Call strike price − stock price + call premium]

- **Maximum Reward**   [Stock price − call premium]

- **Breakeven**   [Stock price − call premium]

7.3.4 Greeks

Key:
Expiration ....
Today – 6 months ———
Time(t) – 1 month – – –

Risk Profile
As the stock falls, we make profits. As the stock rises, our risk is contained by the bought call.

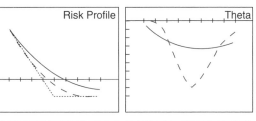

Theta
Time decay is harmful to the position because we are long in options.

Delta
Delta (speed) is negative and peaks as we get deep ITM.

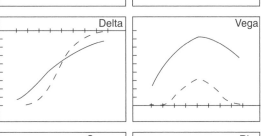

Vega
Volatility is helpful to the position because we are long in options.

Gamma
Gamma (acceleration) peaks positively around the strike price.

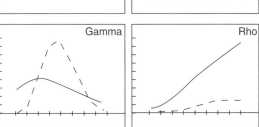

Rho
Higher interest rates are generally helpful to the position.

7.3.5 Advantages and Disadvantages

Advantages

- Replicate a put and profit from declining stocks with no capital outlay.
- Limited risk if the stock rises.
- Uncapped reward until the stock falls to zero.

Disadvantages

- More complex than simply buying puts.
- Time decay will erode the value of the call you buy, while buying a long-term call will detrimentally affect your risk profile. Use the call as insurance against the stock rising.

7.3.6 Exiting the Trade

Exiting the Position

- If the share rises above the strike price, you will make a limited loss.
- If the share falls below the stock price (plus premium you paid), you will make a profit.
- For any exit, you can either buy the stock or sell the call or both. If the share falls and you believe that it may rise afterwards, then you can just buy the stock and wait for the call to regain some of its value before selling that, too.

Mitigating a Loss

- You have already mitigated your losses by buying the calls to insure your long stock position.

7.3.7 Example

ABCD is trading at $34.17 on June 1, 2004.

Short 1,000 shares of stock at $34.17.

Buy 10 August 2004 35 strike calls at $2.76.

Net Credit	Stock price − premium bought $34.17 − $2.76 = $31.41 $31,410
Maximum Risk	Call premium + call strike − stock price $2.76 + $35.00 − $34.17 = $3.59 $3,590
Maximum Reward	Stock price − premium bought $34.17 − $2.76 = $31.41 $31,410
Breakeven	Stock price − premium bought $34.17 − $2.76 = $31.41

Notice how low the maximum risk is: just $3,590 compared to the net credit of $31,410. That's the effect of the insurance you've bought for only $2.76 (or $2,760).

Now let's see what would happen if we tried a higher strike call.

Short 1,000 shares of stock at $34.17.

Buy 10 August 2004 40 strike calls at $1.29.

Net Credit	Stock price − premium bought $34.17 − $1.29 = $32.88 $32,880
Maximum Risk	Call premium + call strike − stock price $1.29 + $40.00 − $34.17 = $7.12 $7,120
Maximum Reward	Stock price − premium bought $34.17 − $1.29 = $32.88 $32,880
Breakeven	Stock price − premium bought $34.17 − $1.29 = $32.88

The higher call strike is cheaper, but it gives us less insurance. Our breakeven is also friendlier with the higher call strike trade, so you should buy as much insurance as you think you'll need. The more insurance you require, the more expensive it will be, but the less risk you'll be taking.

7.4 Long Call Synthetic Straddle

Proficiency	Direction	Volatility	Asset Legs	Max Risk	Max Reward	Strategy Type
Expert	Neutral	High	■ Short Stock ■ Two Long Calls	Capped	Uncapped	Capital Gain

7.4.1 Description

Straddles can be created "synthetically"—in other words, instead of buying calls and puts together, we create the same risk profile by combining calls or puts with a long or short position in the stock.

The Long Call Synthetic Straddle involves buying calls and counteracting them with a short stock position. To create the straddle shape, we must buy twice the number of calls. So for every 100 shares we short, we must buy two call contracts, which represent 200 shares of the stock. You may notice that the Long Call Synthetic Straddle is similar to the Synthetic Call, except that here we buy twice the number of calls.

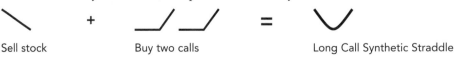

Sell stock   Buy two calls   Long Call Synthetic Straddle

Steps to Trading a Long Call Synthetic Straddle

1. Short the stock (if trading U.S. stocks, sell 50 shares for every call contract you buy).

2. Buy two ATM calls per 100 shares you sell. If the current stock price isn't near the nearest strike price, then it's better to choose the nearest ITM strike (lower than the current stock price).

Steps In

- Actively seek chart patterns that appear like pennant formations, signifying a consolidating price pattern.

- Try to concentrate on stocks with news events and earnings reports about to happen within two weeks.

- Choose a stock price range you feel comfortable with. Some traders prefer a middle range between $20.00 and $60.00.

Steps Out

- Manage your position according to the rules defined in your Trading Plan.

- Exit either a few days after the news event occurs if there is no movement or after the news event if there has been profitable movement.

- If the stock thrusts up, sell the calls (making a profit for the entire position) and wait for a retracement to profit from the short stock.

- If the stock thrusts down, buy back the stock (making a profit for the entire position) and wait for a retracement to profit from the calls.

- Try to avoid holding the option into the last month; otherwise, you'll be exposed to serious time decay.

7.4.2 Context

Outlook

- With a long Synthetic Straddle, your outlook is **neutral** in terms of direction, but you're looking for increasing volatility in the stock so that the stock price moves beyond your breakeven points on either side.

Rationale

- To execute a net credit direction neutral trade, where you expect the stock to behave with increasing volatility in either direction.

- If the stock rises explosively, you will make money from your calls, which rise faster than your short stock position falls.

- If the stock falls, you will make profit from your short stock position, which increases in value faster than your calls lose value beyond the price you paid for the calls.

Net Position

- If you're trading stocks, this is a **net credit** trade because you are selling the stock and paying only a fraction of that credit for the Long Call options.

- Your maximum risk is limited if the stock does not move decisively.

Effect of Time Decay

- Time decay is harmful to the value of your Long Calls. You need time for the stock to move explosively.

Appropriate Time Period to Trade

- We want to combine safety with prudence on cost. Therefore, the optimum time period to trade straddles is with three months until expiration, but if the stock has not moved decisively, sell your position when there is one month to expiration. *Be wary of holding a Straddle into the last month.*

Selecting the Stock

- Choose from stocks with adequate liquidity, preferably over 500,000 Average Daily Volume (ADV).

- Actively seek chart patterns that appear like pennant formations, signifying a consolidating price pattern.

- Try to concentrate on stocks with news events and earnings reports about to happen within two weeks.

- Choose a stock price range you feel comfortable with. For some traders, that's between $20.00 and $60.00.

Selecting the Options

- Choose options with adequate liquidity; open interest should be at least 100, preferably 500.

- **Strike**—As close to ATM as possible.

- **Expiration**—Preferably around three months.

7.4.3 Risk Profile

■	**Maximum Risk**	Limited to: [(contracts * value per point) / number of sold shares] * [call premium paid] + [call strike price] − [stock price sold]
■	**Maximum Reward**	[Uncapped]
■	**Breakeven Down**	[Stock price − (call premium * 2)]
■	**Breakeven Up**	[Stock price + (call premium * 2)] − [(2 * (stock price − strike price))]

7.4.4 Greeks

Key:
Expiration   ....
Today – 3 months ————
Time(t) – 1 month – – –

Risk Profile
If the stock price remains around the strike price, we make our maximum loss. If it moves explosively in either direction, we make profits.

Delta
Delta (speed) is at its greatest when the position is making money in either direction. The negative Delta is purely an indication of direction; i.e., making profit as the stock falls.

Gamma
Gamma (acceleration) peaks positively around the strike price.

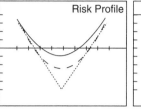

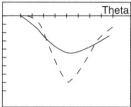

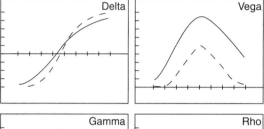

Theta
Time decay is harmful to the position because we are long in options.

Vega
Volatility is helpful to the position because we are long in options.

Rho
Higher interest rates are generally helpful to the position when the stock rises.

7.4.5 Advantages and Disadvantages

Advantages

- Profit from a volatile stock moving in either direction.
- Capped risk.
- Uncapped profit potential if the stock moves.
- No capital outlay.

Disadvantages

- Significant movement of the stock and option prices is required to make a profit.
- Bid/Ask Spread can adversely affect the quality of the trade.
- Psychologically demanding strategy.

7.4.6 Exiting the Trade

Exiting the Position

■   If the share has moved decisively, then you simply unravel the trade by selling your call options and buying back the stock.

Mitigating a Loss

■   Unravel the position as described previously.

7.4.7 Example

ABCD is trading at $35.07 on June 2, 2004.

Short 500 shares of stock at $35.07.

Buy 10 August 2004 35 strike calls at $3.00.

Net Credit	Stock price − (2 * premium bought) **$35.07 − $6.00 = $29.07**
Maximum Risk	[(Contracts * value per point) / number of sold shares] * call premium paid] + [call strike price] − [stock price sold] **([(10 * 100) / 500] * $3.00) + $35.00 − $35.07 = $5.93**
Maximum Reward	Uncapped
Breakeven Down	Stock price − (2 * premium bought) **$35.07 − $6.00 = $29.07**
Breakeven Up	[Stock price + (call premium * 2)] − [(2 * (stock price − strike price))] **[$35.07 + ($3.00 * 2)] − [(2 * ($35.07 − $35.00))] = $40.93**

7.5 Long Put Synthetic Straddle

Proficiency	Direction	Volatility	Asset Legs	Max Risk	Max Reward	Strategy Type
Expert	Neutral	High	■ Long Stock ■ Two Long Puts	Capped	Uncapped	Capital Gain

7.5.1 Description

As we saw in Section 6.4, straddles can be created "synthetically." In other words, instead of buying calls and puts together, we create the same risk profile by combining calls or puts with a long or short position in the stock.

The Long Put Synthetic Straddle involves buying puts and counteracting them with a Long Stock position. To create the Straddle shape, we have to buy twice the number of puts. So for every 100 shares we buy, we have to buy two put contracts, which represent 200 shares of the stock. The Long Stock position replicates the action of buying the same number of calls as puts. Because we're buying stock to counteract the long puts in this case, the Long Put Synthetic Straddle is an expensive strategy, requiring a large net debit.

Buy stock   Buy two puts   Long Put Synthetic Straddle

Steps to Trading a Long Put Synthetic Straddle

1. Buy the stock (if trading U.S. stocks, sell 50 shares for every put contract you buy).

2. Buy two ATM puts per 100 shares you buy. If the current stock price isn't near the nearest strike price, then it's better to choose the nearest ITM strike (higher than the current stock price).

Steps In

- Actively seek chart patterns that appear like pennant formations, signifying a consolidating price pattern.

- Try to concentrate on stocks with news events and earnings reports about to happen within two weeks.

- Choose a stock price range you feel comfortable with. Some traders prefer a middle range between $20.00 and $50.00.

Steps Out

- Manage your position according to the rules defined in your Trading Plan.

- Exit either a few days after the news event occurs if there is no movement, or after the news event if there has been profitable movement.

- If the stock thrusts up, sell the stock (making a profit for the entire position) and wait for a retracement to profit from the puts.

- If the stock thrusts down, sell the puts (making a profit for the entire position) and wait for a retracement to profit from the stock.

- Never hold into the last month.

7.5.2 Context

Outlook

- With a long Synthetic Straddle, your outlook is **neutral** in terms of direction, but you're looking for increasing volatility in the stock so that the stock price moves beyond your breakeven points on either side.

Rationale

■ To execute a direction neutral trade where you expect the stock to behave with increasing volatility in either direction.

■ If the stock rises explosively, you will make money from your long stock position, which will rise faster than your Long Put position falls.

■ If the stock falls, you will profit from your Long Put position, which will increase in value faster than your long stock position loses value beyond the price you paid for the puts.

Net Position

■ This is a **net debit** trade because you are buying the stock and the puts.

Effect of Time Decay

■ Time decay is harmful to the value of your Long Puts. You need time for the stock to move explosively.

Appropriate Time Period to Trade

■ We want to combine safety with prudence on cost. Therefore, the optimum time period to trade straddles is with three months until expiration, but if the stock has not moved decisively, you should sell your position when there is one month to expiration. *Be wary of holding a Straddle into the last month.*

Selecting the Stock

■ Choose from stocks with adequate liquidity, preferably over 500,000 Average Daily Volume (ADV).

■ Actively seek chart patterns that appear like pennant formations, signifying a consolidating price pattern

■ Try to concentrate on stocks with news events and earnings reports about to happen within two weeks.

■ Choose a stock price range you feel comfortable with. For some traders, that's between $20.00 and $50.00.

Selecting the Options

■ Choose options with adequate liquidity; open interest should be at least 100, preferably 500.

■ **Strike**—As close to ATM as possible.

■ **Expiration**—Preferably around three months.

7.5.3 Risk Profile

■ **Maximum Risk**   Limited to: [((contracts * value per point) / number of bought shares] * put premium paid)] + [stock price] − [put strike price]

■ **Maximum Reward**   [Uncapped]

■ **Breakeven Down**   [Put strike + (put premium * 2)] + [(put strike − stock price)]

■ **Breakeven Up**   [Stock price + (2 * put premium)]

7.5.4 Greeks

Key:
Expiration   ············
Today − 3 months   ————
Time(t) − 1 month − − −

Risk Profile
If the stock price remains around the strike price, we make our maximum loss. If it moves explosively in either direction, we make profits.

Delta
Delta (speed) is at its greatest when the position is making money in either direction. The negative Delta is purely an indication of direction; i.e., making profit as the stock falls.

Gamma
Gamma (acceleration) peaks positively around the strike price.

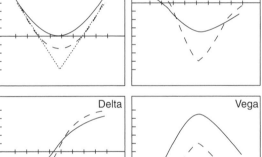

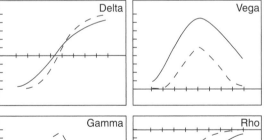

Theta
Time decay is harmful to the position because we are long in options.

Vega
Volatility is helpful to the position because we are long in options.

Rho
Higher interest rates are generally unhelpful to the position when the stock falls.

7.5.5 Advantages and Disadvantages

Advantages

■ Profit from a volatile stock moving in either direction.

■ Capped risk.

■ Uncapped profit potential if the stock moves.

Disadvantages

■ Significant movement of the stock and option prices is required to make a profit.

■ Bid/Ask Spread can adversely affect the quality of the trade.

■ Psychologically demanding strategy.

■ Expensive.

7.5.6 Exiting the Trade

Exiting the Position

■ If the share has moved decisively, then you simply unravel the trade by selling your put options and the stock.

Mitigating a Loss

■ Unravel the position as described previously.

7.5.7 Example

ABCD is trading at $35.07 on June 2, 2004.

Buy 500 shares of stock at $35.07.

Buy 10 August 2004 35 strike puts at $2.85.

Net Debit	Stock price + (2 * put premium) **$35.07 + $5.70 = $40.77**
Maximum Risk	[((Contracts * value per point) / number of bought shares] * put premium paid)] + [stock price] − [put strike price] **[(10 * 100) / 500] * $2.85) + $35.07 − $35.00 = $5.77**
Maximum Reward	Uncapped
Breakeven Down	[Put strike + (put premium * 2)] + [(put strike − stock price)] **$35.00 − $5.70 + ($35.00 − $35.07) = $29.23**
Breakeven Up	[Stock price + (put premium * 2)] **[$35.07 + $5.70] = $40.77**

Let's compare the results of the Long Put Synthetic Straddle with the Long Call Synthetic Straddle.

	Long Put Synthetic Straddle	Long Call Synthetic Straddle
Net Debit / Net Credit	$40.77 net debit	$29.07 net credit
Maximum Risk	$5.77	$5.93
Maximum Reward	Uncapped	Uncapped
Breakeven Down	$29.23	$29.07
Breakeven Up	$40.77	$40.93

As we can see, the Long Put version is more expensive but has slightly less risk, and also the breakevens are narrower, which is preferable for Long Straddles.

If we had the choice of the two here, we'd be more inclined to go with the long put version, even if it means a net debit.

7.6 Short Call Synthetic Straddle

Proficiency	Direction	Volatility	Asset Legs	Max Risk	Max Reward	Strategy Type
(i)	(w)	(~)	(/) + (~) + (~)	(skull)	(l)	(bank)
Expert	Neutral	Low	■ Long Stock ■ Two Short Calls	Uncapped	Capped	Capital Gain

7.6.1 Description

We know that straddles can be created "synthetically." Well, so can short straddles, though I wouldn't recommend them for inexperienced traders.

Instead of selling calls and puts together, we create the same risk profile by combining short calls or puts with a long or short position in the stock.

The Short Call Synthetic Straddle involves selling calls and counteracting them with a long stock position. To create the short straddle shape, we have to sell twice the number of calls. So for every 100 shares we buy, we have to sell two call contracts, which represent 200 shares of the stock.

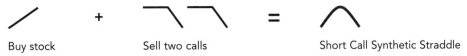

Buy stock   Sell two calls   Short Call Synthetic Straddle

Steps to Trading a Short Call Synthetic Straddle

1. Buy the stock (if trading U.S. stocks, buy 50 shares for every call contract you sell).

2. Sell two ATM calls per 100 shares you buy. If the current stock price isn't near the nearest strike price, then it's better to choose an OTM strike (higher than the current stock price).

    Steps In

    ■ Try to ensure that the trend is rangebound and identify clear areas of support and resistance.

    ■ Try to ensure that no news is coming out imminently for the stock.

    Steps Out

    ■ Manage your position according to the rules defined in your Trading Plan.

    ■ Close the losing side by unraveling the relevant side if the stock breaks in either direction.

- Unravel the entire trade if the position is profitable and you think news may emerge about the underlying stock.

7.6.2 Context

Outlook

- With a Short Synthetic Straddle, your outlook is **direction neutral**—you are looking for no movement in the stock and reducing volatility.

Rationale

- To execute a direction neutral trade where you expect the stock to be range-bound and behave with reduced volatility.

Net Position

- If you're trading stocks, this is a **net debit** transaction because you are buying the stock and receiving only a fraction of that credit for the Short Call options.

- Your maximum risk is uncapped if the stock moves explosively in either direction.

- Your maximum reward is capped and occurs at the strike price.

Effect of Time Decay

- Time decay is helpful to your Short Call position.

Appropriate Time Period to Trade

- One month or less.

Selecting the Stock

- Choose from stocks with adequate liquidity, preferably over 500,000 Average Daily Volume (ADV).

- Try to ensure that the trend is rangebound and identify clear areas of support and resistance.

- Try to ensure that no news is coming out imminently for the stock.

Selecting the Options

- Choose options with adequate liquidity; open interest should be at least 100, preferably 500.

- **Strike**—As close to ATM as possible, but preferably slightly OTM (higher than the current stock price).

- **Expiration**—Preferably one month or less.

7.6.3 Risk Profile

- **Maximum Risk**   [Uncapped]

- **Maximum Reward**   [((Contracts * value per point) / number of bought shares) * call premium] + [call strike price] − [stock price]

- **Breakeven Down**   [Stock price − (call premium * 2)]

- **Breakeven Up**   [Stock price + (call premium * 2)] − [(2 * (stock price − strike price))]

7.6.4 Greeks

Key:
Expiration   ············
Today − 1 month   ————
Time(t) − 5 days – – –

Risk Profile
If the stock price remains around the strike price, we make our maximum profit. If it moves explosively in either direction, we make uncapped losses.

Delta
Delta (speed) is at its greatest when the position is losing money in either direction. The negative Delta is purely an indication of direction.

Gamma
Gamma (acceleration) peaks inversely around the strike price.

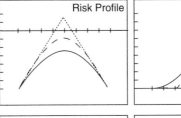
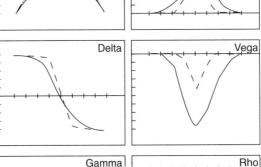
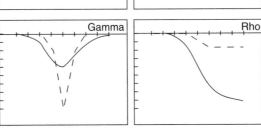

Theta
Time decay is helpful to the position because we are short in options.

Vega
Volatility is harmful to the position because we are short in options.

Rho
Higher interest rates are generally unhelpful to the position when the stock rises.

7.6.5 Advantages and Disadvantages

Advantages

- Profit from a rangebound stock.

Disadvantages

■ Uncapped risk if the stock moves in either direction.

■ Capped reward.

■ Expensive trade because you have to buy the stock.

■ High-risk strategy, not for novices or intermediates.

7.6.6 Exiting the Trade

Exiting the Position

■ If the stock remains below the call strike, then the short options will expire worthless at expiration, and you will keep the premium. You can then either sell the stock or re-create the position with next month's sold calls. Alternatively, you can set up another strategy involving being long in the stock.

Mitigating a Loss

■ If the stock moves explosively upwards before expiration, you will be exercised, meaning that you will have to deliver double the amount of stock you hold.

■ At the beginning of the trade, you will have predefined your stop loss areas.

■ If the stock hits the upper price band, triggering your stop loss, then you should buy back at least one of the calls. You will then have created a "covered call." Alternatively, you can unravel the entire spread.

■ If the stock hits the lower price band, triggering your stop loss, then you should sell the stock, provided that your account permits you to trade naked options. Alternatively, you can unravel the entire spread by buying back the sold calls and selling the bought stock.

7.6.7 Example

ABCD is trading at $35.07 on June 2, 2004.

Buy 500 shares of stock at $35.07.

Sell 10 June 2004 35 strike calls at $1.55.

Net Debit	Stock price − (2 * premium bought) **$35.07 − $3.10 = $31.97**
Maximum Risk	Uncapped
Maximum Reward	[((Contracts * value per point) / number of bought shares] * call premium) + [call strike price] − [stock price] **[((10 * 100) / 500) * $1.55] + [$35.00 − $35.07] = $3.03**
Breakeven Down	Stock price − (2 * premium bought) **$35.07 − $3.10 = $31.97**
Breakeven Up	[Stock price + (call premium * 2)] − [(2 * (stock price − strike price))] **[$35.07 + ($1.55 * 2)] − [(2 * ($35.07 − $35.00))] = $38.03**

7.7 Short Put Synthetic Straddle

Proficiency	Direction	Volatility	Asset Legs	Max Risk	Max Reward	Strategy Type
Expert	Neutral	Low	■ Short Stock ■ Two Short Puts	Uncapped	Capped	Income

7.7.1 Description

As we just saw in Section 6.6, we can create Short Straddles synthetically, though again, I wouldn't necessarily recommend it for inexperienced traders.

The Short Put Synthetic Straddle involves selling puts and counteracting them with a Short Stock position. To create the Short Straddle shape, we have to sell twice the number of puts. So for every 100 shares we sell, we have to sell two put contracts, which represent 200 shares of the stock.

This strategy creates a large net credit in our accounts and as such can be considered an income strategy.

Sell stock   Sell two puts   Short Put Synthetic Straddle

Steps to Trading a Short Put Synthetic Straddle

1. Sell the stock (if trading U.S. stocks, sell 50 shares for every put contract you sell).

2. Sell two ATM puts per 100 shares you buy. If the current stock price isn't near the nearest strike price, then it's better to choose an OTM strike (lower than the current stock price).

Steps In

■ Try to ensure that the trend is rangebound and identify clear areas of support and resistance.

■ Try to ensure that no news is coming out imminently for the stock.

Steps Out

■ Manage your position according to the rules defined in your Trading Plan.

■ Close the losing side by unraveling the relevant side if the stock breaks in either direction.

■ Unravel the entire trade if the position is profitable and you think news may emerge about the underlying stock.

7.7.2 Context

Outlook

■ With a Short Synthetic Straddle, your outlook is **direction neutral**—you are looking for no movement in the stock and reducing volatility.

Rationale

■ To execute a direction neutral trade where you expect the stock to be rangebound and behave with reduced volatility.

Net Position

■ This is a **net credit** trade because you are selling both the stock and the put options, thereby receiving money into your account.

■ Your maximum risk is uncapped if the stock moves explosively in either direction.

■ Your maximum reward is capped and occurs at the strike price.

Effect of Time Decay

■ Time decay is helpful to your short put position.

Appropriate Time Period to Trade

■ One month or less.

Selecting the Stock

■ Choose from stocks with adequate liquidity, preferably over 500,000 Average Daily Volume (ADV).

■ Try to ensure that the trend is rangebound and identify clear areas of support and resistance.

■ Try to ensure that no news is coming out imminently for the stock.

Selecting the Options

■ Choose options with adequate liquidity; open interest should be at least 100, preferably 500.

- **Strike**—As close to ATM as possible, but preferably slightly OTM (lower than the current stock price).

- **Expiration**—Preferably one month or less.

7.7.3 Risk Profile

- **Maximum Risk**   [Uncapped]

- **Maximum Reward**   [((Contracts * value per point) / number of sold shares) * put premium sold] + [stock price sold − put strike price]

- **Breakeven Down**   [Stock price − (2 * put premium)]

- **Breakeven Up**   [Stock price + (2 * put premium)] − [2 * (stock price − put strike)]

7.7.4 Greeks

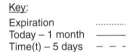

Key:
Expiration   ....
Today − 1 month ———
Time(t) − 5 days   − − −

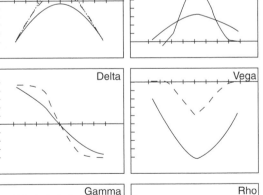

Risk Profile
If the stock price remains around the strike price, we make our maximum profit. If it moves explosively in either direction, we make uncapped losses.

Delta
Delta (speed) is at its greatest when the position is losing money in either direction. The negative Delta is purely an indication of direction.

Gamma
Gamma (acceleration) peaks inversely around the strike price.

Theta
Time decay is helpful to the position because we are short in options.

Vega
Volatility is harmful to the position because we are short in options.

Rho
Higher interest rates are generally helpful to the position when the stock falls.

7.7.5 Advantages and Disadvantages

Advantages

- Profit from a rangebound stock.

- No capital outlay.

- Substantial net credit received.

Disadvantages

- Uncapped risk if the stock moves in either direction.

- Capped reward.

- High-risk strategy, not for novices or intermediates.

7.7.6 Exiting the Trade

Exiting the Position

- If the stock remains above the put strike, then the short options will expire worthless at expiration, and you will keep the premium. You can then either buy back the stock or re-create the position with next month's sold puts. Alternatively, you can set up another strategy involving being short in the stock.

Mitigating a Loss

- If the stock moves explosively downwards before expiration, you will be exercised at that time, meaning that you will have to buy double the amount of stock you shorted.

- At the beginning of the trade, you will have set your stop loss.

- If the stock hits the upper price band, triggering your stop loss, then you should consider buying back the stock. You will then be short in two puts, which you may have to buy back or hedge in order to avoid an unlimited risk position. Alternatively, you can simply unravel the entire spread.

- If the stock hits the lower price band, triggering your stop loss, then you should buy back your sold puts. If you buy back just half of your sold puts, you will have created a "Covered Put" risk profile. However, this still exposes you to unlimited losses, so it is best to simply unravel the entire position and take your stop loss.

7.7.7 Example

ABCD is trading at $35.07 on June 2, 2004.

Sell 500 shares of stock at $35.07.

Sell 10 June 2004 35 strike puts at $1.25.

Net Credit	Stock price + (2 * premium bought) $35.07 − $2.50 = $37.57
Maximum Risk	Uncapped
Maximum Reward	[((Contracts * value per point) / number of sold shares) * put premium] + [stock price − put strike price] [(10 * 100) / 500) * $1.25] + [$35.07 − $35.00] = $2.57
Breakeven Down	Stock price − (2 * put premium) $35.07 − $2.50 = $32.57
Breakeven Up	[Stock price + (2 * put premium)] − [2 * (stock price − put strike)] [$35.07 + ($1.25 * 2)] − [(2 * ($35.07 − $35.00))] = $37.43

Let's compare the results of the Short Put Synthetic Straddle with the Short Call Synthetic Straddle.

	Short Put Synthetic Straddle	Short Call Synthetic Straddle
Net Debit / Net Credit	$37.57 net credit	$31.97 net debit
Maximum Risk	Uncapped	Uncapped
Maximum Reward	$2.57	$3.03
Breakeven Down	$32.57	$31.97
Breakeven Up	$37.43	$38.03

As we can see, the Short Call version is more expensive but has slightly less risk, and also the breakevens are wider apart, which is preferable for short straddles.

If we had the choice of the two here, we'd be more inclined to go with the Short Call version, even if it means a net debit.

7.8 Long Synthetic Future

Proficiency	Direction	Volatility	Asset Legs	Max Risk	Max Reward	Strategy Type
Expert	Bullish	N/A	■ Short Put ■ Long Call	Uncapped	Uncapped	Capital Gain

7.8.1 Description

We can synthetically create the risk profile or a long stock by selling ATM puts and buying ATM calls. The net result is a very inexpensive, nil cost, or even net credit trade that precisely mimics the long stock or long future position.

Sell put + Buy call = Long Synthetic Future

Steps to Trading a Long Synthetic Future

1. Sell an ATM put.
2. Buy an ATM call with the same strike and expiration date.

   Steps In

   ■ Try to ensure that the trend is upward and identify a clear area of support.

   Steps Out

   ■ Manage your position according to the rules defined in your Trading Plan.
   ■ Play the strategy just as you would if you'd simply bought the stock. The difference is that with a Long Synthetic Future, you can leg out of the trade, maximizing your trading opportunity.
   ■ Never hold the long option into the last month before expiration.

7.8.2 Context

Outlook

   ■ With Long Synthetic Futures, your outlook is **bullish.**

Rationale

   ■ To simulate the action of buying a stock, but to do so with a fraction of the cost. This also simulates the action of taking a long position in a future.

Net Position

   ■ This is usually a **net debit** trade. It can depend on how close the strike price is to the stock price and whether it is above or below the stock price.
   ■ Your risk on the trade itself is uncapped on the downside until the stock falls down to zero.

Effect of Time Decay

   ■ Time decay is harmful to your Long Synthetic Future trade, but with this strategy, you are hedging time decay by buying and selling near the money options, so the effect is minimal. What you lose from the Long Call time value, you benefit from the Short Put position.

Appropriate Time Period to Trade

   ■ Generally, you will be using this strategy in conjunction with another trade. It is generally more sensible to use this as a longer-term trade.

Selecting the Stock

   ■ Choose from stocks with adequate liquidity, preferably over 500,000 Average Daily Volume (ADV).
   ■ Try to ensure that the trend is upward and identify a clear area of support.

Selecting the Options

- Choose options with adequate liquidity; open interest should be at least 100, preferably 500.

- **Strike**—As close to ATM as possible (same for both legs).

- **Expiration**—Any time period can work, though remember that the long call will suffer from time decay, particularly in the final month to expiration, so it's best to choose expirations of two months or more. Use the same expiration for both legs.

7.8.3 Risk Profile

- **Maximum Risk**   [Strike price + net debit]

- **Maximum Reward**   [Uncapped]

- **Breakeven**   [Strike price + net debit]

7.8.4 Greeks

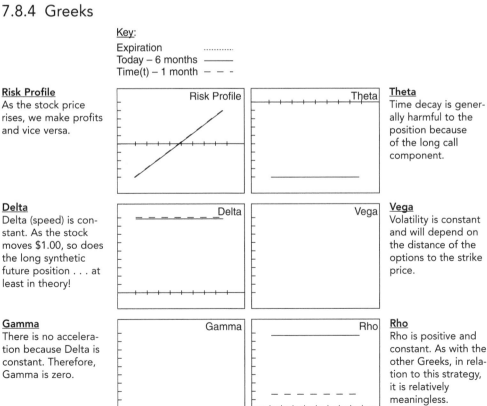

Key:
Expiration   ············
Today – 6 months ————
Time(t) – 1 month – – –

Risk Profile
As the stock price rises, we make profits and vice versa.

Risk Profile

Theta

Theta
Time decay is generally harmful to the position because of the long call component.

Delta
Delta (speed) is constant. As the stock moves $1.00, so does the long synthetic future position . . . at least in theory!

Delta

Vega

Vega
Volatility is constant and will depend on the distance of the options to the strike price.

Gamma
There is no acceleration because Delta is constant. Therefore, Gamma is zero.

Gamma

Rho

Rho
Rho is positive and constant. As with the other Greeks, in relation to this strategy, it is relatively meaningless.

7.8.5 Advantages and Disadvantages

Advantages

■ Create a long stock position with virtually zero capital outlay.

■ Capped risk down to the stock falling to zero (though this could be argued the other way too; i.e., uncapped risk down to zero!).

■ Uncapped profit potential if the stock appreciates.

Disadvantages

■ No leverage or protection created by the position.

■ No dividend entitlement.

■ Bid/Ask Spread can adversely affect the quality of the trade.

7.8.6 Exiting the Trade

Exiting the Position

■ With this strategy, you can simply unravel the spread by selling your calls and buying back the puts.

■ You can also exit just your profitable leg of the trade and hope that the stock moves to favor the unprofitable side later on. For example, if the share has moved decisively upwards, thus making the Long Calls profitable, you will sell the calls and make a profit on the entire trade, but you will be left with almost valueless Short Puts. Having now sold the calls, you will secure your position by buying back the depleted puts.

Mitigating a Loss

■ Sell the position if the stock breaks down through your predetermined stop loss.

7.8.7 Example

ABCD is trading at $35.69 on June 2, 2004.

Sell November 2004 35 strike puts at $3.60.

Buy November 2004 35 strike calls at $4.60.

Net Debit	[Bought call − sold put] **$4.60 − $3.60 = $1.00**
Maximum Risk	[Strike price + net debit] **$35.00 + $1.00 = $36.00**
Maximum Reward	Uncapped
Breakeven	[Strike price + net debit] **$35.00 + $1.00 = $36.00**

7.9 Short Synthetic Future

Proficiency	Direction	Volatility	Asset Legs	Max Risk	Max Reward	Strategy Type
		N/A	![put]+![call]	![Max Risk]	![Max Reward]	![Capital Gain]
Expert	Bearish		■ Long Put ■ Short Call	Uncapped	Uncapped	Capital Gain

7.9.1 Description

The precise opposite of a Long Synthetic Future, we can synthetically create the risk profile or a short stock position by buying ATM puts and selling ATM calls. The net result is a virtually nil cost or even net credit trade that precisely mimics the short stock or short future position.

Buy put   Sell call   Short Synthetic Future

Steps to Trading a Short Synthetic Future

1. Buy an ATM put.
2. Sell an ATM call with the same strike and expiration date.

   Steps In

   ■ Try to ensure that the trend is downward and identify a clear area of resistance.

   Steps Out

   ■ Manage your position according to the rules defined in your Trading Plan.

   ■ Play the strategy just as you would if you'd simply shorted the stock. The difference is that with a Short Synthetic Future, you can leg out of the trade, maximizing your trading opportunity.

   ■ Never hold the long option into the last month before expiration.

7.9.2 Context

Outlook

   ■ With Short Synthetic Futures, your outlook is **bearish.**

Rationale

   ■ To simulate the action of shorting a stock. This also simulates the action of taking a short position in a future.

Net Position

■ This is usually a **net credit** trade. It can depend on how close the strike price is to the stock price and whether it is above or below the stock price.

■ Your risk on the trade itself is uncapped on the upside as the stock rises.

Effect of Time Decay

■ Time decay helps your Short Synthetic Future trade, but with this strategy, you are hedging time decay by buying and selling near the money options, so the effect is minimal. What you lose from the Long Put time value, you benefit from the Short Call position.

Appropriate Time Period to Trade

■ Generally, you will be using this strategy in conjunction with another trade. It is generally more sensible to use this as a shorter-term trade, though at the same time you should consider the effect of time decay on the long put leg.

Selecting the Stock

■ Choose from stocks with adequate liquidity, preferably over 500,000 Average Daily Volume (ADV).

■ Try to ensure that the trend is downward and identify a clear area of resistance.

Selecting the Options

■ Choose options with adequate liquidity; open interest should be at least 100, preferably 500.

■ **Strike**—As close to ATM as possible (same for both legs).

■ **Expiration**—Any time period can work, though remember that the Long Put will suffer from time decay, particularly in the final month to expiration, so it's best to choose expirations of two months or more. Use the same expiration for both legs.

7.9.3 Risk Profile

■ **Maximum Risk**   [Uncapped]

■ **Maximum Reward**   [Strike price + net credit] (or − net debit)

■ **Breakeven**   [Strike price + net credit] (or − net debit)

7.9.4 Greeks

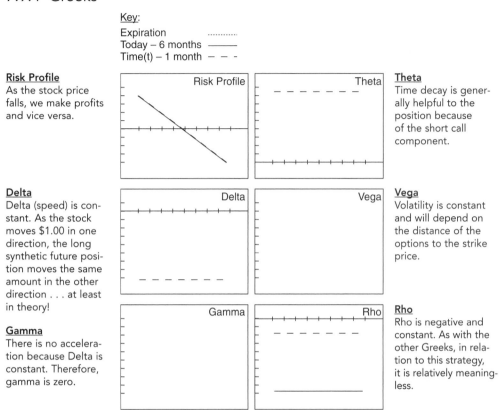

Key:

Expiration   ············
Today – 6 months ————
Time(t) – 1 month – – –

Risk Profile
As the stock price falls, we make profits and vice versa.

Delta
Delta (speed) is constant. As the stock moves $1.00 in one direction, the long synthetic future position moves the same amount in the other direction . . . at least in theory!

Gamma
There is no acceleration because Delta is constant. Therefore, gamma is zero.

Theta
Time decay is generally helpful to the position because of the short call component.

Vega
Volatility is constant and will depend on the distance of the options to the strike price.

Rho
Rho is negative and constant. As with the other Greeks, in relation to this strategy, it is relatively meaningless.

7.9.5 Advantages and Disadvantages

Advantages

- Create a short stock position with the ability to leg in and out of the call or put as appropriate.

- Uncapped profit potential as the stock declines to zero (though this could equally be described as being capped reward after the stock has fallen to zero!).

Disadvantages

- No leverage or protection created by the position.

- Uncapped risk potential if the stock rises.

- Bid/Ask Spread can adversely affect the quality of the trade.

7.9.6 Exiting the Trade

Exiting the Position

■   With this strategy, you can simply unravel the spread by selling your puts and buying back the calls.

■   You can also exit just your profitable leg of the trade and hope that the stock moves to favor the unprofitable side later on. For example, if the share has moved decisively downwards, thereby making the long puts profitable, you will sell the puts and make a profit on the entire trade, but you will be left with almost valueless short calls. Having now sold the puts, you will secure your position by buying back the depleted calls.

Mitigating a Loss

■   Sell the position if the stock rises up through your predetermined stop loss.

7.9.7 Example

ABCD is trading at $35.38 on June 2, 2004.

Buy August 2004 35 strike puts at $2.60.

Sell August 2004 35 strike calls at $2.80.

Net Credit	[Sold call − bought put] **$2.80 − $2.60 = $0.20**
Maximum Risk	Uncapped
Maximum Reward	[Strike price + net credit] **$35.00 + $0.20 = $35.20**
Breakeven	[Strike price + net credit] **$35.00 + $0.20 = $35.20**

7.10 Long Combo

Proficiency	Direction	Volatility	Asset Legs	Max Risk	Max Reward	Strategy Type
Expert	Bullish	N/A	■ Short Put ■ Long Call	Uncapped	Uncapped	Capital Gain

7.10.1 Description

The Long Combo is a variation of the Long Synthetic Future. The only difference is that we sell OTM (lower strike) puts and buy OTM (higher strike) calls.

The net effect is an inexpensive trade, similar to a Long Stock or Long Futures position, except there is a gap between the strikes.

Sell put   Buy call   Long Combo

Steps to Trading a Long Combo

1. Sell an OTM (lower strike) put.

2. Buy an OTM (higher strike) call with the same expiration date.

   Steps In

   ■ Try to ensure that the trend is upward and identify a clear area of support.

   Steps Out

   ■ Manage your position according to the rules defined in your Trading Plan.

   ■ Play the strategy just as you would if you'd simply bought the stock. The difference is that with a Long Combo, you can leg out of the trade, maximizing your trading opportunity.

   ■ Never hold the long option into the last month before expiration.

7.10.2 Context

Outlook

■ With Long Combos, your outlook is **bullish.**

Rationale

■ To simulate the action of buying a stock but to do so with a fraction of the cost. This also simulates the action of taking a long position in a future except for the flat middle part between the strikes.

Net Position

■ This is usually a **net debit** trade. It can depend on where the call and put strikes are in relation to the stock price.

■ Your risk on the trade is uncapped on the downside until the stock falls down to zero.

Effect of Time Decay

- Time decay is harmful to your Long Combo trade, but with this strategy, you are hedging time decay by buying and selling near the money options, so the effect is minimal. What you lose from the Long Call time value, you benefit from the Short Put position.

Appropriate Time Period to Trade

- Generally, you will be using this strategy in conjunction with another trade. It is generally more sensible to use this as a longer-term trade.

Selecting the Stock

- Choose from stocks with adequate liquidity, preferably over 500,000 Average Daily Volume (ADV).

- Try to ensure that the trend is upward and identify a clear area of support.

Selecting the Options

- Choose options with adequate liquidity; open interest should be at least 100, preferably 500.

- **Put Strike**—One strike OTM (lower than current stock price).

- **Call Strike**—One strike OTM (higher than current stock price).

- **Expiration**—Any time period can work, though remember that the long call will suffer from time decay, particularly in the final month to expiration, so it's best to choose expirations of two months or more. Use the same expiration for both legs.

7.10.3 Risk Profile

- **Maximum Risk**   [Lower strike + net debit]
- **Maximum Reward**   [Uncapped]
- **Breakeven**   With net debits: [higher strike + net debit]

    With net credits: [lower strike − net credit]

7.10.4 Greeks

Key:
Expiration   ....
Today – 6 months ————
Time(t) – 1 month – – –

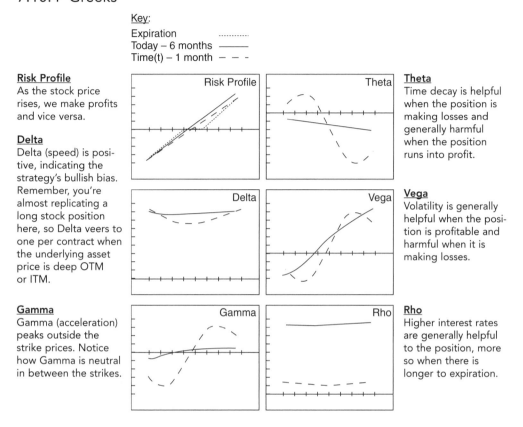

Risk Profile
As the stock price rises, we make profits and vice versa.

Delta
Delta (speed) is positive, indicating the strategy's bullish bias. Remember, you're almost replicating a long stock position here, so Delta veers to one per contract when the underlying asset price is deep OTM or ITM.

Gamma
Gamma (acceleration) peaks outside the strike prices. Notice how Gamma is neutral in between the strikes.

Theta
Time decay is helpful when the position is making losses and generally harmful when the position runs into profit.

Vega
Volatility is generally helpful when the position is profitable and harmful when it is making losses.

Rho
Higher interest rates are generally helpful to the position, more so when there is longer to expiration.

7.10.5 Advantages and Disadvantages

Advantages

- Create something similar to a long stock position with virtually zero capital outlay.

- Capped risk down to the stock falling to zero (though this could be argued the other way too; i.e., uncapped risk down to zero!).

- Uncapped profit potential if the stock appreciates.

Disadvantages

- No leverage or protection created by the position.

- No dividend entitlement.

- Bid/Ask Spread can adversely affect the quality of the trade.

7.10.6 Exiting the Trade

Exiting the Position

- With this strategy, you can simply unravel the spread by selling your calls and buying back the puts.

- You can also exit just your profitable leg of the trade and hope that the stock moves to favor the unprofitable side later on. For example, if the share has moved decisively upwards, thereby making the Long Calls profitable, you will sell the calls and make a profit on the entire trade, but you will be left with almost valueless short puts. Having now sold the calls, you will secure your position by buying back the depleted puts.

Mitigating a Loss

- Sell the position if the stock breaks down through your predetermined stop loss.

7.10.7 Example

ABCD is trading at $35.25 on June 2, 2004.

Sell November 2004 30 strike puts at $1.65.

Buy November 2004 40 strike calls at $2.35.

Net Debit	[Bought call − sold put] **$2.35 − $1.65 = $0.70**
Maximum Risk	[Lower strike + net debit] **$30.00 + $0.70 = $30.70**
Maximum Reward	Uncapped
Breakeven	[Higher strike + net debit] **$40.00 + $0.70 = $40.70**

7.11 Short Combo

Proficiency	Direction	Volatility	Asset Legs	Max Risk	Max Reward	Strategy Type
Expert	Bearish	N/A	■ Long Put ■ Short Call	Uncapped	Uncapped	Capital Gain

7.11.1 Description

The Short Combo is the precise opposite of a Long Combo. Instead of nearly replicating the Long Stock (or Futures) position, we nearly replicate the Short Stock (or Futures) position by buying OTM puts and selling OTM calls.

The net result is a virtually nil cost or even net credit trade that has uncapped risk potential as the stock rises.

Buy put   Sell call   Short Combo

Steps to Trading a Short Combo

1. Buy an OTM (lower strike) put.

2. Sell an OTM (higher strike) call with the same expiration date.

    Steps In

    ▦ Try to ensure that the trend is downward and identify a clear area of resistance.

    Steps Out

    ▦ Manage your position according to the rules defined in your Trading Plan.

    ▦ Play the strategy just as you would if you'd simply shorted the stock. The difference is that with a Short Combo, you can leg out of the trade, maximizing your trading opportunity.

    ▦ Never hold the long option into the last month before expiration.

7.11.2 Context

Outlook

▦ With Short Combos, your outlook is **bearish.**

Rationale

▦ To simulate the action of shorting a stock. This also simulates the action of taking a short position in a future except for the flat middle part between the strikes.

Net Position

▦ This is usually a **net credit** trade. It can depend on how the strike prices are positioned compared to the stock price.

▦ Your risk on the trade itself is uncapped on the upside as the stock rises.

Effect of Time Decay

■ Time decay helps your Short Combo trade, but with this strategy, you are hedging time decay by buying and selling near the money options, so the effect is minimal. What you lose from the Long Put time value, you benefit from the Short Call position.

Appropriate Time Period to Trade

■ Generally, you will be using this strategy in conjunction with another trade. It is generally more sensible to use this as a shorter-term trade, though at the same time you should consider the effect of time decay on the Long Put leg.

Selecting the Stock

■ Choose from stocks with adequate liquidity, preferably over 500,000 Average Daily Volume (ADV).

■ Try to ensure that the trend is downward and identify a clear area of resistance.

Selecting the Options

■ Choose options with adequate liquidity; open interest should be at least 100, preferably 500.

■ **Put Strike**—One strike OTM (lower than current stock price).

■ **Call Strike**—One strike OTM (higher than current stock price).

■ **Expiration**—Any time period can work, though remember that the Long Put will suffer from time decay, particularly in the final month to expiration, so it's best to choose expirations of two months or more. Use the same expiration for both legs.

7.11.3 Risk Profile

■ **Maximum Risk**   [Uncapped]

■ **Maximum Reward**   [Lower strike + net credit] (or less net debit)

■ **Breakeven**   With net debits: [lower strike − net debit]

With net credits: [higher strike + net credit]

7.11.4 Greeks

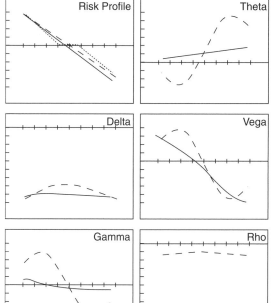

Risk Profile
As the stock price falls, we make profits and vice versa.

Delta
Delta (speed) is negative, indicating the strategy's bearish bias. Remember, you're almost replicating a short stock position here, so Delta veers to −1 per contract when the stock price is deep ITM or OTM.

Gamma
Gamma (acceleration) peaks outside the strike prices. Notice how Gamma is neutral in between the strikes.

Theta
Time decay is helpful when the position is making losses and generally harmful when the position runs into profit.

Vega
Volatility is generally helpful when the position is profitable and harmful when it is making losses.

Rho
Rho is negative and constant. As with the other Greeks, in relation to this strategy, it is relatively meaningless.

7.11.5 Advantages and Disadvantages

Advantages

- Create something similar to a short stock position with virtually zero capital outlay and the ability to leg in and out of the call or put as appropriate.

- Capped risk down to the stock falling to zero (though this could equally be described as being uncapped risk as the stock falls to zero!).

- Uncapped profit potential if the stock appreciates.

Disadvantages

- No leverage or protection created by the position.

- Uncapped risk potential if the stock rises.

- Bid/Ask Spread can adversely affect the quality of the trade.

7.11.6 Exiting the Trade

Exiting the Position

■   With this strategy, you can simply unravel the spread by selling your puts and buying back the calls.

■   You can also exit just your profitable leg of the trade and hope that the stock moves to favor the unprofitable side later on. For example, if the share has moved decisively downwards, thus making the Long Puts profitable, you will sell the puts and make a profit on the entire trade, but you will be left with almost valueless Short Calls. Having now sold the puts, you will secure your position by buying back the depleted calls.

Mitigating a Loss

■   Sell the position if the stock rises up through your predetermined stop loss.

7.11.7 Example

ABCD is trading at $35.10 on June 2, 2004.

Buy August 2004 30 strike puts at $0.90.

Sell August 2004 40 strike calls at $1.00.

Net Credit	[Sold call − bought put] $1.00 − $0.90 = $0.10
Maximum Risk	Uncapped
Maximum Reward	[Lower strike + net credit] $30.00 + $0.10 = $30.10
Breakeven	[Higher strike + net credit] $40.00 + $0.10 = $40.10

7.12 Long Box

Proficiency	Direction	Volatility	Asset Legs	Max Risk	Max Reward	Strategy Type
Expert	Neutral	High	■ Short Put ■ Long Call ■ Long Put ■ Short Call	Capped	Capped	Capital Gain

7.12.1 Description

The Long Box is a complex strategy that can (in some jurisdictions) have beneficial effects for tax planning from year to year. If your incentive for this strategy is a tax play, you should consult with your tax advisor beforehand to evaluate whether or not it is valid where you live.

The strategy involves creating a lower strike Long Synthetic Future and countering it with a higher strike Short Synthetic Future. The long and short positions cancel each other out, and we're left with a straight horizontal line. The trick is to ensure that the sum of our net purchases is less than the sum of our net sales in order to make a profit. Remember, there are four legs in this strategy, two longs and two shorts, and the strategy is typically a net debit because we're buying ITM options and selling OTM options.

Some traders who are sitting on vast capital gains will seek to close out the loss-making legs of the strategy just before the end of the tax year, thereby setting off those losses against their gains and reducing their capital gains tax bill for that year. However, we need to remember that any open short positions are generally treated as 100% gains until the position is closed.

High volatility is good for the Long Box, particularly if we're looking to conduct the type of trade outlined previously, where we leg in and out. Ideally, we want a big fall followed by a big rise, or vice versa, and we leg out in accordance with our original motivation for doing the trade in the first place.

| Sell lower
strike put | Buy same
strike call | Buy higher
strike put | Sell same
strike call | Long Box |

Steps to Trading a Long Box

1. Sell one lower strike (OTM) put.
2. Buy same strike (ITM) call.
3. Buy one higher strike (ITM) put.
4. Sell same strike OTM call.

Steps In

- Identify clear areas of support and resistance that the stock, being volatile enough, will fluctuate between.

Steps Out

- Manage your position according to the rules defined in your Trading Plan.

- Remember that the Long Box is a combination of other strategies, so it can be unraveled in two-leg chunks.

- You can unravel the position as parts of the trade become profitable or loss-making. Remember for tax purposes that a short option is taxed as a 100% gain until you buy it back to close the position, so this position should be handled with care, and professional advice is highly recommended.

- Never hold the long options into the last month before expiration.
  Remember to include all the commissions in your calculations.

7.12.2 Context

Outlook

- With long boxes, your outlook is **direction neutral.** You expect a lot of movement in the stock price, preferably between definable areas of support and resistance.

Rationale

- With long boxes, you are looking to execute a form of arbitrage where the profit is assured, known, and unaffected by market moves.

- You are volatility neutral per se, but there can be potential tax advantages to legging out of the loss-making side first. Professional advice is a must here.

- If you examine what you've done here, you have simply combined a Long Synthetic Future with a Short Synthetic Future at a higher strike. These two combined effectively cancel each other out, and the idea is to capture a profit due to mispricing in the market.

Net Position

- This is typically a **net debit** trade because we're buying ITM options and selling OTM options.

- Your maximum risk is the net debit or net credit less the difference between the strikes. Your maximum reward is the same. With this trade, you can only have one or the other.

Effect of Time Decay

- Time decay is generally helpful because you take your maximum profits at expiration.

Appropriate Time Period to Trade

- It's preferable to trade this strategy on a medium-term basis, preferably around three months, in order to accommodate large swings in price.

Selecting the Stock

- Choose from stocks with adequate liquidity, preferably over 500,000 Average Daily Volume (ADV).

- Identify clear areas of support and resistance that the stock, being volatile enough, will fluctuate between.

Selecting the Options

■ Choose options with adequate liquidity; open interest should be at least 100, preferably 500.

■ **Lower Strike**—Create the Long Synthetic Future element below the current stock price.

■ **Higher Strike**—Create the Short Synthetic Future element above the current stock price.

■ **Expiration**—Preferably around three months or less. Use the same expiration date for all legs.

7.12.3 Risk Profile

■ **Maximum Risk**   [Net credit received or net debit paid] − [Difference between strikes]

■ **Maximum Reward**   [Difference between strikes] − [Net credit received or net debit paid]

■ **Breakeven**   N/A

7.12.4 Greeks

Key:
Expiration   ············
Today − 3 months ─────
Time(t) − 1 month − − -

Risk Profile
The Long Box will either make a certain profit or a certain loss if all legs are closed simultaneously.

Risk Profile

Theta

Theta
Time decay is generally helpful because we take our maximum profits at expiration.

Delta
Delta (speed) is zero.

Delta

Vega

Vega
Volatility does not affect the trade because your profits are locked in and static.

Gamma
Gamma (acceleration) is zero.

Gamma

Rho

Rho
Higher interest rates are generally unhelpful because you have locked in your profits and are waiting to take them.

7.12.5 Advantages and Disadvantages

Advantages

■ Can be used as a tax hedge if entered and exited correctly either side of a tax year.

■ Should be placed in such a way to be virtually risk-free, although as a tax hedge, you'd need to leg out in stages.

■ Can be used to create an arbitrage opportunity.

Disadvantages

■ Requires a large number of contracts to be worth doing.

■ Complicated trade requiring the assistance of your broker or accountant.

■ Bid/Ask Spread can adversely affect the quality of the trade.

7.12.6 Exiting the Trade

Exiting the Position

■ With this strategy, you can simply unravel the spread by buying back the options you sold and selling the options you bought in the first place.

■ Advanced traders may leg up and down or only partially unravel the spread as the underlying asset fluctuates up and down. In this way, the trader will be taking smaller incremental profits before the expiration of the trade.

Mitigating a Loss

■ Unravel the trade as described previously.

■ Advanced traders may choose to only partially unravel the spread leg-by-leg and create alternative risk profiles. There is no point in doing the trade unless you have locked in a certain profit, or unless you have another reason for locking in a deliberate loss.

7.12.7 Example

ABCD is trading at $34.92 on June 2, 2004.

Sell August 2004 30 strike puts at $1.00.

Buy August 2004 30 strike calls at $6.00.

Buy August 2004 40 strike puts at $6.20.

Sell August 2004 40 strike calls at $1.20.

Net Debit	[Bought options − sold options] $12.20 − $2.20 = $10.00
Maximum Risk	[Net debit − difference between strikes] $10.00 − $10.00 = $0.00
Maximum Reward	[Difference between strikes − net debit] $10.00 − $10.00 = $0.00
Breakeven	N/A

So, in this real-life trade, we can make neither a profit nor a loss! But, by legging out as the stock price fluctuates, we may be able to make incremental profits when we close each leg or set of legs.

Taxation for Stock and Options Traders

Introduction

U.S. tax laws concerning trading, and options in particular, are absurdly complicated, so to avoid many sleepless nights, you should hire a decent tax consultant for your annual investment P&L.

In this chapter, we'll attempt to uncover some of the mysteries of the U.S. tax system; however, the summaries are meant to highlight the complications of the rules and steer you toward the appropriate professional advice.

Overall, it's sound practice to concentrate on perfecting your Trading Plan first and worry about the tax later. On the whole, we shouldn't mind paying tax on our trading activities because typically this means that we've been profitable. Unfortunately, the authorities do seem to indulge in a "heads-we-win, tails-you-lose" mentality, whereby your losses will be offset at unfavorably low rates and your gains will be charged at unfavorably high rates wherever possible!

The main purpose of this book is to explain the strategies themselves. Having a sound and well-rehearsed Trading Plan is the key to our success. We can become proficient at playing just one stock, chart pattern, or indicator. The best traders are typically great at one or two things, upon which their Trading Plan is constructed. Specialization is vital to your trading success because it gives you clarity of thought from the planning stage right through to the execution process. If you trade well, then you can "enjoy" paying the tax advisors . . . and even the tax. Ultimately, tax is a headache well worth having because in most cases it means you're making money!

8.1 Tax on Stocks

8.1.1 Simple Capital Gains Tax

In the U.S., taxation on capital gains comes into two categories:

■ Long-term gains for those assets held over one year.

■ Short-term gains for those assets held for less than one year.

Long-term gains are taxed at 15% and short-term gains at 35%.

> Short-term capital losses
> can be netted off long-term
> capital gains. The net (gain)
> is taxable at 15%.

Time Asset Held	Tax Treatment	Tax Rate %
>= 12 months	**Long term**	15%
< 12 months	**Short term**	35%

Example 8a

January 20, 2003	You buy 1,000 shares of ABCD at $20.00 →	$20,000
January 20, 2004	You sell 1,000 shares of ABCD at $25.00 →	$25,000
	Gain →	$5,000
Deemed a long-term investment; therefore, tax rate = 15%		

Example 8b

January 20, 2003	You buy 1,000 shares of ABCD at $20.00 →	$20,000
January 18, 2004	You sell 1,000 shares of ABCD at $25.00 →	$25,000
	Gain →	$5,000
Deemed a short-term investment; therefore, tax rate = 35%*		

  * Short-term capital gains are taxed at your marginal rate. For higher-rate taxpayers, this is 35% in the U.S., although this is scheduled to rise in 2010.

So far, so good . . . but that's about as good as it gets! From now on, things begin to get more complicated.

8.1.2 Shorting Stocks

When you short an asset, the mechanism involves your broker *borrowing* the stock in order for you to "sell" it without having owned it in the first place. In order to reverse the position, you effectively buy back the asset that you sold short.

There are times where we may have multiple positions open on the same security or index. Why could this be the case? Well, we could be long a stock on the weekly chart but also doing a short-term positional trade on the dailies. Whatever the case, it's possible for us to have both long and short positions on the same security. For these types of situations, regardless of how we're classifying the individual trades, the tax classification may conspire against our better interests by treating the long and short positions of the same security as *"constructive sales."*

Example 8c

January 20, 2004	You buy 1,000 shares of ABCD at $20.00
March 18, 2004	You short 1,000 shares of ABCD at $25.00

Even though you may have meant to keep two open positions on this stock (one long position and one short position), this sequence of transaction could be treated as a *constructive sale*, and you may be liable to short-term capital gains tax on the $5,000 "gain." The treatment will depend upon the timing of the two transactions, price differentials, and how you close each position, though it is not straightforward.

8.1.3 Wash Sales (or Bed and Breakfast)

Many tax authorities have wizened up to the investors' attempt to mitigate their tax gains by making the most of their losses. For example, say you have an investment portfolio of several stocks, but you are sitting on a pile of losses on one particular stock that you want to retain for the medium to long term. What you would do is sell the loss-making stock to take advantage of those losses now and buy it straight back the next day (or soon afterwards). In the old days, if you did this towards the end of a tax year, you could utilize those losses and set them off in that tax year against your other profits.

Unfortunately the benefits of bed and breakfasting have been eliminated all around the world in various ways. In the U.S., if you own stock, sell it, and then buy it back within 30 days, this is considered to be a "wash sale." The capital loss is not recognized and therefore cannot be set off against other gains.

How would you attempt to get around this? By selling a naked ITM put, which would mean you'd own the stock again as soon as you're exercised. Alas, the "wash sales" rule covers this practice too, though its precise mechanisms need to be examined by your tax advisor, as do other options scenarios.

8.2 Tax on Options

8.2.1 Long Options

For capital gains tax, long (owned) options are treated the same way as described previously in terms of long-term and short-term gains or losses. The activation of a chargeable gain/loss is triggered either by the disposal or the expiration of the option.

Three things can happen when you buy an option:

1. It expires OTM and therefore is worthless, meaning a 100% loss.

2. You sell the option for a profit or a loss.

3. It expires ITM and you exercise your right to buy (call) or sell (put) the underlying asset.

These three situations give rise to different taxation situations:

1. If the option expires OTM, it is worthless, meaning you have made a 100% loss. In the absence of another related position, you would be able to set off that 100% loss against other gains.

2. If you sell the option for a profit or loss, you will be subject to the long-term or short-term capital gains rules as set out earlier, depending on whether you held the option for more than 12 months.

3. If you exercise a call option, then you will be buying stock. The cost of the call option you bought is added to the strike price at which you're buying the stock, and the holding period for the stock starts on the day after exercise.

Example 8d

August 20, 2003	You buy ten $30.00 strike LEAP call option contracts of ABCD stock expiring in January 2005 for $5.00.	$5,000
January 21, 2005	The stock is worth $40.00, meaning your call option expires with $10.00 of Intrinsic Value. This is a profit of $5,000 on your original investment that you made 17 months ago (i.e., far enough away to have made this a long-term investment).	
	Instead of selling the option the day before expiration and making $5,000 profit with only 15% tax to pay, you decide to exercise the option.	
	This means you now own the stock at $30.00 (the strike price), plus the $5.00 you paid for the LEAP call option; i.e., a net cost of $35.00. However, the holding period of the stock is deemed to begin the day after exercise, meaning the clock only starts on January 22, 2005. This means that until January 22, 2006, this is deemed to be a short-term investment, taxable at 35%. If you decided to sell the stock while it was still at $40,000, you'd still make your $5,000 profit, but you'd be paying 35% on that, as opposed to the 15% you'd have paid if you'd simply sold the option the day before expiration. That's $1,000 of your profit wasted by not understanding the tax situation.	

4. If you exercise a put option, then you will be selling stock. The cost of the put option you bought is subtracted from the strike price at which you're selling the stock, and the holding period for the position starts on the day after exercise.

8.2.1.1 Exercising Options

When we exercise an option early, we forego any time value that is remaining within the option premium. Typically this would be a naïve thing to do. However, being aware of the intricate tax provisions enables us to consider possible occasions where early exercise may be beneficial.

Example 8e

June 2, 2004	You buy ten $20.00 strike call option contracts of ABCD stock expiring in January 2005 for $5.50.	$5,500
December 21, 2004	The stock price is now $30.00. Your calls are worth $11.00 with one month left to expiration. Your unrealized profit is $5.50 ($5,500 in real dollars).	
	You're happy with the profit, but you want to hold the stock for the long term and defer the tax on the profitable option trade.	
January 20, 2005	ABCD shares are still at $30.00, but the option is now only worth $10.00 (time value has evaporated). You exercise your right to buy 1,000 ABCD shares at $20.00.	
	The basis for tax on the stock is now $20.00 plus the $5.50 you paid for the call option. The clock starts on your new investment tomorrow. Now you have to wait until January 21, 2006 in order for the profit to be taxed at the lower (long-term investment) rate.	

Was the wait worth it? Well, only the future action of the share price will tell. If it continues to rise, then that 20% tax differential between short- and long-term investments may become substantial. If ABCD falls, then you may have forfeited a perfectly decent profitable trade purely in order to save yourself some tax.

In summary, the rule is don't let the tail wag the dog. Unless there is a spectacular reason to do otherwise, base your investment decisions around your Trading Plan. Base your Trading Plan around fundamental, technical, news, options and any other indicators you feel are appropriate. Certainly be aware of tax implications, but don't let tax get in the way of a coherent trading plan.

8.2.2 Short Options

In the U.S., short options are not taxable when the position is opened. Closing the position (or the expiration of the option) always creates a *short-term* gain or loss regardless of how long the position was open. In other words, even if you shorted an option with over 12 months left to expiration, and it expires worthless, you're liable to a *short-term* capital gains tax liability. Outside the U.S., shorting a position can incur an immediate chargeable gain.

Short Calls

If a call is exercised, the writer is obliged to deliver the underlying stock. The capital gains tax for the short stock position is based on the strike price *plus* the premium received.

Short Puts

If a put is exercised, the writer is obliged to buy the underlying stock. The capital gains tax for the long stock position is based on the strike price plus the premium received. Note that the stock holding period (for tax purposes) starts the day after exercise.

8.2.3 Offsetting Positions

Consider a Straddle.

Example 8f

December 21, 2004	ABCD is priced at $25.00. There's an earnings report due in five days, and you're convinced there's going to be a surprise. You're not sure which way the market will respond, only that there'll be a significant jump either way. You buy a $25.00 strike March 2005 Straddle, paying $2.45 for the calls and $2.15 for the puts, meaning a total investment of $4.60.	$5,500
December 31, 2004	Earnings were a bonanza, and the Street was completely caught by surprise. ABCD shares have jumped $10.00 to $35.00, and your Straddle has more than doubled in value.	
	Your puts are now worth only $0.15, and your calls are worth $12.15.	
	If you sold your puts, you'd expect to be able to claim the $2.00 loss in this tax year. If you hold onto the calls, you'd expect to pay the CGT on those gains in the next tax year. The problem is that the IRS considers the two legs of the Straddle as "offsetting" each other. Therefore, you will not be able to benefit from the loss you made on the put until you close the other side of the straddle; i.e., the profitable calls.	

The rules of Offsetting Positions state that where two positions offset each other to create substantial diminution of risk, then certain tax restrictions apply to the setting off of one side's losses against the other side's gains. This rule is vital to understand if you're considering a Long Box strategy, which in certain cases can be used as a brilliant tax strategy, depending on the tax legislation of the jurisdiction you're trading in.

8.2.4 Synthetic Call (Also Known as a Married Put)

With this strategy, you're insuring the purchase of stock by also acquiring a put. The bought put caps your losses in case the stock descends into freefall, but it adds to the basis cost of the trade.

For tax purposes, if the stock and put are acquired on the same day, then the position is taken as a whole. If the put expires, then the premium is added to the cost basis of the stock. Regarding the Offsetting rules (described previously), there is still some uncertainty as to the treatment of this strategy.

8.2.5 Covered Calls

Being such a popular strategy, we might hope and expect the tax rules concerning covered calls to be easily interpreted and straightforward. No such luck! In the U.S., the taxation rules governing covered calls are complicated and require considerable analysis.

8.2.5.1 Qualified Status

Covered calls are categorized as either "Qualified" or not qualified. "Qualified" status means that, for tax purposes, the stock *may* be considered a long-term investment if the appropriate conditions prevail. Unqualified covered calls result in the stock being taxed as a short-term investment as far as gains are concerned.

The determination of "Qualified" status for a Covered Call is dependent on the following criteria:

- Time to expiration.

- The strike price in relation to the stock price, where the strike price is In the Money (ITM).

Out of the Money (OTM) Covered Calls

Writing OTM covered calls presents no complications and does not affect the status of the stock. Therefore, if you hold the stock for more than 12 months, writing OTM calls along the way, when you come to sell the stock, it will be considered a long-term investment and gains will be taxed at the long-term investment rate.

In the Money (ITM) Covered Calls

Complications arise with ITM covered calls. As mentioned, there are two main criteria governing "Qualified" status: time to expiration and strike price.

Generally, "Qualified" status relies on the fact that:

- The option must have more than 30 days to expiration.

- The strike price must be the first available strike below (ITM) the stock's closing price the day before the trade was entered.

Example 8g

June 2, 2004	You buy 1,000 shares of ABCD stock at $36.50 and sell ten $35.00 strike July calls. Is this Qualified or not?

■ Days to expiration > 30.

■ The strike price is the first available strike below $36.50.

Therefore, this *does* qualify as a Qualified Covered Call.

Example 8h

June 2, 2004	You buy 1,000 shares of ABCD stock at $36.50 and sell ten $30.00 strike June calls. Is this Qualified or not?

■ Days to expiration < 30.

■ The strike price is not the first available strike below $36.50.

Therefore, this *does not* qualify as a Qualified Covered Call.

However, where there are more than 90 days to expiration, the rules become even more confusing, and this requires a table for explanation.

Table 8a

In the Money "Qualified" Covered Calls

Previous Day Stock Close	Time to Expiration	Lowest Qualifying Strike*
Less than or equal to $25.00	More than 30 days	One strike below previous day stock close unless strike is less than 85% of the stock price.
$25.01 to $60.00	More than 30 days	One strike below previous day stock close.
$60.01 to $150.00	31–90 days	One strike below previous day stock close.
$60.01 to $150.00	More than 90 days	■ Two strikes below previous day stock close. ■ Not more than $10.00 ITM.
Greater than $150.00	31–90 days	One strike below previous day stock close.
Greater than $150.00	More than 90 days	Two strikes below previous day stock close.

* If the opening stock price on the day the option is written is more than 10% higher than the previous day's close, then the opening price is used to determine the lowest acceptable strike price.

Example 8i

December 21, 2003	You buy 1,000 shares of ABCD stock at $36.50.	$36,500
October 20, 2004	ABCD is now at $40.00. You write a $30.00 strike January 2005 call for a $13.50 premium.	
	This is an unqualified covered call now.	
January 21, 2005	With ABCD still at $40.00, the ITM $30.00 strike call is exercised.	
	At what rate are you taxed?	
	Well, you held ABCD stock for 10 months before you wrote an ITM call against it. Because the position was unqualified, your stock holding period was suspended at 10 months. When the written ITM call is exercised in January, for tax purposes, the stock holding period is still suspended at 10 months, even though you've actually held the stock for 14 months. Therefore, the profits are taxed as a short-term investment; i.e., at the higher rate.	

The bad news is that there are plenty more rules concerning trading taxes in the U.S., even on covered calls alone. Calendar and Diagonal spreads are excellent strategies, which can augment the returns of covered calls. The anti-straddle rules can, in theory, interpret the individual legs of the trade as offsetting. You are well advised to seek the appropriate consultants who can help you not only understand the rules for your preferred strategies but also consider how you self-audit your trading results. The better organized you are at the time of your trades, the less time you'll have to spend at the end of each year going over each and every trade.

A

Strategy Table

Strategy	Execution	Benefits	Disadvantages	Component Parts	Risk Profile
Long Call	Buy a call.	Capped risk; uncapped reward; better leverage than stock purchase.	Can lose entire stake if the call expires OTM (out of the money).		
Long Put	Buy a put.	Capped risk; uncapped reward; better leverage than straight stockshorting.	Can lose entire stake if the put expires OTM (out of the money).		
Short Call (naked)	Sell a call.	Short-term income strategy.	Uncapped risk and capped reward.		
Short Put (naked)	Sell a put.	Short-term income strategy.	Uncapped risk and capped reward.		
Covered Call	Buy stock and sell call.	Protected income strategy. Profit assured if stock remains static or rises. Calls can be sold on a monthly basis to generate income.	Uncapped risk and capped reward.		
Collar	Buy stock, buy ATM put, and sell OTM call.	Can be a riskless strategy if executed correctly with the right stock.	Net debit out of your account. Works best for long-term trades where you leave it alone.		

Strategy	Execution	Benefits	Disadvantages	Component Parts	Risk Profile
Covered Put	Sell stock (short) and sell put.	Net credit into your account.	Uncapped risk and capped reward.		
Synthetic Call	Buy stock and buy put.	Capped risk and uncapped reward. Good insurance tactic.	Expensive strategy.		
Synthetic Put	Short stock and buy call.	Capped risk and uncapped reward.	More complex than simply buying puts.		
Covered Short Straddle	Buy stock and sell put and call with same strike and expiration date.	Enhanced income (compared with Covered Call).	Very high risk and capped reward. Not recommended.		
Covered Short Strangle	Buy stock and sell lower strike put and higher strike call with same expiration date.	Enhanced income (compared with Covered Call).	Very high risk and capped reward. Not recommended.		
Bull Call Spread	Buy lower strike calls and sell higher strike calls (same expiration).	Capped risk; lower breakeven point than simply buying a call.	Capped reward.		
Bull Put Spread	Buy lower strike puts and sell higher strike puts (same expiration).	Capped risk; lower breakeven point than simply buying a put; net credit into your account.	Capped reward.		

Strategy	Execution	Benefits	Disadvantages	Component Parts	Risk Profile
Bear Call Spread	Sell lower strike calls and buy higher strike calls (same expiration).	Capped risk; bearish income strategy.	Capped reward.	*[graphical component parts]*	*[graphical risk profile]*
Bear Put Spread	Sell lower strike puts and buy higher strike puts (same expiration).	Capped risk.	Capped reward.	*[graphical component parts]*	*[graphical risk profile]*
Bull Call Ladder	Buy lower strike calls, sell higher strike calls, and sell even higher strike calls (all same expiration).	Cheap strategy.	Uncapped risk if stock rises sharply; confusing as to whether this is a bullish or bearish strategy.	*[graphical component parts]*	*[graphical risk profile]*
Bull Put Ladder	Buy lower strike puts, buy higher strike puts, and sell even higher strike puts (all same expiration).	Uncapped reward as the stock falls.	Expensive; confusing as to whether this is a bullish or bearish strategy.	*[graphical component parts]*	*[graphical risk profile]*
Bear Call Ladder	Sell lower strike calls, buy higher strike calls, and buy even higher strike calls (all same expiration).	Uncapped reward as the stock rises.	Expensive; confusing as to whether this is a bullish or bearish strategy.	*[graphical component parts]*	*[graphical risk profile]*

Strategy	Execution	Benefits	Disadvantages	Component Parts	Risk Profile
Bear Put Ladder	Sell lower strike puts, sell higher strike puts, and buy even higher strike puts (all same expiration).	Cheap strategy.	Uncapped risk as the stock falls; confusing as to whether this is a bullish or bearish strategy.		
Straddle	Buy puts and calls with same strike price and expiration.	Capped risk; profitable if stocks rises or falls significantly; uncapped reward.	Expensive; low volatility required for entry whereas high volatility required once you are in.		
Short Straddle	Sell puts and calls with same strike and expiration.	Net credit into your account; profitable if stock shows low volatility and does not move.	Uncapped risk on either side.		
Strangle	Buy lower strike puts and buy higher strike calls (same expiration).	Capped risk; profitable if stocks rises or falls significantly; uncapped reward.	Low volatility required for entry whereas high volatility required once you are in.		
Short Strangle	Sell lower strike puts and sell higher strike calls (same expiration).	Net credit into your account; profitable if stock shows low volatility and does not move.	Uncapped risk on either side.		

Strategy	Execution	Benefits	Disadvantages	Component Parts	Risk Profile
Strip	Buy two puts and one call with same strike and expiration.	Capped risk; profitable if stocks rises or falls significantly; uncapped reward.	Expensive; low volatility required for entry whereas high volatility required once you are in.	(diagram)	(diagram)
Strap	Buy one put and two calls with same strike and expiration.	Capped risk; profitable if stocks rises or falls significantly; uncapped reward.	Expensive; low volatility required for entry whereas high volatility required once you are in.	(diagram)	(diagram)
Long Call Butterfly	Buy one lower strike call, sell two middle strike calls, and buy one higher strike call. All strikes evenly apart.	Capped risk and a cheap strategy to enter; can be very profitable if stock shows low volatility after you are in.	Capped reward; awkward to adjust.	(diagram)	(diagram)
Long Put Butterfly	Buy one lower strike put, sell two middle strike puts, and buy one higher strike put. All strikes evenly apart.	Capped risk and a cheap strategy to enter; can be very profitable if stock shows low volatility after you are in.	Capped reward; awkward to adjust.	(diagram)	(diagram)
Short Call Butterfly	Sell one lower strike call, buy two middle strike calls, and sell one higher strike call. All strikes evenly apart.	Capped risk; profitable if stock shows high volatility after you are in.	Capped reward; awkward to adjust.	(diagram)	(diagram)

Strategy	Execution	Benefits	Disadvantages	Component Parts	Risk Profile
Short Put Butterfly	Sell one lower strike put, buy two middle strike puts, and sell one higher strike put. All strikes evenly apart.	Capped risk; profitable if stock shows high volatility after you are in.	Capped reward; awkward to adjust.		
Modified Call Butterfly	Buy one lower strike call, sell two middle strike calls, and buy one higher strike call. Middle strike closer to higher strike than to lower strike.	Capped risk and a cheap strategy to enter; can be very profitable if stock shows low volatility or rises modestly after you are in.	Capped reward; awkward to adjust.		
Modified Put Butterfly	Buy one lower strike put, sell two middle strike puts, and buy one higher strike put. Middle strike closer to higher strike than to lower strike.	Capped risk and a cheap strategy to enter; can be very profitable if stock shows low volatility or rises modestly after you are in.	Capped reward; awkward to adjust.		
Call Ratio Backspread	Sell one or two lower strike calls and buy two or three higher strike calls. Buy greater number of higher strike calls in ratio of 0.67 or less.	Capped risk; uncapped and highly geared reward if stock rises significantly.	Lots of volatility required after entry and in the right direction (upwards) for your trade to be profitable.		

Strategy	Execution	Benefits	Disadvantages	Component Parts	Risk Profile
Put Ratio Backspread	Buy two or three lower strike puts and sell one or two higher strike puts. Buy greater number of lower strike puts in ratio of 0.67 or less.	Capped risk; uncapped and highly geared reward if stock falls significantly.	Lots of volatility required after entry and in the right direction (downwards) for your trade to be profitable.		
Ratio Call Spread	Buy lower strike call and sell greater number of higher strike calls (ratio of 0.67 or less).		Uncapped risk; capped reward.		
Ratio Put Spread	Buy higher strike put and sell greater number of lower strike puts (ratio of 0.67 or less).		Uncapped risk; capped reward.		
Long Call Condor	Buy lower strike call, sell middle strike call, sell next middle strike call, and buy higher strike call. All strikes evenly apart.	Capped risk and a cheap strategy to enter; can be very profitable if stock remains rangebound after you are in.	Capped reward; awkward to adjust.		

Strategy	Execution	Benefits	Disadvantages	Component Parts	Risk Profile
Long Put Condor	Buy lower strike put, sell middle strike put, sell next middle strike put, and buy higher strike put. All strikes evenly apart.	Capped risk and a cheap strategy to enter; can be very profitable if stock remains rangebound after you are in.	Capped reward; awkward to adjust.		
Short Call Condor	Sell lower strike call, buy middle strike call, buy next middle strike call, and sell higher strike call. All strikes evenly apart.	Capped risk; profitable if stock shows high volatility after you are in.	Capped reward; awkward to adjust.		
Short Put Condor	Sell lower strike put, buy middle strike put, buy next middle strike put, and sell higher strike put. All strikes evenly apart.	Capped risk; profitable if stock shows high volatility after you are in.	Capped reward; awkward to adjust.		
Long Call Synthetic Straddle	Sell one stock and buy two ATM calls.	Capped risk; profitable if stock rises or falls significantly; uncapped reward; cheaper than doing a normal Straddle.	Low volatility required for entry whereas high volatility required once you are in.		

Strategy	Execution	Benefits	Disadvantages	Component Parts	Risk Profile
Long Put Synthetic Straddle	Buy one stock and two ATM puts.	Capped risk; profitable if stocks rises or falls significantly; uncapped reward.	Even more expensive than normal Straddle; low volatility required for entry, whereas high volatility required once you are in.	*(diagram: / + ⌐ + ⌐)*	*(diagram: ∪ curve)*
Short Call Synthetic Straddle	Buy one stock and sell two ATM calls.	Profitable if stock shows low volatility and does not move.	Uncapped risk on either side; expensive because you are buying the stock.	*(diagram: / + ⌐ + ⌐)*	*(diagram: ∩ curve)*
Short Put Synthetic Straddle	Sell one stock and two ATM puts.	Cheap strategy that brings in a net credit to your account; profitable if stock shows low volatility and does not move.	Uncapped risk on either side; large margin required.	*(diagram: / + ⌐ + /)*	*(diagram: ∩ curve)*
Long Iron Butterfly	Buy lower strike put, sell mid strike put, sell next mid strike call, and buy higher strike call. (Middle strikes can be the same.)	Cheap strategy that brings in a net credit to your account; capped risk; profitable if stock doesn't move much; capped risk.	Capped reward; margin required.	*(diagram: _⌐ + ⌐_ + _⌐ + ⌐_)*	*(diagram: ∨-shaped capped curve)*

Strategy	Execution	Benefits	Disadvantages	Component Parts	Risk Profile
Short Iron Butterfly	Sell lower strike put, buy mid strike put, buy next mid strike call, and sell higher strike call. (Middle strikes can be the same.)	Capped risk.	Expensive strategy.		
Calendar Call	Buy long-term call and sell shorter-term call (same strikes).	Capped risk; can sell the shorter-term calls on a monthly basis in order to generate income.	Capped reward; can become loss-making if the underlying asset rises too much.		
Calendar Put	Buy long-term put and sell shorter-term put (same strikes).	Capped risk; can sell the shorter-term calls on a monthly basis in order to generate income.	Capped reward; can become loss-making if the underlying asset rises too much.		
Diagonal Call	Buy long-term lower strike call and sell shorter-term higher strike call.	Capped risk; can sell the shorter-term calls on a monthly basis in order to generate income.	Capped reward.		
Diagonal Put	Sell shorter-term lower strike put and buy longer-term higher strike put.	Capped risk; can sell the shorter-term calls on a monthly basis in order to generate income.	Capped reward.		

Strategy	Execution	Benefits	Disadvantages	Component Parts	Risk Profile
Guts	Buy lower strike calls and higher strike puts.	Capped risk; profitable if stocks rises or falls significantly; uncapped reward.	Expensive because you're buying ITM options.		
Short Guts	Sell lower strike calls and higher strike puts.	Net credit into your account; profitable if stock shows low volatility and does not move.	Uncapped risk on either side.		
Long Synthetic Future	Buy ATM call and sell ATM put.	Simulates going long on a stock with no or very little net debit or credit.	Same leverage as the underlying.		
Short Synthetic Future	Sell ATM call and buy ATM put.	Simulates going short on a stock with no or very little net debit or credit.	Same leverage as the underlying.		
Long Combo	Sell OTM (lower) put and buy OTM (higher) call.	Almost simulates going long on a stock with no or very little net debit or credit.	Same leverage as the underlying.		
Short Combo	Buy OTM (lower) put and sell OTM (higher) call.	Almost simulates going short on a stock with no or very little net debit or credit.	Same leverage as the underlying.		

Strategy	Execution	Benefits	Disadvantages	Component Parts	Risk Profile
Long Box	Buy one low strike call, sell one same strike put; sell one higher strike call, and buy one same higher strike put; all same expiration dates.	Create a completely hedged position where the ultimate profit is known with certainty ahead of time.	Complicated, requires many contracts to be effective. Bid/Ask spread makes it difficult to guarantee a profitable position.		

Glossary

American Stock Exchange (AMEX)　Securities Exchange that handles approximately 20% of all securities trades within the U.S.

American-Style Option　An option contract that can be exercised at any time before the expiration date. Stock options are American style.

Arbitrage　Where the simultaneous purchase and disposal of a combination of financial instruments is such that a guaranteed profit is made automatically.

Ask　The price that you buy at and the price that market makers and floor brokers are willing to sell at. The Ask stands for what the market makers and floor traders ask you to pay for the stock (or options or other instrument).

At the Opening Order　An order that specifies execution at the market opening or else it is cancelled.

ATM (At the Money)　Where the option exercise price is the same as the asset price.

Automatic Exercise　The automatic exercise of an ITM (In the Money) option by the clearing firm at expiration.

Backspread　A spread where more options (calls or puts) are bought than sold (the opposite of a Ratio Spread).

Bear Call Ladder　A strategy using calls where the trader sells a lower strike call and buys a higher strike call and another higher strike call.

Bear Call Spread　A bearish net credit strategy using calls where the trader buys a higher strike call and sells a lower strike call. The higher strike call will be cheaper, hence the net credit. Bear Call spreads have limited risk and reward, and are more profitable as the underlying asset price falls.

Bear Put Ladder　A spread using puts where the trader sells a lower strike put and buys a higher strike put and another higher strike put.

Bear Put Spread   A net debit spread using only puts where the trader buys a higher strike put and sells a lower strike put. The higher strike put will be more expensive, hence the net debit. Bear Put spreads have limited risk and reward, and are more profitable as the underlying asset falls.

Bid   The price the trader sells at and the price that market makers and floor traders are willing to buy at. The Bid stands for the price at which the market maker will bid for your stock (or options or other instrument).

Bid – Ask Spread   The difference between the bid and asked prices. Generally you will buy at the Ask and sell at the Bid. The Ask is always higher than the Bid.

Breakeven   The point(s) at which a risk profile of a trade equals zero.

Breakout   Where a price chart emerges upwards beyond previous price resistance.

Broker   A person who charges commission for executing a transaction (buy or sell) order.

Bull   Someone who expects the market to rise.

Bull Call Ladder   A spread using only calls where the trader buys a lower strike call and sells a higher strike call and another higher strike call.

Bull Call Spread   Long-term bullish strategy involving buying low strike calls and selling the same number of higher strike calls with the same expiration date.

Bull Market   A rising market over a period of time (usually a few years).

Bull Put Ladder   A spread using puts where the trader buys a lower strike put and sells a higher strike put and another higher strike put.

Bull Put Spread   Short-term bullish strategy involving buying lower strike puts and selling higher strike puts with the same expiration date.

Butterfly Spread   Three-legged direction neutral low volatility strategies involving either all call legs or all put legs. Suitable for rangebound stocks.

Buy on Close   An order stipulating to buy the security at the close of the trading session.

Buy on Open   An order stipulating to buy the security at the opening of the trading session.

Buy Stop   A buy order where the price stipulated is higher than the current price. The rationale here is that the buyer believes that if the security breaks a certain resistance then the security will continue to rise.

Buy-Write   A bullish strategy involving buying a stock and selling near term ATM or OTM call options to generate regular income. See "Covered Call."

Calendar Spread   Two-legged option trade involving buying a long-term option and selling a shorter-term option with the same strike price. A Calendar Spread must involve either all call or all put legs; you cannot mix calls and puts together for this strategy.

Call Option   The right, not the obligation, to buy an underlying security at a fixed price before a predetermined date.

Call Premium   The price of a call option.

Call Ratio Backspread   Bullish strategy involving selling one or two lower strike calls and buying two or three higher strike calls.

Capital Gain   The profit realized from buying and selling an asset.

Capital Loss   The loss taken from buying and selling an asset unprofitably.

Chicago Board Options Exchange (CBOE)   The largest equity options exchange in the world.

Chicago Board of Trade (CBOT)   The oldest commodity exchange in the U.S. Known for listings in T-bonds, notes, and a variety of commodities.

Chicago Mercantile Exchange (CME)   An exchange in which many types of futures contracts are traded in an open outcry system.

Class of Options   Options of the same type, style, and underlying security.

Clearing House   A separate institution to establish timely payment and delivery of securities.

Close   The last price quoted for the day.

Closing Purchase   A transaction that closes an open short position.

Collar   A low-risk bullish strategy involving buying a stock, buying near the money puts, and selling out of the money calls.

Closing Sale   A transaction that closes an open long position.

Commission   A charge made by the broker for arranging the transaction.

Commodity   A tangible good that is traded on an exchange—for example, oil, grains, metals.

Commodity Futures Trading Commission (CFTC)   An institution charged with ensuring the efficient operation of the futures markets.

Condor Spread   Four-legged direction neutral low volatility strategy involving either all call legs or all put legs. Suitable for rangebound stocks.

Contract   A unit of trading for an option or future.

Correction   A post-rise decline in a stock price or market.

Covered Call   A bullish strategy involving buying or owning a stock and selling near term ATM or OTM calls to generate regular income. See "Buy-Write."

Covered Put   A bearish strategy involving shorting stock and shorting a near term put option to create regular income. Considered a high-risk strategy.

Covered Short Straddle   A bullish strategy involving buying (or owning) a stock and selling near term puts and calls at the same strike price and expiration date. This is a risky strategy, involving almost certain exercise of the put or call and a significant downside risk if the stock price falls.

Covered Short Strangle   A bullish strategy involving buying (or owning) a stock and selling near-term OTM puts and OTM calls at the same expiration date. This is a risky strategy, involving significant downside risk if the stock price falls.

Credit Spread   Where the simultaneous buying and selling of options creates a net credit into your account (i.e., you receive more for the ones you sell than those you buy).

Day Order   An order good for the day only.

Day Trade   The acquisition and disposal of an asset in the same day.

Day Trading   A trading style where positions are closed by the end of every day.

Debit Spread   Where the simultaneous buying and selling of options creates a net debit from your account (i.e., you pay more for the ones you buy than those you sell).

Deep In the Money (DITM) calls   Where the price of the underlying security is far greater than the Call Strike Price.

Deep In the Money (DITM) puts   Where the price of the underlying security is far less than the Put Strike Price.

Delayed Time Quotes   Quotes that are delayed from real time.

Delta   The amount by which an option premium moves divided by the dollar-for-dollar movement in the underlying asset.

Delta Hedge   A strategy designed to protect the investor against directional price changes in the underlying asset by engineering the overall position Delta to zero.

Delta Neutral   Where a spread position is engineered so that the overall position Delta is zero.

Derivative   A financial instrument whose value is "derived" in some way from the value of an underlying asset source.

Diagonal Spread   Two-legged option trade involving buying a long-term option and selling a shorter-term option with a higher strike price. A Calendar Spread must involve either all call or all put legs; you cannot mix calls and puts together for this strategy.

Discount Brokers   Low commission brokers who simply place orders and do not provide advisory services.

Dividend   A payment made by an organization to its owners (shareholders), hopefully from profits.

Dow Jones Industrial Average (DJIA)   An index of 30 blue chip stocks traded on the New York Stock Exchange (NYSE). This index is often considered a bellwether of overall market sentiment.

Downside Risk   The potential risk of a trade if prices decline.

End of Day   The close of the trading day when prices settle.

EPS   Earnings per share. The amount of profits of an organization divided by the number of outstanding shares.

Equity Options   Same as Stock Options.

European Style Option   An option that cannot be exercised before the expiration date.

Exchange   Where an asset or derivative is traded.

Exchange Rate   The price at which one currency can be converted into another currency.

Execution   The process of completing an order to trade a security.

Exercise   The activation of the right to buy or sell the underlying security.

Exercise (Strike) Price   The price at which an asset can be bought or sold by the buyer of a call or put option.

Expiration   The date at which the option's ability to be exercised ceases.

Expiration Date   The last day on which an option can be exercised.

Extrinsic Value (Time Value)   The price of an option less its intrinsic value. Out of the Money Options are entirely made up of Extrinsic (or Time) Value.

Fair Market Value   An asset's value under normal circumstances.

Fair Value   The theoretical value calculation of an option using a pricing technique such as Black-Scholes options pricing formula.

Fill   An order that has been executed.

Fill Order   An order that must be filled immediately or cancelled.

Fill or Kill   An order where a precise number of contracts must be filled or the order is cancelled.

Floor Broker   A member of an exchange who is paid to execute orders.

Floor Trader   An exchange member who trades on the floor of the exchange for his or her own account.

Fundamental Analysis   Analysis of a stock security that is based on the ability of the organization to generate profits for its shareholders. Such analysis embraces earnings, PE Ratios, EPS, Net Assets, Liabilities, customers, etc.

Futures Contracts   Agreement to buy or sell an underlying security at a predetermined date at an agreed price. The difference between futures and options is that with options, the buyer has the right, not the obligation. With futures, both parties are obliged to fulfill their part of the bargain.

Gamma   The speed by which Delta changes compared with the speed by which the underlying asset is moving.

Good till Cancelled Order (GTC)   An order that continues until either it is filled or cancelled specifically by the trader.

Guts   A volatility strategy involving buying In the Money (ITM) calls and ITM puts. High volatility is required after the position is opened to make this a profitable strategy.

Hedge   A term for reducing the risk of one position by taking other positions with options, futures, or other derivatives.

Historical Volatility   A measure of the price fluctuation of an asset averaged out over a period of time. A typical and popular period would be 21–23 trading days.

Index   A group of assets (often in a similar class of sector or market capitalization) that can be traded as a single security.

Index Options   Options on the indexes of stocks or other securities.

Interest Rates   The rate at which borrowed money is charged by the lender, usually annualized into a percentage figure.

In the Money (ITM)   Where you can exercise an option for a profit.

In the Money (ITM) calls   ITM calls are where the current stock price is greater than the Call Strike Price.

In the Money (ITM) puts   ITM puts are where the current stock price is less than the Put Strike Price.

Intrinsic Value   The amount by which an option is in the money.

Iron Butterfly   See "Long Iron Butterfly" or "Short Iron Butterfly."

LEAPs   Long-term Equity AnticiPation Securities. These are long-term stock options with expirations up to three years in the future. LEAPs are available in calls and puts and are American-style traded options.

Leg   One side or component of a spread.

Leg In/Leg Out   Legging into a spread entails the completion of just one part of a spread with the intention of completing the other parts at more favorable prices later on. Legging out of a spread entails the opposite, whereby you exit your spread one part at a time with the intention of doing so at more favorable prices as the underlying security moves in the anticipated direction.

LIFFE   London International Financial Futures and Options Exchange. Now known as Euronext.liffe.

Limit Order   An order to buy at a set price that is at or below the current price of the security. An order to sell at a set price that is at or above the current price of the security.

Liquidity   The speed and ease with which an asset can be traded. Cash has the most liquidity of all assets, whereas property (real estate) is one of the most illiquid assets. Volume is the measure of liquidity for stocks, and Open Interest is the measure of liquidity for options. See *Open Interest*.

Long   Being long means that you are a buyer of a security.

Long Call   Buying a call option.

Long Call Butterfly   A three-leg direction neutral strategy requiring low volatility, involving buying a low strike call, selling two middle strike calls with the same strike price, and buying a higher strike call.

Long Call Condor   A four-leg direction neutral strategy requiring low volatility, involving buying a low strike call, selling two middle strike calls with different strike prices, and buying a higher strike call.

Long Call Synthetic Straddle   A two-leg direction neutral strategy requiring high volatility, involving buying two ATM calls for every 100 shares (U.S. stock options) sold, thereby replicating the risk profile of a Long Straddle.

Long Combo   A bullish strategy involving selling OTM puts and buying OTM calls in order to partially replicate a long stock position.

Long Iron Butterfly   A direction neutral strategy constructed by combining a Bull Put Spread with a Bear Call Spread or by combining a narrow Short Strangle with a wider Long Strangle.

Long Put   A bearish strategy, buying put options.

Long Put Butterfly   A three-leg direction neutral strategy requiring low volatility, involving buying a low strike put, selling two middle strike puts with the same strike price, and buying a higher strike put.

Long Put Condor   A four-leg direction neutral strategy requiring low volatility, involving buying a low strike put, selling two middle strike puts with different strike prices, and buying a higher strike put.

Long Put Synthetic Straddle   A two-leg direction neutral strategy requiring high volatility, involving buying two ATM puts for every 100 shares (U.S. stock options) bought, thereby replicating the risk profile of a Long Straddle.

Long Stock   Buying shares.

Long Synthetic Future   Buying calls and selling the same amount of puts with the same strike and expiration date, effectively forming the same risk profile of buying a stock but with almost no cost.

Margin   An amount paid by the account holder (either in cash or "marginable securities") that is held by the brokerage against non-cash or high-risk investments, or where the brokerage has lent the account holder the means to undertake a particular trade.

Market Capitalization   The number of outstanding shares multiplied by the value per share.

Market if Touched (MIT) Order   An order that becomes a market order if the price specified is reached.

Market Maker   A trader or trading firm that buys and sells securities in a market in order to facilitate trading. Market makers make a two-sided (bid and ask) market.

Market on Close Order   An order that requires the broker to achieve the best price at the close or in the last five minutes of trading.

Market on Open Order   An order that must be executed at the opening of trading.

Market Order   Trading securities immediately at the best market prices in order to guarantee execution.

Market Price   The most recent transaction price.

Married Put   See "Covered Put."

Modified Call Butterfly   A neutral to bullish strategy similar to a Long Call Butterfly, except that the OTM bought calls have a strike price nearer to the central strike price of the sold calls.

Modified Put Butterfly   A neutral to bullish strategy similar to a Long Put Butterfly, except that the ITM bought puts have a strike price nearer to the central strike price of the sold puts.

Naked   Selling naked options refers to a sold options contract with no hedge position in place. Such a position leaves the option seller (writer) exposed to unlimited risk.

NASDAQ   National Association of Securities Dealers Automated Quotations system. This is a computerized system providing brokers and dealers with securities price quotes.

Near the Money (NTM)   Where the underlying asset price is close to the Strike Price of an option.

New York Stock Exchange (NYSE)   The largest stock exchange in the U.S.

OEX   Standard & Poor's 100 Stock Index.

Offer   The lowest price at which someone is willing to sell. You also can refer to the "Ask" of a Bid-Ask Spread. See "Ask."

On the Money (At the Money)   See "ATM (At the Money)."

Open Interest   The total number of options or futures contracts that are not closed or delivered on a particular day. This is a measure of an option's liquidity. A higher number of "open" contracts indicates greater liquidity. Greater liquidity affords us greater efficiency in closing our open positions.

Open Outcry   Verbal system of floor trading still used at many exchanges (e.g., the CME and CBOT).

Opening   The beginning of the trading session at an exchange.

Opportunity Cost   The risk of an investment expressed as a comparison with another competing investment.

Option   A security that gives the buyer the right, not the obligation, to buy (call) or sell (put) an underlying asset at a fixed price before a predetermined date.

Option Premium   The price of an option.

Option Writer   The seller of an option (usually naked).

Out of the Money (OTM)   Where the option has no intrinsic value and where you cannot exercise an option for a profit.

Out of the Money (OTM) calls   OTM calls are where the current stock price is less than the Call Strike Price.

Out of the Money (OTM) puts   OTM puts are where the current stock price is greater than the Put Strike Price.

Position Delta   The sum of all positive and negative Deltas within a hedged trade position.

Premium   The price of an option.

Price Bar   The visual representation of a securities price fluctuation for a set period of time. Price bars can be for as little as one minute (or less) and as much as one year (or more).

Put Calendar   A neutral to bullish strategy involving buying longer expiration puts and selling shorter expiration puts with the same strike price.

Put Diagonal   A neutral to bullish strategy involving buying longer expiration puts and selling shorter expiration puts with a higher strike price.

Put Option   The right, not the obligation, to sell an underlying security at a fixed price before a predetermined date.

Put Ratio Backspread   Bearish strategy involving selling one or two higher strike puts and buying two or three lower strike puts.

Quote   The price being bid or offered by a market maker for a security.

Ratio Backspread   A strategy using all puts or all calls, whereby the trader buys OTM options in a ratio of 3:2 or 2:1 to the ITM options he sells. In this way, the trader is always long in more options than those he is short in.

Ratio Call Spread   A bearish strategy that involves the trader being short in more options than those he is long in, at a ratio of 3:2 or 2:1. In this way, the trader will have an unlimited risk profile with only limited profit potential.

Ratio Put Spread   A bullish strategy that involves the trader being short in more options than those he is long in, at a ratio of 3:2 or 2:1. In this way, the trader will have an unlimited risk profile with only limited profit potential.

Real Time   Data that is updated and received tick by tick.

Resistance   A price threshold on a price chart that is thought to be difficult for the price to burst up through because of past price movements.

Return   The income profit on an investment, often expressed as a percentage.

Rho   The sensitivity of an option price to interest rates. Typically, call options increase in value as interest rates rise, and puts decrease in value as interest rates rise.

Risk   The potential loss of a trade.

Risk-Free Rate   The interest chargeable on Treasury Bills (T-Bills) is generally known as the Risk-Free Rate; this rate is used as a component part of the theoretical valuation of options model.

Risk Profile   The graphic depiction of a trade, showing the potential risk, reward, and breakeven points as the underlying security price deviates within a range of prices.

Securities and Exchange Commission (SEC)   Organization that regulates the securities markets in order to protect investors.

Security   An instrument that can be traded—e.g., stocks, bonds, etc.

Selling Short   Selling a security that you don't actually own beforehand. You will eventually have to buy it back, hopefully at a reduced price, thus making profit.

Series (Options)   Option contracts of the same class (underlying asset), same strike price, and same expiration date.

Shares   Units of ownership in a company or organization.

Short   Selling a security that you don't actually own.

Short Call   A bearish strategy involving the short selling of call options.

Short Call Butterfly   A three-leg direction neutral strategy requiring high volatility, involving selling a low strike call, buying two middle strike calls with the same strike price, and buying a higher strike call.

Short Call Condor   A four-leg direction neutral strategy requiring high volatility, involving selling a low strike call, buying two middle strike calls with different strike prices, and buying a higher strike call.

Short Call Synthetic Straddle   A two-leg direction neutral strategy requiring low volatility, involving selling two ATM calls for every 100 shares (U.S. stock options) bought, thereby replicating the risk profile of a Short Straddle.

Short Combo   A bearish strategy involving buying OTM puts and selling OTM calls in order to partially replicate a short stock position.

Short Guts   A low volatility strategy involving selling In the Money (ITM) calls and ITM puts. Low volatility is required after the position is opened to make this a profitable strategy.

Short Iron Butterfly   A direction neutral strategy constructed by combining a Bull Call Spread with a Bear Put Spread or by combining a narrow Long Strangle with a wider Short Strangle.

Short Put   A bullish strategy, selling put options usually OTM (with a strike price below the current stock price).

Short Put Butterfly   A three-leg direction neutral strategy requiring high volatility, involving selling a low strike put, buying two middle strike puts with the same strike price, and selling a higher strike put.

Short Put Condor   A four-leg direction neutral strategy requiring high volatility, involving selling a low strike put, buying two middle strike puts with different strike prices, and selling a higher strike put.

Short Put Synthetic Straddle   A two-leg direction neutral strategy requiring low volatility, involving selling two ATM puts for every 100 shares (U.S. stock options) sold, thereby replicating the risk profile of a Short Straddle.

Short Stock   Selling shares short.

Short Straddle   A low volatility direction neutral trade that involves simultaneously selling a call and put at the same strike price and with the same expiration date. Requires the underlying asset to be rangebound to make the trade profitable.

Short Strangle   A low volatility direction neutral trade that involves simultaneously selling a call and put at different strike prices (the put strike being lower than the call strike—i.e., both OTM) and with the same expiration date. Requires the underlying asset to be rangebound in order to make the trade profitable.

Short Synthetic Future   Selling calls and buying the same amount of puts with the same strike and expiration date, effectively forming the same risk profile of shorting a stock but with no net credit.

Short Selling   Selling a security that you don't actually own beforehand. You will eventually have to buy it back, hopefully at a reduced price, thus making profit.

Sigma   Generally a term used to represent volatility. It is generally represented as a percentage. The term "one sigma level" refers to the actual change in the underlying asset price.

Small-Cap Stocks   Smaller (and sometimes newer) companies that are associated with high risk and high potential rewards. Can be illiquid to trade with large bid-ask spreads.

Speculator A trader who aims to make profit by correctly assessing the direction of price movement of the security. Generally distinguished from investors in that speculators are associated with short-term directional trading.

Spread The difference between the bid and ask of a traded security. Also, a trading strategy that involves more than one leg to create a (hedged) position. A price spread is the difference between the high and the low of a price bar.

Stock A share of a company's stock is a unit of ownership in that company.

Stock Exchange or Stock Market An organized market where buyers and sellers are brought together to trade stocks.

Stock Split Where a company increases the amount of outstanding stock, thus increasing the number of shares, reducing the value per share. Generally a sign that the stock has been rising and management's way of assisting the liquidity in the stock.

Stop Orders Buy Stops: where the order price is specified above the current value of the security. Sell Stops: where the order price is specified below the current value of the security.

Straddle A neutral trade that involves simultaneously buying a call and put at the same strike price and with the same expiration date. Requires the underlying asset to move in an explosive nature (in either direction) in order to make the trade profitable.

Strangle A neutral trade that involves simultaneously buying a call and put at different strike prices (the Put Strike being lower than the Call Strike—i.e., both OTM) and with the same expiration date. Requires the underlying asset to move in an explosive nature (in either direction) in order to make the trade profitable.

Strap A neutral to bullish trade that involves simultaneously buying two calls and a put with the same strike price and expiration date. Requires the underlying asset to move in an explosive nature (preferably upwards) in order to make the trade profitable.

Strike Price (Exercise Price) The price at which an asset can be bought or sold by the buyer of a call or put option.

Strip A neutral to bearish trade that involves simultaneously buying two puts and a call with the same strike price and expiration date. Requires the underlying asset to move in an explosive nature (preferably downwards) in order to make the trade profitable.

Support A price threshold on a price chart that is thought to be difficult for the price to fall through because of past price movements.

Synthetic Call Buying a share and a put, or going long a future and a put, replicating the risk profile shape of a Long Call.

Synthetic Put Buying a call and shorting a stock or future, replicating the risk profile shape of a Long Put.

Synthetic Long Stock Buying a call and shorting a put with the same strike and expiration date.

Synthetic Short Call   Shorting a put and shorting a stock or future.

Synthetic Short Put   Shorting a call and buying a stock or future.

Synthetic Short Stock   Shorting a call and buying a put with the same strike and expiration date.

Synthetic Straddle   Combining stocks (or futures) with options to create a delta neutral trade.

Technical Analysis   Using charts, charting techniques, and indicators (such as prices, volume, moving averages, stochastics, etc.) to evaluate likely future price movement.

Theoretical Value (Options)   The fair value calculation of an option using a pricing technique such as Black-Scholes options pricing formula.

Theta (Decay)   The sensitivity of an option price to the variable of time. Remember that options only have a finite life (until expiration), so Theta is an extremely important sensitivity to consider.

Tick   The least amount of price movement recorded in a security. Before decimalization, the lowest was 1/32 of a dollar.

Time Premium   The non-intrinsic component of the price of an option.

Time Value (Extrinsic Value)   The price of an option less its intrinsic value. Out of the Money and At the Money options are entirely made up of Extrinsic (or Time) Value.

Trading Plan   The step-by-step process in which you select your chosen securities, define your entry and exit points, and execute your strategy. No trade should ever be made without a proper trading plan in place. Your trading plan is like a business plan for each trading decision.

Triple Witching Day   The third Friday in March, June, September, and December when U.S. stock options, index options, and futures contracts all expire at the same time. The effect of this is often increased volume and volatility as traders look to close short and long positions.

Type   The classification of an option—either a call or a put.

Uncovered Option   A short position where the writer does not have the underlying security (or call option) to hedge the unlimited risk position of his naked position.

Underlying Asset/Instrument/Security   An asset that is subject to purchase or disposal upon exercise.

Upside   The potential for a price to increase.

Vega   The sensitivity of an option price to volatility. Typically, options increase in value during periods of high volatility.

Volatility   The measure of the fluctuation in the price movement in a security over a period of time. Volatility is one of the most important components in the theoretical valuation of an option price. Historical Volatility: the standard deviation of the underlying security (closing) price movement over a period of time (typically

21–23 days). Implied Volatility: the calculated component derived from the option price when using the Black-Scholes Option Pricing model. If there is a significant discrepancy between Implied and Historical Volatility, then there is the opportunity for the trader to take advantage of it.

Volatility Skew   Whereby deep OTM options tend to have higher Implied Volatilities than ATM options. When there are discrepancies, the trader can make trades whose profits are determined by volatility action as opposed to directional price action.

Volume   The number of underlying securities traded on their particular part of the exchange. Where price direction and volume bars are aligned in the same direction, then this is a bullish sign (i.e., it means that prices are rising with increased volume or that prices are falling with decreased volume). Where price direction diverges from volume bars, then this is a bearish sign (i.e., prices rising with falling volume or prices falling with rising volume).

Whipsaw   Where a price swing ensures a losing scenario for both sides of a position.

Witching Day   When two or more classes of options and futures contracts expire.

Writer   Someone who sells an option.

Yield   The rate of return of an investment, expressed as a percentage.

Zeta   An option price's sensitivity to Implied Volatility.

Index

E

K–L

N

W–Z

FT Press
FINANCIAL TIMES

In an increasingly competitive world, it is quality
of thinking that gives an edge—an idea that opens new
doors, a technique that solves a problem, or an insight
that simply helps make sense of it all.

We work with leading authors in the various arenas
of business and finance to bring cutting-edge thinking
and best-learning practices to a global market.

It is our goal to create world-class print publications
and electronic products that give readers
knowledge and understanding that can then be
applied, whether studying or at work.

To find out more about our business
products, you can visit us at www.ftpress.com.